T0418767

Mapping Medea

Cover image and frontispiece Costume design for Médée for the opera *Thésée* by Jean-Baptiste Lully, by Jean Louis Fesch (undated, *c.* 1770–8). Courtesy of Bibliothèque nationale de France.

Mapping Medea

Revolutions and Transfers 1750–1800

Edited by
ANNA ALBREKTSON AND
FIONA MACINTOSH

OXFORD
UNIVERSITY PRESS

OXFORD
UNIVERSITY PRESS

Great Clarendon Street, Oxford, OX2 6DP,
United Kingdom

Oxford University Press is a department of the University of Oxford.
It furthers the University's objective of excellence in research, scholarship,
and education by publishing worldwide. Oxford is a registered trade mark of
Oxford University Press in the UK and in certain other countries

Published in the United States of America by Oxford University Press
198 Madison Avenue, New York, NY 10016, United States of America

British Library Cataloguing in Publication Data
Data available

Library of Congress Control Number: 2023936213

ISBN 978-0-19-288419-0

DOI: 10.1093/oso/9780192884190.001.0001

Printed and bound in the UK by
Clays Ltd, Elcograf S.p.A.

Links to third party websites are provided by Oxford in good faith and
for information only. Oxford disclaims any responsibility for the materials
contained in any third party website referenced in this work.

Acknowledgements

This volume grew out of a conference held in Uppsala and Stockholm from 25–27 April 2018, entitled, 'Placing Medea: Transfer, Spatiality, and Gender in Europe 1750–1800'. The conference was generously funded by 'Literature as a Leading Research Area', the Faculty of Humanities, Stockholm University, and the Sven och Dagmar Saléns Stiftelse. For their kind support of the conference, we would like to thank warmly the following: both Literature and Theatre Studies colleagues within the Department of Culture and Aesthetics at Stockholm University; the research network AGORA at Uppsala University; and the Interdisciplinary Eighteenth-Century Seminar at Uppsala. We would especially like to mention Eric Cullhed, Katherine Heavey, Ingela Nilsson, Sabrina Norlander Eliasson, Vera Sundin, Erik Zillén, and Ann Öhrberg for their contributions to the conference; and we are enormously appreciative of the administrative support of Love Andersson, Joanna Bong Lindström, Mattias Arreborn, and Torbjörn Wilson. None of this would have been possible without funding from Riksbankens Jubileumsfond (RJ), the Swedish Foundation for Humanities and Social Sciences, for the project 'Moving Medea: The Transcultural Stage in the Eighteenth Century'.

At OUP, as ever, we are truly grateful to Charlotte Loveridge for her unstinting support and for her belief in this project; to Jamie Mortimer and Alex Hardie-Forsyth for their patience and management skills. Alice Ahearn has done a hugely professional job on the bibliography, for which we are extremely grateful, not least because it was undertaken at a very challenging time. We would especially like to thank Otto Fischer and Marie-Christine Skuncke for invaluable suggestions concerning translations from German and French. Finally, all colleagues at the APGRD have been, as ever, tirelessly supportive; and especial thanks are due to Claire Kenward, who has generously contributed both her extensive knowledge of Medea in performance and its iconographic tradition to this volume.

Contents

Theatre   193
Zoé Schweitzer

AFTERTHOUGHTS

10. Medea—Sorceress or Woman? *c.* 1750 and Beyond   209
Roland Lysell

Bibliography   223
Index   251

List of Illustrations

List of Contributors

Anna Albrektson (fka Cullhed) is Professor of Literature at Stockholm University. She holds a PhD from Uppsala University, and has been a fellow at SCAS and a Research Fellow of the Swedish Academy. She has published on eighteenth- and nineteenth-century European poetry and poetics, as well as Swedish sentimental literature. Currently, she is engaged in an ecocritical project about representations of nature in Sweden 1780–1840. Her project 'Moving Medea: The Transcultural Stage in the Eighteenth Century' has been funded by Riksbankens Jubileumsfond (RJ). Albrektson is a former President of the Swedish Society for Eighteenth-Century Studies.

Petra Dotlačilová holds a PhD in Dance Studies from the Academy of Performing Arts in Prague (2016) and a PhD in Theatre Studies from Stockholm University (2020). In her research, she specializes on European dance history and theatrical costume of the sixteenth to nineteenth century. She participated in research projects Performing Premodernity at SU, and Ritual Design on the Ballet Stage (1650–1760) at the University of Leipzig. Currently, she is leading a research project The Fabrication of Performance: Processes and Politics of Costume-Making in the 18th Century, funded by Swedish Research Council (2021–2024), and conducted in collaboration with Centre de musique baroque de Versailles.

Edith Hall is Professor of Classics Durham, and Co-Founder and Consultant Director of Oxford University's Archive of Performances of Greek & Roman Drama (APGRD). She has published more than thirty books on classical civilization and its continuing presence in modernity, including *Adventures with Iphigenia in Tauris: A Cultural History of Euripides' Black Sea Tragedy* (2013). Her *Medea: A Life in Five Acts* is forthcoming with Yale University Press. She is the recipient of the Erasmus Medal of the European Academy and Honorary Doctorates from the Universities of Athens and Durham. In 2022 she was elected Fellow of the British Academy and in 2023 was awarded the Classical Association Prize.

Jörg Krämer is Professor of German Literature at Erlangen-Nürnberg University. He is also a professional flute soloist, and combines his expertise in literature, music, and theatre culture in his research. In 1998 he published a two-volume work on the German *Singspiel* of the eighteenth century, *Deutschsprachiges Musiktheater im späten 18. Jahrhundert: Typologie, Dramaturgie und Anthropologie einer populären Gattung*, and has recently published a collection of essays about the theoretical and methodological challenges of working with *Musiktheater*, musical drama. His critical edition of Gotter's and Benda's melodrama *Medea* (the 1784 version) was published in 2018.

Anthony John Lappin is Lecturer in Spanish at the University of Stockholm, after holding posts at the University of Manchester and the National University of Ireland,

Maynooth. His research interests stretch from Late Antiquity to the modern period, with particular interest in translation and textual criticism (most recently, Fernando Pessoa and Lope de Vega, respectively), and he is currently investigating the rise of the individual through performance- and reading-cultures.

Roland Lysell is Emeritus Professor of Literary History at Stockholm University. He has published books and articles about Swedish and Scandinavian authors such as Strindberg, Ibsen, Ekelund, and Lindegren. His specialisms are Romanticism (Atterbom, Stagnelius, Almqvist, Shelley, Keats) and Literary Modernism and his approach is broadly hermeneutic. He is also a theatre critic and drama historian.

Fiona Macintosh is Professor of Classical Reception, Director of the Archive of Performances of Greek and Roman Drama (APGRD) and Fellow of St Hilda's College, University of Oxford. She author of *Dying Acts: Death in Ancient Greek and modern Irish Tragic Drama* (1994), *Greek Tragedy and the British Theatre 1660–1914* (2005, with Edith Hall), *Sophocles' Oedipus Tyrannus* (2009), and *Performing Epic or Telling Tales* (2020, with Justine McConnell). She has edited nine APGRD volumes, including *Medea in Performance* (2000), *The Ancient Dancer in the Modern World* (2010), *Choruses, Ancient and Modern* (2012), and *Epic Performances from the Middle Ages into the Twenty-First Century* (2018).

Larisa Nikiforova is a Professor at the Department of Philosophy, History and Theory of Art at the Vaganova Ballet Academy (St Petersburg). She is a member of the Russian Union of Artists (Art-critic department) and the Russian Society for Eighteenth-Century Studies. Her publications include: *Palace of Baroque: The Interpretation with the Help of Rhetoric* (2003), *The Palace in Russian Culture* (2006), *The Edifices of Power: Cultural History of Palaces* (2011), *The Iconography of Dignity and Choreographed Poses in Russian Portraiture of the 18th Century* (2018), and *Portrait with a Black Page in Eighteenth-Century Russian Art and the Cultural Transfer of Signs* (2019).

Zoé Schweitzer is Associate Professor of Comparative Literature at Saint-Étienne University and a member of IHRIM (UMR-5317), and has worked on the theoretical challenges and the scenic effects of dramatic transgression from Antiquity to contemporary theatre. She is interested, in particular, in the relations between spectacle and aesthetic and ethical requirements. Her latest book is entitled *La Scène cannibale. Pratiques et théories de la transgression au théâtre (XVIᵉ–XXIᵉ siècle)* [*The Cannibal Scene. Practices and Theories of Transgression in the Theatre (16th–21st centuries)*] (2021).

1

Mapping Medea

Revolutions and Transfers 1750–1800

Anna Albrektson and Fiona Macintosh

The late eighteenth century witnessed multiple Medeas on the stages of Europe, in the Americas, and across the Russian empire, both to the east and to the south. Performances took place in Moscow and São Paulo, in London and Lisbon, in Gotha, Stuttgart, and Venice. Whilst Euripides' tragedy of 431 BCE and Seneca's tragedy from the first century CE are the two major points of departure for these late eighteenth-century receptions, Medea did not enter the stage solely as the protagonist of tragic drama at this time. In addition to the more traditional re-figurations, such as Richard Glover's tragedy *Medea* (published 1761, premiered 1767), the transgressive woman of Graeco-Roman antiquity was regularly at the forefront of political, aesthetic, and particularly generic, debate and innovation during this period.

Medea's complex tale of betrayal and bloody revenge was especially popular throughout the course of the long eighteenth century in musical theatre, which experimented with 'a wealth of mixed and intermediate stages of speaking and singing, as well as the most diverse combination forms of music and text.'[1] From Marc-Antoine Charpentier's 1693 *Médée*, with libretto by Thomas Corneille, to François Benoît Hoffmann's and Luigi Cherubini's grand opera *Médée* (1797), operatic Medeas always pushed aesthetic boundaries: deploying not only astonishing vocal range to mirror the emotional tumult of the protagonist, these Medea operas also exploited all the technological possibilities afforded by a century of scenic innovation. The experimental forms that provided exciting new ways to bring Medea to the world stage included the *ballet d'action* by Jean-Georges Noverre, *Médée et Jason* (1763), with its innovative blend of music, somatic movement, and emotional expressiveness. Medea also contributed significantly to the highly successful combination of spoken word and musical accompaniment in the emergent form of melodrama when

---

[1] Krämer (2018), xxvii.

Anna Albrektson and Fiona Macintosh, *Mapping Medea: Revolutions and Transfers 1750–1800* In: *Mapping Medea: Revolutions and Transfers 1750–1800*. Edited by: Anna Albrektson and Fiona Macintosh, Oxford University Press.

Friedrich Wilhelm Gotter and Georg (Jiří) Benda's landmark *Medea* appeared in 1775. Medea was at the forefront of this particular eighteenth-century theatrical innovation and was equally in the vanguard of developments in puppet theatre and the burlesque.

During the same decades, scenarios, libretti, and scores for these radical performances, and accounts of their classical origins and subsequent receptions, were printed, reissued, translated, revised, illustrated, and circulated throughout Europe and the colonies. Some Medeas of the late eighteenth century didn't actually reach the stage at all but remained highly influential as printed texts, such as the Swedish author Bengt Lidner's opera libretto *Medea* from 1784 and Friedrich Maximilian von Klinger's two Medea tragedies (1787 and 1791). Medea intrigued, enthralled, and shocked audiences in all her guises at this time—on the page as much as in performance—and we find prose versions, based on Ovid's *Metamorphoses* as well as on medieval romances, also in wide circulation and adapted to local and transnational contexts. Likewise, Medea made her presence felt in treatises arguing for revolutionary changes in theatre theory and practice. The character of Medea, for example, becomes crucial to the reinterpretation of Aristotle's categories of pity and horror, in several languages, as well as to the new ideals of acting developing during the century. She becomes embroiled in debates about the baroque and is seen to embody many aspects of the eighteenth-century sublime.

This volume seeks to examine the reasons why Medea attracted the attention of authors, audiences, actresses, and rulers in Europe and its dominions from 1750 to 1800, and to what purposes. As migrant and iconoclast, Medea crosses a number of eighteenth-century borders: linguistic, cultural, national, temporal, spatial, aesthetic, ethical, and generic. This is a pivotal moment in the reception of Medea: the moment when the Senecan Medea begins to cede ground permanently to Euripides' version, as she contributes to the early discourse around the Woman Question. It may well appear counterintuitive that Medea should appeal to a generation of playwrights whose primary goal was the representation of sentimental motherhood and feminine vulnerability on European stages dominated by bourgeois tragedy and the pursuit of theatrical naturalism. Yet the fact that late eighteenth-century playwrights, poets, composers, and choreographers all turned to one of the most problematic characters of Graeco-Roman antiquity offers a unique opportunity to study the remarkable flexibility of the reception process. If the designation 'witch' is a hangover from pre-Enlightenment sectarian discourse, the Senecan Medea not surprisingly begins to recede in the background and only occasionally finds her voice outside the realms of serious, spoken theatre.[2] From 1750 onwards, it is versions of Medea's womanhood that provide the principal object of interest. In a very real sense, it is between 1750 and 1800 that contemporary understandings of Medea emerge.

By studying the figure of Medea within the revolutionary context of the late eighteenth century, it is possible to address the negotiations between court culture and the emergent metropolitan cultural centres, as well as the role of antiquity in national, imperial, and colonial politics at this time. Furthermore, the generic range of eighteenth-century performance culture can be explored with the same protagonist as common denominator. Medea herself therefore functions as a case study reflecting a wider context of cultural change in the late eighteenth century.

Medea at the Hands of Colonial Europe

The resonance of Medea during the revolutionary decades of the late eighteenth century is generated mainly from the events in Corinth, the subject matter of Euripides' and Seneca's tragedies. However, the pre-history of Colchis, Medea's native land, is also the object of deep interest. As Apollonius Rhodius' *Argonautica* (third century BCE) recounts, Medea flees her homeland Colchis in the Black Sea region, armed with the Golden Fleece and Jason as husband, betraying her family and killing her brother in the process. After further power struggles in Greece, with Medea acting as her husband's helper, the couple and their two sons are then forced to seek refuge in Corinth. Euripides' and Seneca's tragedies begin at this point with Jason's plan to divorce Medea and marry the local princess. Medea is to be exiled by King Creon, and plans her revenge on the perjurer Jason. She kills the young princess with a poisoned wreath and robe, Creon dies trying to save his daughter, and Medea stabs her own two sons to death. At the end of Euripides' tragedy, Medea flees on the chariot of her grandfather Helios to exile in Athens.

The eighteenth-century Medea is in many ways perpetual migrant— literally within the repertoire of travelling players, but also because she is embedded in a world of flux, transformation, and revolution. Lully's *Thésée* (1675), based on Ovid's retelling in the *Metamorphoses*, not surprisingly enjoyed considerable prominence during this period. For *Thésée* replays, albeit in a slightly different key, the broadly similar events in Athens that

[2] For early modern Medeas, see Wygant (2007); Heavey (2015); Pollard (2017).

involve a love triangle in which Medea is again the third party. The *tragédie lyrique* also includes Médée's acts of terrifying revenge that necessitate (another) exodus in a dragon-drawn chariot. Yet Medea's story also entered the eighteenth-century stage in a light-hearted manner. The frequent performances of Cavalli's 1649 opera *Giasone* brought not only scenes of incantation and madness to eighteenth-century audiences, but also a complicated amorous plot with a happy ending that draws, amongst other ancient sources, on Ovid's letters from Hypsipyle and Medea in his *Heroides*. In this opera version, Jason in Colchis stands between his former love interest Isifile (Hypsipyle), and Medea. In the end he returns to Hypsipyle, the mother of his two children, while Medea is united with Egeo (Aegeus), the king of Athens. Both *Thésée* and *Giasone* are examples of the wide-ranging ramifications of the story that gain in resonance during their eighteenth-century revivals. In this sense, as Medea plays a prominent part in several myths concerning Colchis, Corinth, and Athens, her migration in geopolitical space sometimes takes her very far away from Euripides' Corinth and very much into the eighteenth-century world of travel and colonization.

This combination of mutability and multiplicity in Medea's story extends beyond the stage. Not surprisingly, the Medea story became entangled with new reports about encounters with indigenous people as the result of colonial and scientific endeavours; and it could also be argued that some eighteenth-century stories were modelled on the ancient Greek myth through a form of inverted displacement.[3] The well-known story of the Amerindian young woman Yarico parallels, in many ways, the myth of Medea; and both eighteenth-century re-figurations are shaped by European global expansion, colonization, and slavery.

The story of Yarico was one of the most widespread tales of the eighteenth century and concerned the relationship between the English trader Thomas Inkle and the 'Indian' Yarico. It first appeared in print in *The Spectator* on 13 March 1711,[4] and 'its appeal', according to Frank Felsenstein, 'is primarily as a myth of the Enlightenment'.[5] In the tale, Inkle, a tradesman on his way to the West Indies, goes ashore in search of provisions on the American mainland. While the rest of the crew is slayed by natives, Inkle is saved by Yarico, a 'Person of Distinction', who hides him and feeds him. The two are drawn to

---

[3] The sexual relations between European men and foreign women 'drew from the narrative arcs of the classical tales of Jason and Medea as well as Dido and Aeneas, myths that inspired audiences' sympathy for the abandoned woman'. Eastman (2012), 142.

[4] On Inkle and Yarico, see Felsenstein (1999); Kunz (2007).   [5] Felsenstein (1999), 40.

each other, they become lovers, Inkle promises to take Yarico to England and to dress her in silk, and together they board the ship heading for Barbados. The story ends abruptly with Inkle selling Yarico into slavery. Her protestations that she is pregnant are in vain: '[...] he only made use of that Information, to rise in his Demands upon the Purchaser'.[6] The story is embedded in a salon setting, as an oral defence of the constancy of women, against a man who states that women are fickle and willingly abandon their love interest as soon as the opportunity arises. The tale of Inkle and Yarico serves to prove that women are constant lovers, and it lays the charge of cruel inconstancy on men.

The eighteenth century saw a remarkable number of adaptations and translations of this story, and it also has precedents of note.[7] Jean Mocquet's early seventeenth-century travelogue is regarded as one of the intertexts, with its even more striking references to the Medea story. Mocquet's couple have a child during the Englishman's extended stay, and the English lover abandons the woman on the shore. When the ship is leaving without her, she tears the child in two, throwing one half after the ship, and keeping the other with her.[8] The horrendous conclusion of Mocquet's tale, and the infanticide, call for comparisons with both Medea's fratricide and her subsequent filicide.[9]

Yarico, who like Medea is daughter of the leader of this society, functions as the helper maiden, using her skills to save the life of the helpless male in the name of love. His offer of marriage turns out to be a false promise, broken as soon as he has achieved what he desires, in this case, safe passage from the wilderness. Carolyn Eastman's study of these seventeenth- and early eighteenth-century tales of intercultural marriages, including Mocquet's horrific travelogue, concludes that the purpose was not only to evoke sympathy for the abandoned women, 'loving, passionate, loyal' as they proved to be. Primarily, 'they warned of almost demonic revenge by spurned native women, thus cementing an association between indigenous peoples and ruthless violence.'[10] During the eighteenth century, however, the Inkle-Yarico stories, like the versions of Medea, increasingly make the indigenous woman a more sympathetic character: as her desire for revenge abates, it is the English trader (like Jason) who is repeatedly described as barbarian.[11]

The German poet Christian Fürchtegott Gellert explicitly referred to Inkle as a barbarian in his poem *Inkle und Yariko* from 1746:

---

[6] Steele (1711).   [7] On Richard Ligon's 1657 travelogue, see Kunz (2007), 29–38.
[8] Eastman (2012), 135–7; Kunz (2007), 21–8.
[9] Eastman notes the 'propensity of those tales to conclude with child murder'. Eastman (2012), 144.
[10] Eastman (2012), 145.   [11] On the inversion of the barbarian, see Albrektson, this volume.

O Inkle! du Barbar, dem keiner gleich gewesen;
O möchte deinen Schimpf ein jeder Welttheil lesen!
[O Inkle, you barbarian, as none before,
O let your disgrace be read by every continent!][12]

Not only is Inkle a barbarian, a designation repeated in several German eighteenth-century versions, but the whole world should read about him to learn a lesson from his conduct.[13] The language of sentimentalism is the perfect medium for this supposedly sincere exclamation of moral outrage. Humankind is seen as the overarching category, and the recognition of every human being is paired with a particular criticism of western greed, slavery, and the atrocities of colonialism. Cruel actions, it is inferred, turn the male European into a barbarian.

Melanie Rohner detects 'negotiations of the barbaric' in the German Inkle and Yarico adaptations of Gellert, Jakob Bodmer, and Samuel Gessner, including their French translations.[14] While there is still a tension in these new versions between the indigenous 'barbarian' Americans—in several versions they kill the ship's crew—and the European barbarian, who is driven by greed, this tension is ultimately erased in the romanticized transfiguration of these versions' conclusions.[15] Now Yarico's cruel revenge disappears, and Inkle mutates into a repentant husband, and in some accounts the happy couple even end up ruling over an ideal society, where money is banned. According to Rohner, these later versions relate directly to Rousseau's criticism of civilization by raising the state of nature, état de nature, to an ideal (Figure 1.1).[16]

The link between these Inkle and Yarico versions and those of Jason and Medea is strengthened by their shared sentimental modes of representation. Ovid's Heroides is an important intertext for eighteenth-century Medea plays as well as for the contemporaneous Inkle and Yarico versions in Britain. As Felsenstein points out: 'In the genre of heroic epistle, the emotions articulated by the disempowered female contain the potential to disturb because of the pendular process by which they reflect extremes of passion and hope in tandem with the most rankling despair.'[17] Offering a stage for the slighted

---

[12] Gellert (2000), 72 (our translation); Rohner (2016), 53; Kunz (2007), 52.

[13] Kunz (2007), 132–7.   [14] Rohner (2016).

[15] For example, in a lost duodrama, Inkle und Yariko by J. F. Schink (1777, music by F. W. Rust) Inkle's uncle intervenes and frees Yarico. Jörg Krämer kindly made us aware of Schink's version, which is discussed in Berlinisches Litterarisches Wochenblatt (13 September 1777, 578–89).

[16] Cf. Felsenstein (1999) on the happy ending of Colman's comic opera, uniting a reformed Inkle and a virginal Yarico in matrimony.

[17] Felsenstein (1999), 29. See also Wiseman (2008); Horowitz (2014).

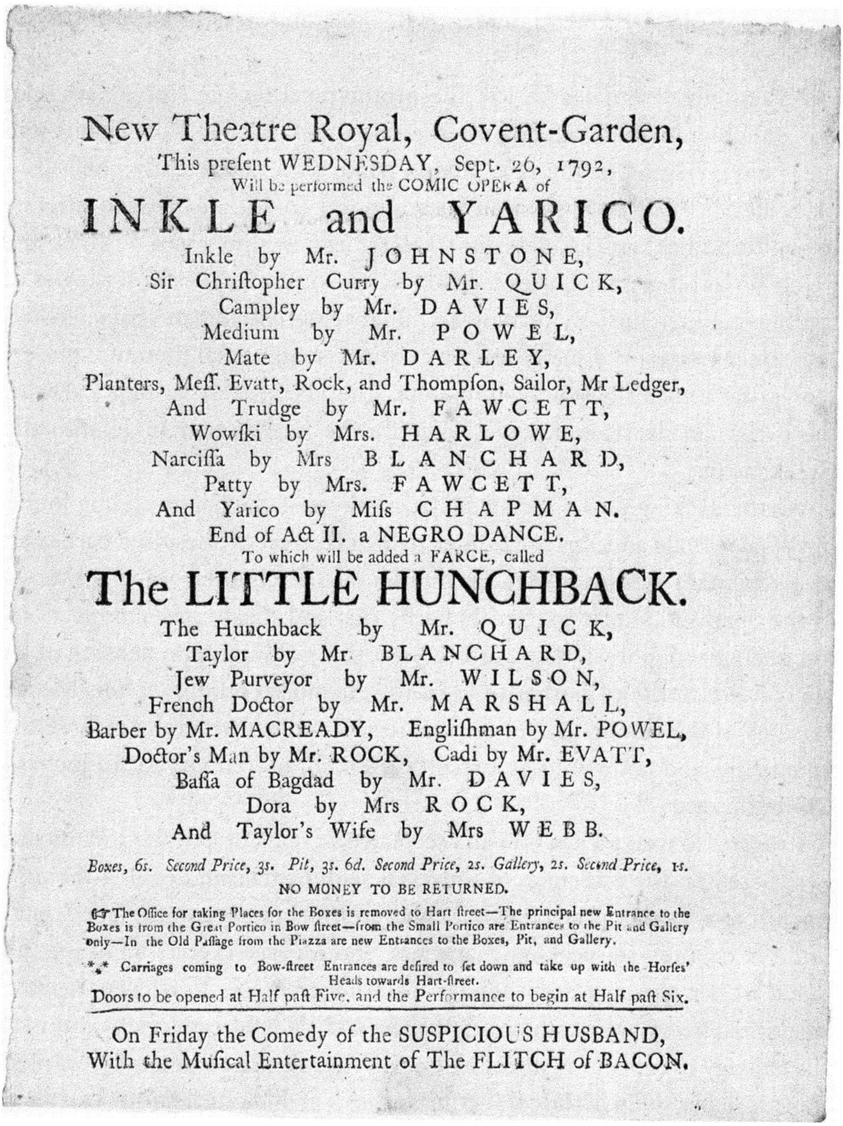

New Theatre Royal, Covent-Garden,
This prefent WEDNESDAY, Sept. 26, 1792,
Will be performed the COMIC OPERA of

INKLE and YARICO.

Inkle by Mr. JOHNSTONE,
Sir Chriftopher Curry by Mr. QUICK,
Campley by Mr. DAVIES,
Medium by Mr. POWEL,
Mate by Mr. DARLEY,
Planters, Meff. Evatt, Rock, and Thompfon, Sailor, Mr Ledger,
And Trudge by Mr. FAWCETT,
Wowfki by Mrs. HARLOWE,
Narciffa by Mrs BLANCHARD,
Patty by Mrs. FAWCETT,
And Yarico by Mifs CHAPMAN.
End of Act II. a NEGRO DANCE.
To which will be added a FARCE, called

The LITTLE HUNCHBACK.

The Hunchback by Mr. QUICK,
Taylor by Mr. BLANCHARD,
Jew Purveyor by Mr. WILSON,
French Doctor by Mr. MARSHALL,
Barber by Mr. MACREADY, Englifhman by Mr. POWEL,
Doctor's Man by Mr. ROCK, Cadi by Mr. EVATT,
Baffa of Bagdad by Mr. DAVIES,
Dora by Mrs ROCK,
And Taylor's Wife by Mrs WEBB.

Boxes, 6s. Second Price, 3s. Pit, 3s. 6d. Second Price, 2s. Gallery, 2s. Second Price, 1s.
NO MONEY TO BE RETURNED.

The Office for taking Places for the Boxes is removed to Hart ftreet—The principal new Entrance to the Boxes is from the Great Portico in Bow ftreet—from the Small Portico are Entrances to the Pit and Gallery only—In the Old Paffage from the Piazza are new Entrances to the Boxes, Pit, and Gallery.

Carriages coming to Bow-ftreet Entrances are defired to fet down and take up with the Horfes' Heads towards Hart-ftreet.
Doors to be opened at Half paft Five, and the Performance to begin at Half paft Six.

On Friday the Comedy of the SUSPICIOUS HUSBAND,
With the Mufical Entertainment of The FLITCH of BACON.

Figure 1.1   Playbill of George Colman's comic opera *Inkle and Yarico* &c

subject, voicing her predicament, and incorporating all human passions, the Ovidian epistolary mode resonated also with emergent dramatic conventions, notably monologic melodrama, 'She-Tragedy', and the domestic and pathetic plays of the eighteenth-century British stage.[18] A direct translation of Ovid's

---

[18] Hall and Macintosh (2005), 64–98. The anonymous reviewer of Schink's and Rust's duodrama in *Berlinisches Litterarisches Wochenblatt* lauds the expression of passions in the drama (and the

verse letter was even incorporated in Benito Rubio y Ortega's *Medea cruel* from 1797.[19]

Felsenstein designates Yarico 'the prototypical female Noble Savage of the Enlightenment';[20] and whilst the colour of Yarico's skin changes in the many versions of the tale, Inkle's white skin consistently conceals a black heart: 'Blackness, then, defines a moral condition that can migrate to white bodies and escalate into greater evil within them.'[21] Thus, the inversion of binary categories tends to be one of the successful strategies of sentimental literature. By turning seemingly external human characteristics into inner traits, in terms of vices or virtues, sentimental literature under-scores the universal view of humanity. The black heart is identical with the barbarian heart, and serves to unite the Englishman Inkle with the Greek Jason.

What is lacking in the Medea plays, however, is the happy ending found in the later Inkle and Yarico versions, which convert the despised barbarian to a repentant husband. Medea's murder of the children was considered in the Spanish context 'extremely barbarous and most cruel', 'too terrible, too uncivilized', phrases that gesture towards a colonial apprehension of an uncivilized world of barbarity.[22] However, most endings of the Medea versions of the second part of the eighteenth century generally include the infanticide, and not always as a result of 'temporary phrenzy', as in Richard Glover's tragedy.[23]

Struggles to turn Medea into an acceptable woman, despite her infanticide, were based on the principles of universal sentimentalism, defining the pro-tagonist as a mother protecting her children from an even worse fate. Scenes with the children as speaking characters, and Medea's expression of the full gamut of her passions, from tender maternal embraces to dagger-wielding infanticidal frenzy, were common in the second half of the eighteenth century.[24] The strategy of explaining infanticide as a benevolent act is noted by Marilyn Francus in her study of the conflicting versions of domestic femininity. When infanticidal mothers in the later eighteenth century could be designated either

performers), not least the natural femininity of Yarico, as a contrast to the shallow young women of his own surroundings, 580–1.

[19] See Lappin, this volume.   [20] Felsenstein (1999), 36.

[21] Nussbaum (2003), 246. On performances of Colman's comic opera and the use of facial blacking by white actresses, see Felsenstein et al. (2014), 691.

[22] See Lappin, this volume, citing Luzán.

[23] See Hall (1999), (2000); and Schweitzer, this volume.

[24] See Lappin, this volume, citing Rubio y Ortega; Cullhed (2017), 96–101.

'good' or 'bad', it became possible to interpret Medea's infanticide 'as an act of love and devotion [...] for it prevented the child from suffering', and thus integrated the tormented mother within the ideal of domesticity.[25]

However, Medea's actions clearly signal, as with the horrific depiction of Mocquet's Yarico, the dangers of intercultural sexual liaisons. As Francus notes, representations of infanticide served a specific aesthetic purpose: 'the reader enjoys the thrill and terror of transgressive acts, but ultimately the horror is explained away and sutured over.'[26] In most late eighteenth-century versions, neither Medea nor Yarico's cultural alterity is relevant. In fact, cultural differences are notably suppressed.[27] Both women behave very much as bourgeois European Christians, and fully support the idea of the sentimental family, envisaged as 'natural'. Yarico on the stage in the 1760s is routinely an embodiment of European family values and her role is routinely taken by European actresses.[28] Whilst Medea's alterity is signalled sartorially, her costume points to her magical powers and her connection to the underworld rather to any geographically remote area of the world.[29] Medea, like Yarico at this time, is deliberately domesticated as ideal bourgeois spouse and it is the barbarity of Jason, as with Inkle, that is underlined in order to provide a sharp critique of western civilization.

Medea and Yarico's outsider status is thus suppressed to such an extent, both visually and textually, that both become mirrors of the desired ideals of European sentimental femininity. Whilst the notion of a civilization based on cruelty and dissimulation inevitably brings in the perspectives of slavery and European atrocities in the New World, Medea and Yarico remain broadly universal 'women' rather than women from 'elsewhere'. Yet however indeterminate is the race of either Medea or Yarico, both women place the world of eighteenth-century global expansion centrally on stage (Figure 1.2).[30]

---

[25] Francus (2012), 80.   [26] Francus (2012), 80.

[27] See Svensson (2009), on the Swedish poet Lidner. She connects his *opéra comique Milot och Eloisa*, set in Batavia, with the Inkle and Yarico story. Her conclusion is that the cultural exchange is completely suppressed. Her interpretation relies on reading of Said, Bhabha, and Nigel Leask's discussion about the 'anxieties of empire'.

[28] Kunz (2007), 109–12; Felsenstein et al. (2014), 691.

[29] See Dotlačilová, this volume. As Krämer points out in this volume, Gotter's and Benda's melodrama *Ariadne auf Naxos* is one of the first examples of performances with Greek costumes, in terms of loosely draped garments.

[30] On the tension between temporal and spatial interpretations of the barbarian, see Vogt (2015). Vogt emphasizes the Christian temporalization of the concept barbarian, in contrast to the basically spatial contrast between Hellenes and barbarians (128–30).

J.M. Moreau le Jeune. Del.   *1780*   *N. De Launay Sculp*

Un Anglais de la Barbade, vend sa Maitresse

Liv. XIV. Pag. 525.

Figure 1.2 'An Englishman from Barbados sells his mistress', from Abbé Raynal, *Histoire des deux Indes*, 1780

The Medea Moment

This volume examines the surge in interest in Medea as a transcultural phenomenon, who functions in various local cultural contexts within the much wider context of Europe and its colonies. Just as in antiquity when the Colchian princess had to learn to become Greek, so too the eighteenth-century Medea adapts generically and morally as she travels to and through these different emergent nation states and their colonial outposts. But the Medea of the Enlightenment, in turn, transforms the lives of the peoples she encounters just as much as she did in ancient mythology. However, it is not just Medea's agency in this migration process that is significant; it is equally important to consider the ways in which the receiving cultures and her new audiences reshaped her within a process of cultural exchange. Medea's ethnic identity allows the tensions between nationalism and universalism in the Enlightenment to come into particularly sharp focus.

The contributors to this volume address the multi-faceted aspects of the revolutionary Medea, not least as a direct consequence of her transcultural iterations in the expanding world under European dominion. Such a study is only possible through interdisciplinary collaboration. It is deliberate that the two editors are an eighteenth-century and a classical reception specialist respectively, and that the contributors are scholars from various national literatures (English, German, French, Spanish, Portuguese, Russian, and Swedish), classical reception, music, dance, and theatre studies. The contributors have consulted a range of archives across continental Europe and Latin America and bring much rare material to critical attention for the first time. It is only by combining these areas of research—both in disciplinary and geographical terms—that any deep synchronic study is made possible; and it is only in concert that the challenging and protean presence of Medea in the late eighteenth century can be properly charted. The editors firmly believe that their respective disciplines need each other: eighteenth-century studies can benefit from the breadth of vision afforded by the diachronic lens of classical reception; and classical reception studies, in turn, need the tight focus and attention to detail afforded by periodicity.

During recent decades, the scholarly interest in Medea has been informed by new theoretical possibilities. A gender perspective, often combined with psychological approaches, has been at the heart of several studies, followed by an increased focus on postcolonial aspects of the myth.[31] Anglophone performance reception studies have also focused on Medea, notably in the publications from Oxford's Archive of Performances of Greek and Roman Drama (APGRD). The APGRD studies combine diachronic performance reception history with interdisciplinary perspectives, and a focus on Medea's iteration between different genres and media.[32] Within the German tradition of cultural studies, an intermedial perspective is similarly adopted.[33]

While these broad studies, along with specialized contributions within national literatures, have enriched the study of Medea, a synchronic focus on 1750 to 1800 offers very specific possibilities. The period is important as a moment of change and revolutions in the western world; and as a result of these transformations and convulsions—cultural as well as political—Medea was inserted, as we have heard, into a world of new encounters and within new cultural and aesthetic frameworks. The decades closing the eighteenth century are understood as starting points for a decidedly more modern society, and are regularly pinpointed as the moment of the formation of the modern self, the invention of humanity, as well as the establishment of a new gender system, and the beginning of bourgeois culture.[34]

Likewise, this is the era of aesthetic upheaval, ushering forth a cult of sensibility, manifest both in the novel and in other genres. The focus on compassion and sympathy was routinely contested, and became a target of satire from the outset; and the ethical ambivalence of the cult of sensibility has become an important area of study.[35] A cult of sentiment, together with new ideas of acting, and a renewed interest in Aristotle's concepts of *phobos* (horror) and *eleos* (pity), paved the way for the centrality of Medea in eighteenth-century theatre.[36] The decades under review in this volume witness yet another shift of focus in the wake of the French Revolution. The study of Medea in Germany points to a powerful critique of the Enlightenment idea of human perfectibility and sentimentalism, and uncovers a return to the mythical aspects of Medea. It is during this period that multiple prefigurations of the modern Medea emerge: a Medea who affords a close investigation of the

---

[31] Corti (1998); Stuttard (2014); Goff and Simpson (2015); Nikoloutsos (2015); Andújar and Nikoloutsos (2020).

[32] Hall et al. (2000); Bartel and Simon (2010); Macintosh et al. (2016).

[33] Luserke-Jaqui (2002); Stephan (2006).

[34] Habermas (1989); Outram (1995); Wahrman (2004); Knott and Taylor (2005); Stuurman (2017).

[35] Csengei (2012).

[36] For the new ideas of acting, see G. E. Lessing, *Hamburgische Dramaturgie*, 30. Stück in Lessing (2010), 331; F. T. M. Baculard d'Arnaud (1782), xviii–xix ('Discours préliminaire' to the tragedy *Coligny*), xiv, xxvi ('Discours préliminaire' to the *drame Le Comte de Comminge*), 172–3 ('Préface' to the tragedy *Fayel*); Engel (1785–6).

emotional range of a female subject and prompts the sympathetic response from an audience; and another, who invites an exploration of the workings of forces beyond the control of the human subject, as they impact both psychologically and ontologically on the protagonist, in particular.

The effects of all these ruptures on Medea are registered not only in performance terms; they are also present in the translations and scholarly readings of Euripides and Seneca, as well in as the popularized Ovidian versions of medieval romances and the enduring popularity of seventeenth-century operas and tragedies. In many ways, this synchronic space provides simultaneity as well as temporal dislocations as Medea's appearances in Paris and St Petersburg, or São Paulo and London, are compared. While Gotter and Benda's melodrama *Medea* premiered in 1775 in Leipzig, in St Petersburg its premiere in the early nineteenth century pre-dated the first performance of Longepierre's 1697 tragedy *Médée*.[37] This reversed order of the performance history makes the question of circulation, translation, adaptation, and non-linear receptions a key feature in how we understand the synchronic framework of this volume.[38] The second half of the eighteenth century can thus be understood as both a pivotal moment that itself entails moments of great change, and also as a period that allows for temporal ambiguities and disruptions. The inclusion of works that originally pre-date 1750 is often essential for the simple reason that in the reading or performance reception processes these texts play key roles between 1750 and 1800. By the same token, it is equally important to incorporate some texts from the early nineteenth century, where the imprint of developments from 1750–1800 are clearly felt. Thus, this fifty-year span offers the possibility of studying not only the neglected or often entirely forgotten micro-histories of reception but also the *longue durée* that is never allowed to disappear from sight. The revolutionary Medea is certainly dressed in corset and panniers, but according to the audience she appeared in 'classical' style.

The tight synchronic focus at a moment of revolutionary change reinforces the need to transgress national literary boundaries, whose very constructions date from this period of newly emergent national consciousness. However, the persistent shared court culture, the powerful concept of the republic of letters, notwithstanding the reliance on an itinerant cast of professionals, including musicians, choreographers, singers, dancers, and practitioners of many kinds in an increasingly bourgeois theatrical world, all meant that

---

[37] See Nikiforova, this volume.   [38] On non-linear receptions, see Ward (2019).

national self-consciousness was more aspirational than a given at this time. The career of Noverre, the choreographer and author of perhaps the most celebrated Medea of this period, offers a powerful example: he worked in Paris, Stuttgart, Vienna, London, and St Petersburg, to name only some of the venues where he staged his dance dramas before applying unsuccessfully for a post at the Swedish court towards the end of his career; and his works were translated into several languages, after first appearing in French. For this very reason, Noverre plays a prominent role in accounts of the French Medea, the German Medea, the Russian Medea, the British Medea, and even the Spanish Medea as she migrates across the Atlantic to the colonies.

Against a backdrop of emergent geopolitical boundaries, Medea resisted both restraint and containment. This volume takes its cue from its subject as it unsettles the borders drawn by nineteenth-century literary historians in their attempts to define national literatures as closed areas of study. Even today, most scholars are trained within national literatures in a specific language, and this volume transgresses orthodox frameworks in its attempt to produce a transnational study of culture.[39] Whilst rejection of national boundaries is at the heart of classical reception theory and practice,[40] and given the dominance in the period of both the idea of and engagement with a republic of letters, a synchronic Medea across languages and nation states grounds this mythical figure simultaneously within the local and the wider contexts. As we have heard, conventional, teleological narratives are often reversed, due to the vagaries of booksellers, copyright laws, and the hazards encountered by touring theatre troupes; and Medea herself is often re-formed as she crosses language, place, and genre. Further, a performance of any one version of *Medea* in London, say, is not identical to the same play in a theatre in Paris. What a synchronic perspective can afford is an awareness of the cultural specificities of each venue, be it a court, theatre, city, or any other kind of cultural space.

The many local spaces of reception in this volume bring out the multiplicity of audiences, and the divergent cultural and political contexts within each of these arenas. Medea found her way into courtly settings no less that she did into theatres with a mainly bourgeois audience, as well as into wider social groups, including those spectators who gathered to watch street performances of folk tales. The volume's aim is to capture the dynamic between the overall

---

[39] For a discussion of a transnational perspective on the study of culture, see Bachmann-Medick (2016).
[40] On the relationships between classical reception, comparative literature, and world literature, see the online APGRD/BCLA seminar, 'Receptions and Comparatisms', Oxford, autumn 2021.

contemporaneity of sources, and the variety of voices sounded in those sources. By joining eighteenth-century specialists from multiple language areas and disciplines, together with the reception perspective from Classics, we proffer multiple reasons why Medea entered the stage so frequently during the period 1750 to 1800.

The Mapping of Medea

The first part of this volume brings the Medea story into the contexts of the expanding empires of the late eighteenth century. The character of Medea intervened in an Enlightenment struggle against tyranny and ethical barbarity, and was routinely appropriated to address matters central to the political revolutions in Europe and in America. In many ways, Medea's presence on the stage served the purpose of framing global issues, at least from a European perspective. Her deeds prompted discussion about the need to demarcate the limits of the human, and, indeed, the limits of femininity, themes that were under constant revision in travel writing of the eighteenth century. Within a context of imperial expansion, as the Yarico and Inkle tales demonstrate, the question of Medea's foreignness and her presumed barbarity was equally a double-edged sword, at times explaining her abhorrent actions, at others discovering that the civilized Greeks represented an even more disturbing degree of barbarity than the supposed outsider. Similarly, Medea's fate was deployed as a critique of colonial oppression and alterity in the versions performed in Brazil and circulating within the Spanish empire. Simultaneously, the story of the Argonauts was invoked during the expansion of the Russian empire, thus turning Medea into a character used both in support of colonial endeavour and in critiques of the suppression of the colonial subject.

Poets and playwrights made use of this powerful protagonist as a cautionary example in multiple contexts. From Moscow to São Paulo, and from London to Madrid, her tale either reinforced or questioned contemporary rule in the eighteenth century and was enriched by intertexts describing European encounters with indigenous peoples. Whilst this is certainly a familiar story in classical reception studies, the very malleability of Medea in this period is unusual. In contrast to an evil Caligula or a virtuous Marcus Aurelius, a murderous Clytemnestra or a self-sacrificing Alcestis, the range of interpretations of the eighteenth-century Medea in this geopolitical context is remarkable. It is the aim of this volume to spell out how a number of these local interpretations of Medea functioned in a world of political revolutions and competing empires.

The eighteenth-century Medea becomes embroiled in different revolutionary processes, not least the print and theatrical revolutions of the period. Erika Fischer-Lichte outlines the struggles between the older precepts of court theatre, where the stage functioned primarily as a mirror of the court, and the ideals of the rising bourgeois theatre of the major cities, where the new forms of acting approximated to the theatre of illusion.[41] The superhuman witch of the sumptuous baroque stage was becoming less popular, and new bourgeois audiences called for stories and passions placed in a recognizable domestic sphere.[42] Medea could thus act as a cunning witch, resorting to dissimulation in order to reach her aims in one version, while being transformed into the tender mother and spouse of the domestic stage in another.

The generic range was also explored and extended during this period, as a means of finding new ways to display and arouse emotions. It is, from our perspective, not surprising that Medea is one of the protagonists of early melodrama, a dramatic genre combining spoken lines, mainly by one single character, and accompanied by music underlining, or contrasting with, the speech.[43] Together with the use of gestures, this genre was highly successful in the German-speaking areas.[44] Medea therefore stood at the forefront of both aesthetic debate and experimental performance.

Some eighteenth-century versions further explored the consequences of the cultural revolution, replacing the ideals of French classicism, or the spectacular baroque opera, with a focus on tearful emotions and on 'depicting the human heart', as Jean-Marie-Bernard Clément put it in the preface to his tragedy Médée (1779). This humanized Medea was confined within a sentimental theatre culture that abstained from showing violence on the stage. However, the violent aspects of the myth had to be handled within the structure of the play, even with a human Medea on stage. Was sentimentality, one could ask, a method of suppressing violence on one level, while displaying it in a far more disturbing manner on another? Or was it just a method of transforming Medea into a less complex character, by focusing solely on her predicament as a woman and mother?

Towards the end of this short, fifty-year period 1750–1800, a renewed interest in Medea's suprahuman aspects came to the fore, as in Klinger's and

---

[41] Fischer-Lichte (2002), chapters 2–3.   [42] Macintosh, this volume.

[43] For a recent overview of melodrama in the eighteenth century, see Hambridge and Hicks (2018).

[44] See the chapters by Hall and Krämer, this volume.

later in Grillparzer's tragedies. In the wake of the French Revolution, the conflict between woman and demi-goddess became apparent, and offered new explanations for the violent vengeance. The humanized Medea was, in this sense, partly succeeded by a counter-Enlightenment Medea who once again reclaimed her divine ancestry: Medea thus ultimately resisted her bourgeois confinement and broke out once more from the narrow dictates of western, Enlightenment typologies. Yet her exit from humanity also indicates a narrowing of the borders of ideal femininity, a tendency that has been identified in research concerning broader cultural contexts.[45] At the turn of the nineteenth century, it is Kreusa who claims position as the ideal woman, while Medea is cast as a monstrous and larger-than-life creature. Thus, each of the two female figures ends up representing polarized and restricted versions of what femininity could entail.

A focus on the aesthetic transgressions of Medea exhibits a parallel to her geopolitical aspects. There is a stunning range of possible interpretations of the character in the sources during this period: to the dynamics between the local and the global perspectives, we can add the dynamics between genres; and there is a very real sense in which the geopolitical and the aesthetic interact and are mutually illuminating. French neo-classical tragedy was increasingly viewed as an example of both arbitrary monarchical power and cultural imperialism, and was routinely contested, not least in German contexts, through the development of the non-courtly, and often explicitly revolutionary genre of melodrama. But a bourgeois Medea was never really 'Medea', the Medea of either Euripides or especially of Seneca, who recovers herself as she hatches her own revenge plot—*Medea superest* (Sen. Med, 166–7). The Medea who effects her own escape *ex machina* took refuge in the opera houses because the proscenium-arch theatres refused to allow her to flee on the vertical axis.[46] In the Spanish-speaking world, the bourgeois sentimental versions never managed to appeal to audiences; and several of the contributions to this volume explore the popular Medeas of chapbooks as well as of puppet theatres where the Medea of mythical marvels prevailed. In sum, these studies of a single and ambiguous character such as Medea allow for very specific examples of the aesthetic upheavals known from a broader history of European aesthetics and drama. In the sources under discussion in this

---

[45] The increase in scientific arguments in relation to the separation of categories, such as gender, or race, in the nineteenth century is also present in research on the eighteenth century. See, for example, Outram (1995), 95.

[46] Cf. Macintosh, this volume.

volume, the humanized Medea stands beside the divine Medea, soaring on high no less than plumbing the depths of human despair.

This collection of essays opens with four chapters offering broad perspectives on the eighteenth-century Medea. Edith Hall begins with a close study of the revolutionary 1775 melodrama by Gotter and Benda, a strikingly new and successful genre, and moves on to examine its reception as a travesty in Vienna, and a tragedy about the Colchians, by the German playwright Klinger, then working in Russia. Hall concludes by placing Medea in her native Georgia, which in 1801 was incorporated within the Russian empire.

Larisa Nikiforova takes up the baton and introduces the vicissitudes of Medea in Russia, including the performance and translation of German and French versions within the transnational court culture. Nikiforova also analyses prose versions for a broader audience, and Russian folklore with obvious parallels to the Greek myth. She highlights the significant ways in which the Colchian story was invoked by Catherine the Great herself. In the Russian context, current political events were scrutinized in the guise of classical myth, combined with indigenous legends, during a century dominated by strong female rulers.

Anthony Lappin's chapter extends the focus westwards, to the imperial Medea of Spain, Portugal, and eventually across the Atlantic to the colonies. It shows the enormous range of the representations of Medea on stage, including in puppet theatres, and lays bare the aesthetic preference for eighteenth-century versions that exploited spectacular stage effects. The sentimental Medea largely remained on the page, but in many ways to a higher degree than in other cultural spaces included in this volume. The sentimental Medea, when she did appear in performance, met with local generic modes, such as the *zarzuela*, originally a court entertainment including speech, song, and music that became a dominant genre during this period. The traditional separation of high-brow and popular audiences within the Spanish and Portuguese world intersected in performances of Medea, with the distance between metropolis and periphery anticipating in many ways the postcolonial Medeas of recent years.

With focus on the shifting use of the concept of the barbarian, Anna Albrektson continues to position the figure of Medea within the context of colonial expansion. Euripides labels Medea a barbarian, but this identity is pinned on Jason in several versions from the 1770s and 1780s, as a sentimental strategy enhancing Medea's position as woman and victim of male cruelty. The idea of the 'ethical barbarian' becomes a cultural commonplace within eighteenth-century literature. By the 1790s, Medea is translated once more into an ethnic barbarian in versions that abandon the Enlightenment idea of human universality. The interplay between Enlightenment discourses, colonial experiences, and aesthetic experimentations forms the context for these often divergent representations of Medea from several European nations.

The second part of the volume turns away from the geopolitical peregrinations of Medea towards a number of case studies reflecting on both the ontological status of Medea and on questions of form. Fiona Macintosh explores Medea's connections with both the baroque and the eighteenth-century sublime, and her concomitant failure to conform to generic and institutional norms in this period. The chapter argues that Noverre's *ballet d'action* is pivotal not simply because it was staged throughout Europe in the last part of the century, but also because it provided a radically different model for tragic drama. It was this new kind of tragedy, informed no less by Euripides than it was by ideas of the theatrical sublime, that enabled Medea's return to serious spoken drama in the playhouses of Europe and the Americas in the following century.

Jörg Krämer traces the multiple iterations of the German Medea, first in her 1770s guise as a woman with an inner drama, and second as divine figure, not only aloof, but also estranged from the human context in Klinger's tragedy of 1787. Krämer argues that the modifications to the German Medea at this time are inextricably linked to wider generic and intermedial transformations. First, Krämer delineates the shift from the unambiguous characters of early opera to the experiments with psychological interiority afforded by the development of 'monodramatic melodrama'; and second, he explores the rejection of sentimentalism found in the new tragedies by Klinger at the turn of the nineteenth century.

Petra Dotlačilová discusses the key, but routinely overlooked, visual means of representing character on stage: costume. Her close analysis of Louis-René Boquet's designs for costumes for Noverre's *ballet d'action Médée et Jason* (1763) underlines how much the new aesthetic trends of the century focus on the human body and its movement. Her observations on costume closely parallel Krämer's identification of an early operatic witch, in contrast to the humanized Medea of some decades later. The sartorial signs of the underworld in the early versions—mainly bats and magical symbols—became less visible in Boquet's later designs. The 1791 design presented Medea in her role as princess, woman, and mother. Dotlačilová's discussion demonstrates just how malleable and durable the specific cultural spaces and genres are.

Zoé Schweitzer's contribution brings French and British texts in conjunction with translations of the classics. How can the infanticidal mother be accepted within an aesthetic of sensibility? As we have seen elsewhere, the constant dialogue with ancient sources, with Horace's *Ars Poetica* and Seneca's tragedy in particular, reveals the adjustments made to Medea in accordance with an early modern understanding of translation practice. Schweitzer unfolds the ambiguity of the translations: they censure violations of *decorum*, both in terms of sexual references and breaches of verisimilitude. Further, Schweitzer argues that the elimination of violence on stage according to sentimental stage practice, in fact, draws even sharper attention paradoxically to the filicide of Medea; and it promotes, moreover, a concomitant taste for suffering. In this way, the double-faced aspects of sensibility in general are explored with help of the figure of Medea.

In Roland Lysell's concluding thoughts, the stage presence of Medea comes to the fore, in twentieth-century productions of the versions by Euripides and Grillparzer. With specific focus on the last years of the eighteenth century, and the beginning of the nineteenth century, Lysell emphasizes the return of the mythical and metaphysical forces in the play. He discusses the move from the humanized eighteenth-century Medea to Klinger's tragedies where the gods are 'evil horror forces', and suggests that these two seemingly opposing Medeas come together in Franz Grillparzer's seminal *Medea* of 1821. Here in this early nineteenth-century tragedy, it is both exile as existential determinant and the ineluctability of the ancient demonic forces that are foregrounded. With Grillparzer, Lysell suggests, the stage is set for the twentieth-century Medea, and her relevance as a psychologically complex figure.

These individual contributions collectively display the centrality of Medea to the period 1750 to 1800. In many ways, Medea acts as vector for the geopolitical pressures of the late eighteenth century, and the numerous performance versions inspired by her demonstrate how the events in ancient Colchis, Corinth, and Athens are reflected in the Enlightenment iterations around the globe. Medea both conditions and becomes the driving force in the aesthetic revolutions—and counter-revolutions—of the period. By the beginning of the nineteenth century, Medea's political and poetological range encompasses proto-feminist sensibility, emotional sensitivity and affect, the divine and the demonic, exile and alterity. The stage is now set for the entrance of a modern Medea—no longer idealized victim of the late eighteenth century but again the exile, haunted by demonic and material forces.

PART I

MEDEA IN AN EXPANDING EIGHTEENTH-CENTURY WORLD

2

Pushing the Boundaries of Operatic Convention and European Identity

Generic and Historical Perspectives on Georg Benda's 1775 *Medea*

Edith Hall

The place is the Theater am Rannstädtertor in Leipzig. The date is 1 May 1775. The audience of Saxe-Gotha courtiers, their honoured guests and culturally aspirational local citizens have gathered to witness the premiere of the new work by the Bohemian Kapelldirektor at the Gotha court, Jiří or Georg Benda (1722–95) (Figure 2.1). It is a *melodrama*, or drama using speech accompanied by music, entitled *Medea*.

The arrival of the famous Seyler theatrical troupe at Gotha means that the performance will be of the highest quality; they have only arrived there by accident because a fire has wrought havoc at Weimar, where they had been engaged previously. The troupe's director, Anton Schweitzer, has already 'catapulted German opera into a new world with his setting of Wieland's serious opera *Alceste* in 1773'.[1]

There is a particular sense of anticipation as the audience wait for the opening of *Medea* because Benda's first and previous *melodrama*, *Ariadne auf Naxos*, earlier the same year, had caused a sensation. Its text was written for the actress Charlotte Brandes, famed for her ability to evoke heartrending pathos, by her husband Johann Christian Brandes. It was in an adventurous new aesthetic form, *melodrama* (i.e. 'sung-dramatic', from the Greek *melos*, 'song' and *drama*, 'action'). The young Princess Luisa herself had developed a fascination with the new operatic genre. She encouraged Benda to write the music for Brandes' *Ariadne*, and she had helped finance the printing of the

[1] Bauman (1985), 18.

Edith Hall, *Pushing the Boundaries of Operatic Convention and European Identity: Generic and Historical Perspectives on Georg Benda's 1775* Medea In: *Mapping Medea: Revolutions and Transfers 1750–1800.* Edited by: Anna Albrektson and Fiona Macintosh, Oxford University Press. © Anna Albrektson and Fiona Macintosh 2023. DOI: 10.1093/oso/9780192884190.003.0002

Figure 2.1 Georg Benda by J. F. Schröter after a drawing by Jacob Wilhelm Mechau

text and the costumes.[2] But this time, even more excitingly, the role of Medea is to be performed by the finest tragic actress in the troupe, the 'overpowering, bone-chilling' Sophie Seyler (Figure 2.2),[3] whose art has been well served by the radically dramatic new libretto written by poet Friedrich Wilhelm Gotter (Figure 2.3), the court archivist.

Benda's *Medea* is one of the more significant musical-theatre realizations of the ancient myth given canonical form by Euripides more than two thousand years earlier. It marked a pivotal moment, during a powerful transnational dialogue on the European continent, about the future form of serious musical theatre. Investigating Benda's *Medea* will lead us on an intricate journey linking France, Germany, Italy, Britain, Austria, and Russia. Several powerful women are involved in this story, besides those actresses Charlotte Brandes and Sophie Seyler; they include the last Holy Roman Empress, Maria Theresa of Austria, and Tsarina Catherine the Great of Russia.

---

[2] Istel (1906), 8, where he also quotes Brandes as writing that Luisa had a particular interest in 'diese neue Gattung Schauspiele'.

[3] Bauman (1985), 115.

Figure 2.2 Sophie Seyler as Merope (1775)

This chapter explores several ways in which Benda's melodrama marked a moment of transition. It stands at or near the head of important cultural developments: in the artistic representation of the psychological intensity of this classical heroine's experience as she works herself up for murder; in its use of the spoken voice in new experimental genres that combine multiple media; in the context of the emergence of the vogue for burlesques of Greek tragedy; and finally, less directly, in the return of Medea, one of the most important of all ancient heroines in opera, to her homeland south of the Caucasian mountains.

Tragedy to Melodrama

First, let us look backwards rather than forwards to keep our focus on the barbarian Medea's ethnicity. She emerged in archaic Greek literature as the foreign wife who aided Jason of Iolcus, when he was sent on the terrifying quest for the Golden Fleece to her homeland on the edge of the known world. The journey took him up the River Phasis, now the Rioni, in Colchis, now western Georgia. She escaped from Colchis with him and returned after many adventures to Greece, where they were forced to settle as exiles in Corinth. There he betrayed her, and undertook a new marriage to the local princess, daughter of the Corinthian king, who is in other, later sources named Creusa.

It was Euripides' tragedy of 431 BCE that dramatized Medea's revenge killing of both the princess and her own two sons, while exploring her psychological journey into the heart of darkness through extraordinary monologues.

Figure 2.3 Friedrich Wilhelm Gotter, engraving by Ernst Ludwig Riepenhausen

And Euripides' tragedy was performed to an audience some of whom had sailed the Black Sea, had met Colchians, and even possessed Colchian slaves in Athens. Some had traded in and eastward of Crimea using hybrid Phasian-Greek coinage, which used the myths involving Colchis as national emblems. Some had seen the fabulously intricate goldwork of the Colchians, including complicated coronets like the one Medea sends, complete with a mechanism for releasing poison, as a wedding present to her rival.[4]

Benda, like many of his contemporary composers and musicians, was originally from Bohemia. He had been sent to Italy by Duke Friedrich III of Saxe-Gotha in 1756 precisely in order to immerse himself in the operatic traditions of Italy and France—Baldassare Galuppi, Tommaso Traetta, Niccolò Piccinni, Giovanni Paisiello, and Christoph Willibald Gluck. The court of the current Duke, the cultured Ernst II, was known for its progressive taste for all things French.[5] But the unexpected arrival of the Seyler troupe, which was soon to become the primary agent for change in the German opera scene of the late eighteenth century, encouraged Benda to compose innovative stage works in the German language.

The new genre of the melodrama was the talk of musical circles in France and Germany at this time. Its genealogy is at least threefold. First, choosing a classical myth such as those of Ariadne and Medea signalled the composer's sense of an aesthetic ancestry extending back to the ancient Greeks. Ever since the founding fathers of opera in the Florentine Camerata had looked to ancient myth, and above all what they mistakenly believed to have been the all-sung form taken by ancient theatrical tragic performances, ancient myth and ancient tragedy had played a crucial role in experiments with all forms of theatre, both musical and spoken. Ancient pantomime or silent danced realization of tragic myth had played an equally seminal role in the emergence of *ballet d'action* (see Macintosh, this volume). Moreover, as Erika Fischer-Lichte has argued, the most familiar classical tragedies have always been favoured when composers and playwrights have wanted to make avant-garde statements about their art or experiment in form.[6]

Second, musically speaking, the principal musical models informing Benda's new use of the spoken word in alignment with music were the two types of baroque recitative accompanied by orchestra rather than just a bass continuo, the *recitativo obbligato* or *stromentato* which used expressive, often very dramatic orchestral interjections, and the calmer, more sustained 'accompanied

---

[4] Hall (2018).   [5] Bauman (1985), 111–12.   [6] Fischer-Lichte (2004).

recitative' (*recitativo accompagnato*). These types of recitative had already become much more sophisticated at the hands of Niccolò Jommelli and Traetta.

Third, poetically speaking, the reflective monologue exploring the subjectivity and interiority of the leading characters, especially female ones, was an influence from French classical tragedy, and therefore ultimately from the private monologues and declamations of ancient Greek and Senecan Latin tragedy which Racine had studied so intently. Over in France, Gluck, who had likewise been brought up in Bohemia, was also experimenting with the relationship between word and music in opera, a project which found fullest consummation in his 1779 *Iphigénie en Tauride*.[7] He sought to emphasize the organic relationship of speech and melody, to create a new aural medium in which neither music nor poetry dominated the other, but rather were complementary. In so doing, he did many things to the parts for the singers analogous to Benda's melodramas. But Gluck retained the chorus and he did so without dispensing wholesale with melody. He discarded castrati and coloratura, wrote clean, singable melodic lines, and banned his singers from using their favourite ornaments like the short passing notes (*appoggiatura*), which broke up the sustained hold on the notes he had written for them.[8] He insisted on simple language without flights of artificial rhetoric or estranging elevation, and, like Benda, thought hard about how music could underline the emotion that the singer was expressing.

Both composers were responding, though differently, to the call for the 'return' to the Greek model recommended in the unofficial manifesto of the operatic reform movement, the polymath Francesco Algarotti's *Saggio sopra l'opera in musica* (1755). Algarotti wrote that if composers followed his advice,

> Then would the Opera be no longer called an irrational, monstrous and grotesque composition: on the contrary, it would display a lively image of the Grecian tragedy, in which, architecture, poetry, music, dancing, and every kind of theatrical apparatus united their efforts to create an illusion of such resistless power over the human mind, that from the combination of a thousand pleasures, formed so extraordinary a one, as in our world has nothing to equal it.[9]

Algarotti's perceived insistence on the classical Greek cultural model was celebrated in the engraving that appeared as a head-piece to his collected

[7] See Hall (2013), 183–205.   [8] Delsarte in Delaumosne (1893) 'Part Fourth'.
[9] Algarotti (1767), 108–9.

works (1791–4). Alongside the theatre masks and the musical instruments, his name is inscribed in ancient Greek letters to symbolize his life's work. His name is not these days very familiar outside specialist eighteenth-century circles, but his contribution to the history of opera, by recommending its reform through a return to the simplicity of Greek tragedy and its persuasive 'total theatre', lay behind all the innovations and experiments in opera in the 1770s.

However, in the case of Benda's *Medea*, that return to the Greeks was additionally complemented by the way in which the three ancient *Roman* innovations in tragic performance also informed the total performance style and experience. Declamation, *tragoedia saltata* or pantomime, and *tragoedia cantata* or solo lyric performance,[10] fuse with Gotter's psychological reading of Euripides' heroine to create a hair-raising new type of tragic voice. 'In this piece', wrote the *deutsche Merkur*, 'Madame Seyler exhausts her whole art of declamation and pantomime'.

Other reviews were equally effusive. Seyler's Medea was very real, and with her true, affective speech she was said to surpass everything that one can say in her praise. She was thought to have brought varieties of volume that penetrated the marrow to make the blood congeal and curdle. She was considered outstanding in the furious passages; and her elevated, noble style, comprehension and feeling, *Empfindung*, were much admired.

Benda's speciality was the effect produced by alternating short sections delivered by instruments and by the spoken voice: for example, at the very beginning of the opera where Medea addresses her house, herself, and the goddess Juno with mounting emotion. Benda only sporadically fuses music and text simultaneously, as for example when Medea talks about *Rache* (revenge) in her opening recitative. At bars 1026–1116 of the full score, he uses poignant, minor arpeggios on the violin when she is remembering her homeland and family. Each burst of highly descriptive music anticipates the emotional content of the short speech that follows it. In one of the climactic moments, music and speech unfold simultaneously, with the music following the flow of the text in such a way that the changes in harmony coincide with crucial words such as 'death', 'sufferings', and 'lightning bolts'.[11]

The piece was emotionally stunning and received instant celebrity.[12] The young composer Christian Gottlob Neefe exclaimed of Benda's two classical melodramas: 'How everything is so new and still so true'.[13] And the aesthetic

---

[10] On all of which, see Hall (2002).
[11] On the interplay of text, music, and gesture, see Betzweiser (2018).
[12] Hodermann (1894), 13–14.   [13] *Theater-Journal für Deutschland* 1777, no. 1, 75.

impact of their popularity was to prove enduring. In *Ariadne* there had been imitations of the sounds of nature to create the atmosphere of Naxos, but in *Medea* the musical effects are directed intensively towards suggesting Medea's tortured psychological journey. The prayer to Hekate, for example, works up to a loud climax where her voice is sounded simultaneously with orchestra and rhythmically closely aligned with it.

Benda's *Medea* marks a new height in the representation of Medea's tortured psyche. As Yixu Lü has shown, earlier German stagings of her myth had gone nowhere near as deeply into the fluctuations of her emotions, which clearly reflect the new aesthetic of *Sturm und Drang* and anticipate the full-blown subjectivities to be explored by Romantic poets and composers. Most, including a *Singspiel* performed at the Rudolstadt court in 1752, had been based on Corneille's 1635 tragedy *Médée*, which had little interest in Medea's consciousness or conscience.[14] The exception had been the ballet *Médée et Jason* choreographed by Jean-Georges Noverre and scored by Jean-Joseph Rodolphe, which despite its French creators had actually premiered at Stuttgart in 1763. It was performed there as an interlude following the first act of *Didone abbandonata*, an enormous opera by Niccolò Jommelli. Lü argues that this *ballet d'action* created the hunger amongst German audiences for a more emotionally developed Medea suited to their taste for *Zärtlichkeit*, the German equivalent of *tendresse*, and yearning for depictions of maternal souls locked in crisis.

Benda's melodrama was certainly an instant hit. It then retained its popularity for twenty-six text editions and more than twenty scores were published between 1775 and 1812.[15] The German conception of Medea never looked back, either. Soon afterwards, there came Friedrich Maximilian Klinger's emotionally tempestuous tragedies *Medea in Korinth* (1787) and *Medea auf dem Kaukasos* (1791). Since Benda, the German-speaking Medea has never, emotionally and expressively speaking, looked back.

But Benda's melodramas also affected the use of the spoken voice in opera on all kinds of themes, not only Medea, permanently. Mozart loved *Medea* after seeing two performances in Mannheim in late 1778. He wrote to his father:

Nothing has ever surprised me so much, for I had always imagined that such a piece would be quite ineffective! You know, of course, that there is no singing in it, only recitation, to which the music is like a sort of obbligato

---

[14] Lü (2010), 148–50.   [15] Lü (2010), 148 with n.1.

accompaniment to a recitative. Now and then words are spoken while the music goes on, and this produces the finest effect.[16]

Mozart carried around Benda's classical melodramas and intended to write a melodrama himself, starring another ancient heroine, the Babylonian queen Semiramis, on whom Voltaire had written a famous tragedy in 1748. But Mozart either never started or never completed *Semiramis*.

Where his fascination with melodrama does emerge is in two sections of *Zaide*, the unfinished *Singspiel*. He may have realized that melodrama, if used throughout a work, might be too restrictive, but that interesting effects might be achieved by occasional passages introduced for specific effects within an opera. In one of the *Zaide* passages, the slave Gomatz is attempting unsuccessfully to sleep. As he begins to drift off, he is accompanied by a calming melody on the oboe, but his distress is represented in phrases from the orchestra which are harshly syncopated. In the second melodramatic section of *Zaide*, the orchestra plays a tempestuous preface to the Sultan's angry aria when he discovers that Zaide has escaped from the harem.

The influence of melodrama extends into the new century. In *Fidelio* (1805), for example, Beethoven prepared his audience for the climactic scene in which Leonore is required to dig her own husband Florestan's grave with a short melodramatic sequence. The musical interjections accompany Florestan as he tosses and turns in his sleep and they also accompany Leonore's terrified shaking fits. In his 1810 music for Goethe's drama *Egmont*, Beethoven used the speech combined with music as Egmont pays his last farewell to life the night before he is executed. Schubert's melodrama, *Die Zauberharfe*, on the other hand, was a singularly unsuccessful attempt of 1820 to set music behind the spoken drama of that title by Georg von Hofmann. But the following year, in 1821, Carl Maria von Weber's instant hit *Der Freischütz*, regarded as the first great German romantic opera, with its libretto by Friedrich Kind, included the most important of early nineteenth-century melodramas, the scene in the wolf's glen at the end of Act II. Max is so desperate to win Agathe in the shooting contest that he stoops to black magic, and it is here that spoken German alternates with song and recitative in a stunningly dark psychological scene. Wagner said that he despised melodrama, but there is no

---

[16] Mozart, in a letter to his father, 12 November 1778 (Mozart, 1985, 631). In response to a revival of Benda's *Ariadne auf Naxos* and Mozart's *Zaide* at the Edinburgh Festival in 2005, Misha Donat, who had long been Senior Music Producer at BBC Radio 3, wrote a fascinating article for the *Guardian* on the future of the spoken voice in opera after Benda. My next section is indebted to his insights. See further Head (2018) and Betzweiser (2018).

doubt how much he learned from this scene. Wagner's musical roots, in many ways, can thus be traced back all the way to Benda.[17]

The tradition was continued by Wagner's arch-rival, Felix Mendelssohn, in his *A Midsummer Night's Dream* music of 1842 and his setting of Sophocles' *Antigone* (1841), which was fully staged not only in Paris and London but in Potsdam, Berlin, Hamburg, Frankfurt, Vienna, Dublin, Edinburgh, and even New York. The 'Mendelssohn' melodrama *Antigone* had numerous cultural consequences and played a seminal role in the emergence of the genre of classical burlesque on the London stage, especially burlesques of Greek tragedy, for which Benda's *Medea* is in many ways a forerunner, as we will see in the next section.[18]

There is a missing link in the chain of aesthetically avant-garde melodrama using classical mythology as a basis for the libretto. The link, as so often in the third quarter of the eighteenth century, is constituted by Jean-Jacques Rousseau. He had first staged his 'lyric scene' *Pygmalion* in Lyon after 19 April 1770.[19] It had been written at a key moment in Rousseau's life: his return to Switzerland after the banning of *Émile* in France.[20] It was enormously popular and performed dozens of times in French- and German-speaking countries, often using a new musical score: indeed, some years later Benda himself was to compose one, and provide a translation. These served as the basis for Goethe's production of the piece in the spring of 1798.

There was a production of *Pygmalion* at the Vienna court theatre in February 1772, followed by one with a score by Anton Schweitzer, the director of the Seyler troupe, performed at Weimar seven or eight times between May 1772 and August 1773. It was almost certainly also performed when the Seyler company arrived in Mannheim.[21] And it was the rapturous applause, which the actor Johann Böck received for his performance as Pygmalion, that inspired Johann Christian Brandes to write a similar piece for his wife Charlotte.[22] Although there had been occasional experiments with German melodrama before,[23] Benda's *Ariadne auf Naxos* is the first to intersperse the

---

[17] Bauman (1985), 20. For the wider context of melodrama from 1790–1820, see the essays in Hambridge and Hicks (2018).

[18] Hall and Macintosh (2005), 316–49.   [19] Waeber (1997), xix; Waeber (2018).

[20] Nielsen (2015), 68. Wokler (1987), 235–378 discusses Rousseau's revolutionary approach to music and the relationship between word and music, born in response to Rameau's theoretical writings and practice, especially in Rousseau's *Essai sur l'origine des langues*.

[21] Nielsen (2015), 68.   [22] Drake (1971), 1059; Nielsen (2015), 54.

[23] Nielsen (2015), 79 n.21. Johann Ernst Eberlin wrote the first German melodrama, *Sigismundus*, between 1753 and 1761.

music frequently between the words, showing the influence of Rousseau's *Pygmalion*.[24]

Why was *Pygmalion* so popular and so instrumental in the invention of German melodrama using classical material? After all, there had been at least five other productions before Rousseau's in eighteenth-century Paris using Ovid's evergreen tale in *Metamorphoses* X of the man who fell in love with the statue he had sculpted.[25] We know little about the premiere except that Madame de la Tourette played Galatea,[26] and that the show subsequently circulated among private Paris audiences before first appearing at the Comédie Française on 30 October 1775.[27] But in her penetrating article, Wendy Nielsen has argued that Rousseau's version did something no other version had done before—namely, remove the supernatural element and place the tale in the human realm completely:

> What distinguishes Rousseau's *Pygmalion* from other versions of the tale is that the sculptor brings his statue to life through the power of his own genius, thus secularizing the act of creation. Venus never appears onstage, and it appears as if Pygmalion's own creative spirit and genius animate the statue [...] the stage directions deal almost exclusively with emotions: 'he gets up impetuously' (209) [...] is seized by fright, feels bitter irony, and an excess of depression before she comes to life. It is a monologue except for the final lines of the play when she speaks her first words (198) 'C'est moi'.[28]

The fascination with the power of the human artist to use emotion to create and even procreate is profoundly eighteenth-century. Nielsen suggests that Rousseau had been inspired by the musical automata of Jacques de Vaucanson which had appeared in 1740–1 in Lyon.[29] That there is a line of descent from Rousseau's sculpted and finally self-sculpting Galatea to Benda's melodramatic Medea is perhaps also detectable in the statue's strident first words, 'C'est moi', which are strikingly reminiscent of Pierre Corneille's *Médée* and the Senecan Medea's '*Medea nunc sum*', from which they all originate.[30]

---

[24] Kravitt (1976), 573.   [25] Nielsen (2015), 71; Waeber (1997), xix.   [26] Istel (1906), 18.

[27] Starring Larive (Jean Mauduit) as Pygmalion and Mlle Raucourt as Galatea.

[28] Nielsen (2015), 71.

[29] Nielsen (2015), 69 and 70: his *Pygmalion* 'can be read as a critique of the materialist view of humanity [...] the lyrical scene underlies the ways in which music and creation allow the artist to express genuine affect'. Rousseau allowed readers of the *Mercure de France* 30 October 1775 to believe he had written the music but it was probably by Horace Coignet. It was believed lost until 1995. It was very popular and appeared at least 139 times by the end of 1799, usually with other music by Arnaud Berquin.

[30] Macintosh, this volume.

Melodrama Burlesqued

The impact of Benda's *Medea* can be also seen in the speed with which it was travestied in Vienna. This had much to do with the cultural direction taken by the court there after the arrival from Naples in 1792 of the very young and dynamic Empress Maria Theresa, the second wife of Emperor Franz II (not to be confused with her namesake, the famous Empress who had died in 1780). Before her death in 1807, still only 34 years old, the young Empress had left an indelible mark on Viennese culture through her enthusiasm for new music. The extent of her contribution as commissioner of new works, connoisseur and arbiter of taste has been meticulously documented by John Rice.[31] She supported many musicians, including Beethoven, Luigi Cherubini, Joseph and Michael Haydn, Johann Simon Mayr, Salieri, and Joseph Weigl.

The young woman, herself a harpist and singer, had a penchant for burlesques and parodies and above all loved the travesties composed by her court orchestra conductor, another Czech musician named Paul Wranitzky.[32] She owned private scores of his burlesque *The Picnic of the Gods* as well as his famous *Macbeth travestirt* and *Medea, ein travestirtes Melodrama*.[33] In the Shakespearean burlesque, first performed at the Theater auf der Wieden in 1796, Wranitzky cast the three witches as two tenors and a baritone, probably enriching the comic effect by the use of falsetto.[34] The primary humorous effect of the *Medea* travesty, however, was derived from importing aspects of contemporary Viennese culture and dialect into a high-brow historical or classical context. In a pioneering essay, Christoph-Hellmut Mahling has showed how closely Wranitzky's 1796 *Medea* parodied Benda's melodrama both textually and musically, while constantly singing bathetic references and modernizations.[35] The closeness of the parody confirms the popularity of the melodrama, which was familiar to Viennese audiences, and indeed was performed at least forty-two times in the Viennese court theatres between 1778 and 1809.

The librettist, who has not been identified but may have been either playwright Joachim Perinet or satirist Joseph Richter, is extremely astute about the style and conventions of the new medium of melodrama. The Viennese audience was expected to recognize that this was specifically a parody of Benda's fashionable *Medea*, but it makes more or less ludicrous alterations to the original libretto and adds some real singing—arias, ensembles, and songs by the supernumerary choruses. Instead of Jason's Corinthian palace, the

---

[31] Rice (2003).   [32] Rice (2003), 154.   [33] Rice (2003), 154.
[34] Rice (2003), 157–8.   [35] Mahling (1993); Rice (2003), 155.

setting is a contemporary Viennese tavern. There are some new added characters, and the catastrophic ending is averted altogether as Medea and Jason reunite, their children unharmed. The characters use Viennese dialect, with liberal scatterings of phrases in French and Italian. Above all they talk about Viennese food, which Maria Theresa, after her Italian upbringing, may have found particularly hilarious.

A sense of the vertiginous veering between Gotter's solemn libretto for Benda and the up-to-date, knowing, sly Viennese flavour of the travesty's script can be gained simply by comparing, as Rice does, the opening texts of each:

Benda/Gotter

Vertrauter Wohnsitz! Vormahls den Schutzgöttern frommer Eintracht, häuslichen Glücks, der unverbrücklichen Treue heilig! […] Haus meines Gatten, der mich von sich stößt! Meiner Kinder—ach, die nicht mehr mein sind! Unglückliche Medea!

[Trusted abode, once sacred to the tutelary gods of innocent concord, of domestic bliss, of unbreakable constancy! […] House of my husband who rejects me, of my children who are no longer mine. Unfortunate Medea!]

Wranitzky

[Wohnsitz meiner vormaligen Freuden! Vormals den Schutzgöttern frommer Eintracht und häuslichen Glückes heilig! O geliebter goldener Kegel! Wie oft fraß ich hier nicht gebackene Händl mit meinem Jason. O unglückliche Medea!

Abode of my former happiness. Once sacred to the tutelary gods of innocent concord and of domestic bliss! O beloved Golden Ninepin! How often did I eat fried chicken here with my Jason! O unfortunate Medea!]

The name of the public house, the colloquial *fraß* and the clearly hysterical reference to the local speciality of fried chicken draw attention, by ludicrous contrast, to the grave, impassioned idiom of the melodrama's opening.

The music does the same. There are plentiful quotations from Benda's score, interspersed with completely new material. But the opening is emphatically identical so that the audience would clearly be led to expect a travesty of the familiar Benda melodrama. There is more reeling, this time of a musical and melodic nature, between tragic orotundity and demotic, almost folksy, simplicity: an example is the lofty tone of the opera seria in Medea's aria 'Wart nur ich Krieg dich schon',[36] and especially in the governess' down-home aria

---

[36] Rice (2003), 157; for musical examples see Mahling (1993), 265–6.

'Mercket doch ihr jungen Herren'. Apparently to accommodate Maria Theresa's taste for toy instruments and amusing props, Wranitzky also added unorthodox instruments played by members of the chorus. These included not only Bavarian folk instruments but also the specific instruction that a roasting spit for cooking meat be used instead of a triangle.

Melodrama in Russia

The success of Benda's *Medea* was such that it reached Russia as well (cf. Nikiforova, this volume). There were regular performances of German operatic works by the resident German Company in St Petersburg from at least as early as December 1777. Although comic works preponderated, the first two German-language serious works known to have been performed were Benda's *Ariadne auf Naxos* in 1779 and *Medea* on 28 January 1781, at the Shliakhetenyi Corps Theatre. For *Medea*, the orchestra of the court was invited to assist, perhaps because it is technically demanding.[37] The significance of this particular revival, out of so many, amongst the very many other re-performances of Benda's celebrated melodrama, is that it provides another prefiguration of perhaps the most important new direction Medea reception was to take not long afterwards—and that is her return to her native land, to the land of Colchis on the River Phasis, or (in modern terms) western Georgia around the River Rioni.

Additionally, in a curious twist, the figure of Friedrich Maximilian von Klinger re-emerges here, the German dramatist whose tragedies included *Medea in Korinth* (1787) and *Medea auf dem Kaukasos* (1791) (see further Krämer, this volume). Although Klinger's tragedies were never performed, they illustrate the extraordinary impact that Benda's melodrama had made on the emotional configuration of Medea. A childhood friend of Goethe, Klinger was central to the *Sturm und Drang* movement—indeed, it was his play by that name which in 1776 had given the tendency its label. He also worked as playwright for the *Seylersche Schauspiel-Gesellschaft* for two years after Benda had parted company with them shortly after the *Medea* melodrama. Klinger went to St Petersburg in 1780 (a year before Benda's *Medea* was performed there), became an officer in the Imperial Russian army and married a woman said to be a natural daughter of Catherine the Great. It is likely that it was his viewpoint on Medea from Russia that enabled him to think up the fascinating plot of *Medea auf dem Kaukasos*, which restores the heroine, in her mature

---

[37] Findeizen (2008).

years long after the Corinthian debacle, to her Georgian homeland (cf. Albrektson, this volume). She tries to dissuade her compatriots from a wild cult involving human sacrifice, but ends up committing suicide before being sacrificed by them instead, in a clear criticism of Goethe's *Iphigenie auf Tauris* in which the heroine persuades Thoas to give up this cruel custom forever.

So, for a German-speaking author who knew Benda's melodrama, based in St Petersburg, Medea could be both an emotionally convincing and redeemable heroine, and an exception to the rule that Georgians are wild, primitive, and bloodthirsty. But those Georgians were about to begin to reclaim Medea for their own. A revitalized sense of Georgian national identity had already begun to emerge in the early eighteenth century with the establishment of the first Georgian-language printing press. The country remained dominated by Persian rule until, in the 1760s, Catherine the Great began to cultivate allies amongst the Georgians in her struggle against the Turks. It was not, however, until 1801 that Russia annexed Georgia and incorporated it within the Russian empire. They dethroned Georgian rulers, dismantled the state, and made Russian the language of the administration.

Catherine's interest in Georgia and the Russian annexation did, however, mean that the classical mythology of the ancient Greeks and Romans began to become much more familiar in Georgia. Some anthologies and studies of Greek myth began to circulate, and ancient authors began to be translated into Georgian via Russian intermediaries.[38] Medea's definitive arrival in the Georgian language was through the enlightened and secularizing *Kalmasoba* or *Teaching through Games* by Ioann Bagrationi, a three-volume Georgian-language encyclopaedia, which he wrote in St Petersburg after the 1801 annexation. Bagrationi sees the potential of the story of Medea and Jason as a story of national interest to his fellow Georgians, and mainly draws on Apollonius' *Argonautica*. It is probably the first Georgian version of the myth to continue the story of Medea beyond the Hellenistic epic and into the events dramatized in Euripides. He presented Medea as a victim and associated her with great tragedy. As Tea Dularidze has argued, Bagrationi was alone amongst Georgian writers at this time who 'even acquainted readers with Euripides' version, which Georgian writers normally tried to avoid'.[39]

---

[38] Many scholarly works were devoted to the study of these issues, by authors such as Korneli Kekelidze, Simon Kaukhchishvili, Ilia Abuladze, and Akaki Urushadze.

[39] Dularidze (2007), 30. Yet the mother who killed her children remained unappealing to Georgian writers and artists until the 1860s, when nationalist feeling led to a reappraisal of the ancient Greek myths about Colchis and Medea. The most famous result was a poem by prominent poet Prince Akaki Tsereteli.

Scholars working in Georgian universities including Tbilisi have recently embarked on an intensive enquiry into Georgian Medeas.[40] The acclaimed 1979 Georgian ballet *Medea*, based on Euripides' tragedy and choreographed by Giorgi Aleksidze, is very much in the spirit of Benda with its focus on the psychological depths of Medea, her anger and jealousy becoming its leading themes. Significantly, the critics considered the performance to be the first successful monodrama in Georgian ballet history.[41]

Via melodrama, and later via burlesque, Benda's Medea transports late eighteenth-century European audiences to new realms—of the mind with her searching interiority; sonically with her searing arias; and spatially as she travels across the continent with her new formal experiments, and finally finds herself back home in her native Georgia.

---

[40] In September 2017 there was a major international conference, *Medea in the Artistic Cultures of the World* organized by Dr Irine Darchia, which included fascinating explorations of the role played by Medea in Georgian culture more recently. In the 1960s, the celebrated Georgian director A. Chkhartishvili staged Euripides' *Medea*, in a production notably sympathetic to the heroine as a victim of foreign interference; an opera, *The Colchian Maiden* by Bidzina Kvernadze, later followed.

[41] Nadareishvili (2007). See https://www.youtube.com/watch?v=aX5pcaN2Zg8 [last accessed 15 February 2023] at 1044.

3

Medea's Russian Images on Stage and in Literature

The Politics and Poetics of Female Characters

Larisa Nikiforova

The literary afterlife of Medea in Russia has received scant attention and, in many ways, Claudio Napoli's monograph is the exception that proves the rule.[1] Napoli refers briefly to the first Russian engagement with the story of Medea in Guido de Colonna's mid-sixteenth-century *Historia destructionis Troiae*; and to the translation of Longepierre's version into Russian in 1819. His focus is on the ancient sources (mainly Euripides' and Seneca's *Medea*) and scholars' and artists' engagements with them; and he finds 'neither a real interest in the exhausted heroine, nor any attempts to understand her drama' before the 1860s, when N. Leskov's novella, *Lady Macbeth of the Mtsensk District* (1865) proved to be 'a complete reflection of the original Medea'.[2] According to Napoli, the general attitude in Russian literature is one of 'silence about Medea', with only occasional interruption; and the eighteenth century, in his view, did not play any significant role in this long history of silence.[3]

Yet in the eighteenth century, Medea did appear on the Russian stage. Her character often served as a metaphor for the transformative force of the soul with alchemical and Masonic allusions.[4] As Radishchev observes in the 1780s, this alchemical and Masonic-inspired soul is represented by the Medea who kills her brother and rejuvenates her father-in-law: 'the new Medea who is capable of dissecting existing images and creating completely new and beautiful ones'.[5] Comparisons and parallels with Medea lent new contours to

---

[1] Napoli (2011).   [2] Napoli (2011), 420.   [3] Napoli (2011), 425.

[4] On the alchemical interpretation of the Medea myth from the sixteenth to the eighteenth century, especially the rejuvenation of Aeson, see Wygant (2007), 37–47. On the role of alchemy in Russian Freemasonry, see Halturin et al. (2015); and for alchemical symbols in eighteenth-century Russian art, see Kleshchevich (2017).

[5] Radishchev (1941), 115.

Larisa Nikiforova, *Medea's Russian Images on Stage and in Literature: The Politics and Poetics of Female Characters*
In: *Mapping Medea: Revolutions and Transfers 1750–1800*. Edited by: Anna Albrektson and Fiona Macintosh,
Oxford University Press. © Anna Albrektson and Fiona Macintosh 2023. DOI: 10.1093/oso/9780192884190.003.0003

other poetic heroines as well: for example, Tsarina of Kazan Söyembikä, from the epic poem by Mikhail Kheraskov 'The Rossiad' (1779), performs mysterious rites in the sacred grove recalling Ovid's Medea from both his *Metamorphoses* and *Heroides*.[6] There are also numerous echoes of Medea in different contexts at this time, but they are scattered and often appear in works that have little connection with each other and have very different roots. In order to get some idea of what the Russians knew about Medea and where their knowledge came from, it is necessary to search far and wide. Greek and Latin texts were available only to a very small educated circle; more often Russians read German and French translations and adaptations because translations of both Euripides' and Seneca's versions into Russian appeared quite late.[7] It was the stage, by contrast, that proved the main locus for Medea's reception in the long eighteenth century in Russia—and all subsequent receptions of the Graeco-Roman classics in the first third of the nineteenth century are strongly dependent on her late eighteenth-century performances on stage.

Introducing Medea

Medea was first introduced to Russian audiences at the end of the fifteenth and the beginning of the sixteenth centuries as a heroine in the translation of Colonna's prose narrative *Historia destructionis Troiae*.[8] The significance of this translation is evident from its inclusion in the so-called *Illustrated Chronicles of Ivan the Terrible*, a ten-volume novel about world and Russian history with over 10,000 pages and more than 16,000 illustrations, which had originally been compiled in the second half of the sixteenth century under the order of Ivan the Terrible.[9] An abridged manuscript edition of the novel was published in 1709 and became a bestseller with thirteen reprints between 1709 and 1824. Since this Russian translation of the *Historia* appeared in the *Chronicles*, it served as a major source of knowledge about Troy in the long

---

[6] Kheraskov (1895), 51–4.

[7] The first full translation of Euripides' *Medea* from Greek into Russian (by P. D. Shestakov) was published in 1863. From 1863 to 1905 seven translations were published. In 1905 the first full translation of Seneca's *Medea* from Latin into Russian (by N. Vinogradov) appeared in print.

[8] Tvorogov (1971), 65 claims that Colonna's prose narrative (first edition, Strasburg, 1489) was translated into Russian *c.* late fifteenth century or early sixteenth century. It was 'accurate, even literal, in some places; it is a word-for-word translation difficult to understand' and so further revisions of the translation were made. There are four manuscript versions of the full translation in Russian, dating from the sixteenth and seventeenth century; and there are additionally five abridged editions, one of which was printed in 1709.

[9] Tvorogov (1972), 168.

eighteenth century and was far more significant than any direct 'acquaintance with Homer's poems'.[10]

Printed editions of the *Historia* did not include any illustrations, and since Medea's presence in the visual arts in Russia is almost non-existent, the illustrations of the sixteenth-century *Chronicles of Ivan the Terrible* proved an invaluable visual source of Russian reception. There are no ethnographic or especially ancient visual traits for the figure of Medea in the illustrations in the *Chronicles*: she is depicted like a Russian tsarina whereas Jason resembles a Russian knight dressed in chain mail and wearing a helmet. The scenes of their meeting appear sequentially: Jason performs his various feats while Medea watches from the top of her secluded tower; and there is even a 'bedroom scene', depicting Medea and Jason sitting on the bed (Figures 3.1–3.4).

Though the images seem formulaic, Medea has clear emotional features and each illustration shows Medea making a different gesture. For example, while watching Jason's feats, she waves her arms with glee, supports her head with her hands, opens her hands in a gesture of defence, and holds her hands together in a gesture of pleading.[11]

Another source for the images was Ovid's *Metamorphoses*, which served as 'an introduction to antiquity [...] as well as to mythology, which was a significant part of a poet's or even an ordinary reader's intelligence'.[12] Ovid's influence on eighteenth-century Russian culture was as extensive as the Renaissance reception of Ovid across the whole of Europe. The only difference was in the way the story became known to the eighteenth-century Russian reader and viewer. Among the earliest adaptations of the *Metamorphoses* was an illustrated edition of 1722, which narrates the main plot in 226 illustrations with short explanatory notes.[13] This Russian illustrated Ovid represents a fine reflection of the European Renaissance iconographic Ovidian tradition;[14] and it introduced the *Metamorphoses* to a wide range of readers and artists, including those who had no reading knowledge of Latin, French, or German.[15] As Llewellyn has demonstrated, it is highly likely that printed Ovid illustrations coexisted with the tradition of oral retellings. This is also likely to be true for Russian speakers,

---

[10]   Maslov (2010), 218.

[11]   A team of anonymous artists worked on the illustrations for each volume: one would do a pencil sketch, another one painted the details, the third would do the colouring. The illustrations follow the text precisely and resemble typical medieval icon paintings—one illustration depicts several episodes and often several different places, separated by mountains, rivers, or buildings and walls. The poses are typical and colours are symbolic. During the same period, masters used western European examples as models. See Amosov (1998), 224–45.

[12]   Berkov (1973), 88.   [13]   *Ovidievy figury v 226 izobrazheniayh* (1722).

[14]   See Kinney and Styron (n.d.): ovid.lib.virginia.edu [last accessed 15 February 2023].

[15]   Llewellyn (1990), 152.

Figure 3.1 Jason on the way to the fire-breathing bulls

since the first more or less complete translations of the *Metamorphoses* did not appear until the 1760s.[16]

The Russian illustrated edition of Ovid is a translation, and almost a replica, of a 1697 Augsburg edition. The illustrations in both the German and Russian editions are taken from the 1676 Paris edition of *Métamorphoses en Rondeaux*, written by Isaac de Benserade, and consist of engravings by Le

---

[16] Llewellyn (1990), 152.

Figure 3.2 Medea rejoices

Brun, Le Clerc, and Chauveau (in the Russian edition, there is no poetic text, just engravings and captions).[17] The book was republished several times and the engravings reappeared in new translations of the *Metamorphoses* from the 1770s–1790s. There are four illustrations of the capture of the Golden Fleece and Jason and Medea's return to Iolcus: first, Jason's sedation of the dragon (Figure 3.5); second, the rejuvenation of Aeson (Figure 3.6); third, Peleus' daughter; and finally, Medea watching the dragon turn to stone.

The first translation of the *Metamorphoses* from French into Russian, which appeared sometime between the 1760s and 1770s, didn't include Medea's story; nor did the first translations made for the Latin summaries of the

[17] Klepikov (1964).

Figure 3.3 Jason between Aeth and Medea

Metamorphoses for schools. The 1794–5 edition 'with remarks and historical explanations' by C. Rembovsky was the first to have a complete prose translation of book 7 of the *Metamorphoses*, which tells Medea's story in full, from her meeting with Jason up to her revenge and escape from Corinth. The Corinthian part of the plot is included (as it is in Ovid's version as well) rather briefly. Still unlike Ovid, who omits certain things, the translator explains everything: on return to Corinth from her voyage, Medea discovers that Jason has married Creusa; Medea takes her revenge on Creon, Creusa, and Jason. Pseudo-Apollodorus' *The Library* served as another encyclopaedia of ancient mythology, when it was translated into Russian and published in 1725, and subsequently appeared in a new translation in 1787.[18] Despite the fact that the

---

[18] Apollodorus (1787).

Figure 3.4 Jason in Medea's bedroom

plot is presented only briefly in the encyclopaedia, both the Colchian and the Corinth stories are included.

Russian Wise Maidens

In Russian literature, there is a love story similar to the Colchian strand of the Medea myth. This is 'The Tale of Peter and Fevronia', written by Hermolaus-Erasmus in the middle of the sixteenth century—around the time that Colonna's *Historia* was translated into Russian.

In the tale, *Knyaz* (a royal or noble Slavic title) Peter receives a mortal wound while fighting a serpent (the Devil). Fevronia alone manages to heal

Figure 3.5 Jason defeats the dragon

his wounds with an ointment, which she herself prepares and she makes the *Knyaz* promise to marry her in return. The characters' social inequality (a *Knyaz* and a peasant woman) is emphasized in the tale but emphasis on a woman's superior skills, in particular, was a novel invention in Russian literature. As in the myth of Medea, this tale involves broken vows, although in reverse order here. The *Knyaz* breaks his promise to marry Fevronia; as a result his body becomes covered with sores. Some years later, however, he marries Fevronia, recovers, and they are never parted. Fevronia's wisdom is shown by her knowledge in preparing the magical ointment, and also by her riddles and miracles that echo the tenets of Christianity. There is also a story version in which Fevronia is exiled by the *boyars* (members of the ruling nobility), and as a result of her wisdom and wit she is able to rescue her husband.

As Rosalind McKenzie has highlighted, 'Fevronia, a sixteenth-century Christianized version of the traditional folkloric Wise Maiden character, engagingly leads her prince successfully through trial and tribulation by dint

Figure 3.6 The rejuvenation of Aeson

of her superior wit and foresight.'[19] Russian Wise Maidens, like Medea, live in 'sunny kingdoms' and they often have golden hair (a substitution for the Golden Fleece). They demonstrate their intelligence by speaking in riddles, knowing incantations and spells, and by providing herbal refreshment. They have the power to heal and rejuvenate and help their weak male partners carry out several impossible acts, thus saving them from death.

Similar characters appear in Russian *bylinas* (epic poems) and folk tales, including Helen the Wise and Vasilisa the Wise (the Greek *basileia* means tsarina). The modern Russian reader knows these tales from childhood, and the long eighteenth-century reader was also acquainted with them. In Garila Derzhavin's poem 'The Tsar Maiden' (1812), the subject of the poem has golden hair, embroiders clothes with gold, and has golden rye in her realm. She rejects all of her suitors, but a foreigner steals her love (with a kiss) swiftly and unexpectedly; and the occasional eroticism notwithstanding,

[19] McKenzie (1998), 43.

the poem follows the general structure of the Wise Maiden tales. There were plans for the choreographer Charles-Louis Didelot working at the Russian Imperial theatre from 1801 to 1832 to stage a ballet entitled 'The Golden Braid or Medea's Youth', but they never materialized.[20] As the title indicates, Didelot had intended to compare the ancient Medea to a Russian Wise Maiden-Tsarina.

Love-struck Medea

Colonna's translation of the *Historia* not only introduced the Russian reader to the famous epic cycle in its medieval version, it also presented plots that were perceived as unusual in Russian literature at that time. The feelings of a woman in love are described here in a highly expressive way, strikingly evocative of passages in the *Argonautica* and very different from contemporary conventions in Russian literature. Indeed, this has been described as the first detailed description of female love in the Russian language.[21] Medea feels a sudden outbreak of passion, emotional shock, and inner struggle relating to her conflicting emotions; and the Russian translator represents the feminine as volatile and sinful, and in need of a man's patronage. According to the translator, women cannot be trusted: Medea's thoughts are in disarray and highly unstable; before marriage, she tries to understand her man's strength and as all substances strive for form, all women strive to possess a man.[22] However, all these feelings and doubts are absent from the printed edition of the *Historia* available to the eighteenth-century reader.[23] Medea's infatuation is mentioned without any extra details: she seems to offer Jason a sort of deal—she will help him and he will take her away, marry her, and remain devoted to her forever.

Engravings in the 1722 illustrated edition of Ovid show Medea as a witch, rather than a suffering woman. She prepares a magic potion, while lifeless Aeson lies at her feet as clouds of smoke rise from a cauldron. She sits upon a

---

[20] Glushkovskij (2010), 400.   [21] Napoli (2011), 415–17.

[22] *Licevoj letopisnyj svod* (2014), 35–6.

[23] Tvorogov (1971) identified the author of this edition as Fedor Zlobin; Rosovetsky (1994) concurs and convincingly attributes several historical-fantastic, adventurous, and fairy-tale novels to this author as well. Little is known about the life of Zlobin except that he was born before 1672, was alive in the first third of the eighteenth century, and in Astrakhan, where his cousin served as archbishop, and in Arkhangelsk. He was, most probably, a church servant. The author of the printed version of the *Historia* not only shortened, but also greatly reworked the text, introducing details about the power of the state, the honour of the tsar, and the causes of wars. He added descriptions of lavish ceremonies and luxurious outfits.

dragon-drawn chariot among the clouds watching Peleus' deceived daughters or the dragon turn to stone. There is only one picture illustrating Medea's agitation—'Jason defeating the dragon guarding the Golden Fleece' (No. 108)—where she stands in a group of women looking at Jason and she alone joins her hands in prayer.[24]

In the Russian translation of the *Historical Library of Diodorus Siculus* (1787), Medea's passions are controlled by the Olympic gods: 'Juno was angry with Pelias and wished Medea to ruin him' (Apollodorus, 1787, 45). This is what the reader learns at the very beginning of the story, when Jason comes to Pelias wearing only one sandal. When Jason and Medea first meet, Medea is 'infected by love' (Apollodorus, 1787, 55), after which she simply acts, without any doubts. Even in Rembovsky's translation of Ovid's *Metamorphoses* (1794–5), which includes the most complete description of Medea's anxiety and doubts available to eighteenth-century Russian readers, Medea still upholds the gods' will: 'Some god won't leave me in peace', she thinks, realizing her inability to extinguish the flames of her passion.[25] At Hecate's altar, almost having pulled herself together, she meets the wonderful Jason, and sees 'something divine' in him. She understands that she must help him; it has been ordained by the gods (p. 181). This weakens the existential motif of female love—it is not her choice, but rather her destiny.

Following Ovid, Rembovsky defines the difference between barbarism and civilization: Medea is in love with a foreigner; she is going to leave 'her savage father and his barbaric land'; she will, instead, live in a wonderful country where politeness and the fine arts rule (p. 185). In Medea's monologues, barbarism is equated with violence: Medea asks herself if she, too, does not possess a barbaric heart/soul: if only she were able to see a young, handsome, honourable man dying without regret.[26] At the same time, in a moment of uncertainty and inner struggle, Medea predicts her future fate: if Jason leaves her one day and gives his heart to another woman, 'he will die ungrateful' (p. 223). Befriending Pelias' daughters, she fakes a quarrel with Jason in order to complain about his ingratitude and in a way that again anticipates the future tragic ending.

Medea the passionate woman in love is thus presented in the eighteenth century without any proto-psychological traits. In Russian translations of the eighteenth century, it is her magical nature and her learning, as well as her

---

[24] *Ovidievy figury* (1722), figs. 108, 111, 112, 119.
[25] Translation by Rembovsky (1794), 181. All subsequent references to this translation appear in parenthesis in the text after the citation.
[26] See further, Albrektson, this volume.

role as instrument of the will of the gods in assisting the Argonauts, that come to the fore. These new features were important too for the political readings of the Colchian strand of the myth that emerge during the second half of the century.

Medea and the Mythology of Power

Before 1768, the few rare stagings of the myth of Medea were always political, even though there were no explicit parallels with contemporary events, in contrast to, say, the allusions to the Emperor during the Holy Roman Empire, or the Habsburg dynasty.[27] However, during the Russian-Ottoman War of 1768–74, the Argonauts and the capture of the Golden Fleece became highly politically relevant.

A notable example of the earlier generalizing reference was *The Capture of the Golden Fleece* (a ballet), which formed part of Francesco Araja's opera *Eudossa incoronata, a sia Teodossio II* and was performed in 1751 in St Petersburg to commemorate the anniversary of Empress Elizabeth Petrovna's coronation. The opera suggests that the audience should recognize Elizabeth in the character of Eudossa ('the tongue spells Eudossa's name, whereas the heart spells Elizabeth's'[28]). There were some easily understood contemporary parallels between the life of the two empresses.[29] According to the librettist Giuseppe Bonecchi, 'on overcoming all the obstacles of cunning, detraction and hatred with her innocence, virtuous Eudossa married Theodosius and received the title of Empress, which she proved worthy of, thanks to her goodness and other talents'.[30] The opera opens with a scene in the Imperial Palace and the final scene portrays Eudossa's wedding and coronation. Bonecchi created *Eudossa's* libretto building on Apostolo Zeno's drama *Athenais* (1709), with some changes and additions.[31] One of the additions was the ballet; and some years later, in 1762, the emblem depicting the Golden Fleece and the inscription 'Intended for a decent one' decorated the Triumphal Arch of Moscow, which framed the solemn entrance for Catherine the Great's coronation.[32]

During the Russian-Ottoman War of 1768–74, references became more explicit, especially in connection with the so-called Orlov revolt, when from 1768–70 the Russian fleet sailed around Europe arriving eventually in the Mediterranean, the home front of the Ottoman empire and defeated the

---

[27] Colavito (2014), 206–17.   [28] Bonecchi (1753).   [29] Luzker (2017).
[30] Bonecchi (1753), 3–5.   [31] Luzker (2017).   [32] Mahotina (2011), 11–12.

Turkish fleet at the Battle of Chesma. Images emerged of these 'New Argonauts'—alluding to the capture of the Golden Fleece and Jason's defeats—reflecting the recent military manoeuvres and the naval victory.[33]

Whilst many poems during the Russian-Ottoman War period portrayed Medea simply as Jason's assistant with magical powers, in several solemn odes, Empress Catherine II is allegorically compared to Medea. If previously Medea had assisted Jason with her magical skills, now with her association with the Empress Catherine the Great, the enemy trembles.[34] In Mikhail Kheraskov's 'Battle of Chesma' (1771), Jason and the Argonauts overcome obstacles by holding a magical branch 'craftily created' by Medea; now 'their branch, their hope, their god is Catherine the Great. She serves as a shield at sea and a fortress on land'.[35]

The preface to the ballet programme 'New Argonauts' (1770), dedicated to the victory at Chios, had a similar message: the Golden Fleece (victory in the naval battle) wasn't won with the help of trickery or cheating; rather, victory comes with the help of a wise naval strategy and the patronage of the Russian Minerva (Catherine the Great). The ancient Jason had Medea's magical branch; now, under Catherine's patronage, new Jasons are crowned with branches of glory.[36] Thus Medea has become one of Minerva's incarnations.

The Golden Fleece was thus considered a metaphor for the naval victory over the Ottoman fleet and occasionally also as a symbol of the annexation of the Crimea. The poet Gavrila Derzhavin in his ode 'Waterfall' (1791–4), for example, wrote that Grigory Potemkin 'had subdued gold-fleeced Colchis', referring to the annexation of the Crimea.[37] This intellectual manoeuvre was likely further supported by the stories of the *Historical Library of Diodorus Siculus* (translated in 1774–5), in which Taurida is presented as Hecate's (often said to be Medea's mother's) kingdom. This was also the last place visited by the Argonauts before they arrived in Colchis.[38]

Medea in Melodrama and Ballet

The Corinthian story about Medea, as a scorned spouse and child-killer, became especially familiar to Russian audiences, as poetical and rhetorical exemplars. While working on Aristotle's *Rhetoric*, Mikhail Lomonosov

---

[33] See further Hall, this volume.
[34] Vasily Maykov, 'Ode on the Taking of Khotin', 1769, see Maikov (1867), 59.
[35] Kheraskov (1961), 170–1.   [36] Angiolini (1770), 3; Nikiforova (2022).
[37] Derzhavin (1864), 469.
[38] See Hall, this volume for Medea in the Crimea; and for Iphigenia, see Hall (2013).

translated a section of Medea's monologue from Seneca's tragedy ('Now I am Medea [...]') for his chapter 'On the passion'. This was the first, and for a long time, the only attempt to translate Seneca's tragedy into Russian.[39] But theatre was the main place where Russian spectators could become acquainted with the tragedy of Medea.

Some elite Russian audience members had already seen different versions of *Medea* performed on the European stage. The portrait of Mlle Clairon as Medea by Charles-André van Loo is known to have been ordered by the Russian duchess Ekaterina Golicyna, the wife of the Russian ambassador to Paris.[40] Additionally, Nikolay Karamzin, when travelling through Berlin in 1789, found much fault with Luísa Todi in the opera *Medea in Colchis* by Johann Gottlieb Naumann. By contrast, in Paris, he admired Mlle Raucourt's performance as 'a perfect Medea' in Corneille's tragedy.[41]

On the Russian stage there were three Medeas—the melodrama, with Friedrich Wilhelm Gotter's libretto and Jiří Antonín Benda's music, Jean-Georges Noverre's ballet, and a tragedy by Hilaire-Bernard de Longepierre. Whilst the ballet programme was printed, the translation of Benda's melodrama remained in manuscript form and only two acts of Longepierre's tragedy were published in piecemeal form in the works of translators, poets, and playwrights. Thus, the Russian audience was not acquainted with the character of an avenging Medea through written texts, only through the theatre. If most European audiences watched these works in the chronological order in which they were written—Longepierre's tragedy (1694), Noverre's ballet (1763), and eventually the Gotter/Benda melodrama (1775)—Russian audiences encountered them in reverse order, with the most psychologically complex melodrama coming first and then extending its influence into the early nineteenth century.

The Russian premiere of the melodrama was in the German theatre of St Petersburg in 1781 and was in German.[42] Despite the novelty of the genre, or perhaps because of it, the single performance went unnoticed, as was the case with several other melodramas staged in the German theatre (including Benda's *Ariadne auf Naxos*, 1808). Gubkina explains this with reference to the specific patriarchal audience of the German theatre, who preferred comedies and *Singspiele* to tragedies.[43] According to Filipp Vigel's memoirs, 'audiences of good taste' didn't visit the German theatre: 'Pastors, chemists, professors

---

[39] Lomonosov (1952 [1744]), 450.   [40] Houssaye (1857), 414.
[41] Karamzin (1984), 236.   [42] See further, chapters by Hall and Krämer, this volume.
[43] Gubkina (2003), 125–6.

and doctors took the seats; their families took the boxes of all tiers; backers, tailors, tinkers occupied the stalls; their apprentices sat in the gallery.'[44] The melodrama received only one subsequent revival in the German theatre in 1808; and in 1819 it was staged at the Empress Dowager Maria Feodorovna's (Sophia Marie Dorothea Auguste Luise von Württemberg by birth) home theatre. There were around ten productions from 1781 to 1830,[45] and they were closely connected with the so-called 'Russian German' circle.

In 1802, Gotter's libretto was translated into Russian and the melodrama was staged twice in Moscow in Maddox's Theatre—on 21 and 26 December 1802. The performances were held as benefits for the married couple Elizaveta and Sila Sandunov. The role of Jason was taken by Sandunov (a Russified version of the Georgian name Silovan Zandukeli), whose younger brother Nikolay Sandunov was the translator; and although the brothers were born and died in Moscow, the family had Georgian roots. There are no sources confirming that the choice of play was stipulated by the sense of national identity or political context. But since Georgia was annexed by the Russian empire in 1801–2, the choice of play may well have been deliberate.

In Nikolay Sandunov's translation, the monologues of Medea, the lines of Jason, the tutor (here in the Russian version called Ifil), and the children all correspond closely to the German text (*Medea*, 1776; *Medea*, 1782; *Medea and Jason*, 1802). But the stage directions are different. Medea does not make her entrance in a cloud-chariot drawn by dragons, but stands alone on stage to deliver her monologue, which means that her magical nature is not apparent at the opening.[46] Jason does not kill himself on stage, although his last line 'My children! My dear children! I follow you in the darkness of eternal night' leaves the audience in no doubt that his death is imminent.

Ballet was added to the Russian version of the melodrama, and even in the poster for the 1802 performance it is called a 'melodrama with ballet'.[47] According to the stage directions, after killing the children, Medea sends the Furies in search of Jason, who subsequently appears on stage surrounded by the dancing Furies, who carry the children's bodies and place them in front of him (*Medea and Jason*, 1802, 25; 28). One possible reason for including the ballet might have been the popularity of Noverre's ballet and its dancing forces of hell. No doubt, melodrama was considered a suitable vehicle for the two actors, but it was decided to enhance it with special effects (although the

---

[44] Vigel (2000), 160–1.   [45] Vsevolodski-Gerngross (1918–37), no numbers.
[46] On the role of the chariot in the representation of Medea's celestial nature see Cullhed (2017).
[47] Chayanova (1927), 243.

manuscript makes no reference to Noverre's collapse of the palace, perhaps owing to the additional costs that this would have entailed).

The Russian premiere of Noverre's *Médée et Jason* itself had taken place in St Petersburg in 1789.[48] Andrey Bolotov, a writer, philosopher, and scholar, remembers the full house on opening night in 1789, and describes the performance as 'the most perfect of its kind' (Bolotov, 1873, 700). The ballet ran for a number of years—it was staged three to four times each year—and remained a box-office hit. At that time, the average total box-office earnings ranged from 400 to 600 rubles a night, sometimes reaching as high as 800 rubles; in the 1790s, Noverre's ballet *Médée et Jason* brought in about 1,000 rubles a night at the box office, sometimes more.[49] Occasionally, the ballet would disappear from the repertoire and then reappear: 'We have turned the heads of the Moscovites', Ivan Valberkh, Gasparo Angiolini's student and Charles Didelot's assistant, wrote about Moscow performance in 1808.[50] It remained in the repertoire until 1831, when it was finally deemed 'an outdated ballet with nothing interesting, but for a couple of worthy scenes'.[51]

In 1789 the performance was mounted by Noverre's student, Charles Le Picq, who had come to Russia in 1787 accompanied by his wife, Gertrude Rossi, a ballet dancer, and by his stepson Carlo, who later became an outstanding architect of the Russian empire style.[52] In 1796, another student of Noverre's, Giuseppe Solomoni, staged *Médée et Jason* in Sheremetev's serf theatre in Moscow; and in 1800 it was performed in the public Moskow's Petrovsky Theatre.[53] Le Picq's pupil, Charles Didelot, revived his master's 1789 staging in 1806; and two years later, Noverre's ballet was again staged in Moscow by Ivan Valberkh, who was Gasparo Angiolini and Charles Le Picq's student and an actor who had played Jason in his teacher's ballet performance. In 1819, Adam Glushkovsky, the pupil of Valberkh and Didelot, revived this version in Moscow;[54] and the ballet was therefore passed bodily from one dance professional to another.

The printed programme of the 1789 performance with parallel text in French and Russian (translated by I. Trediakovsky) has been preserved. It is broadly similar to the programme of the Stuttgart premiere of 1763 (*Médée et Jason*, 1763), but has some differences. First of all, there is a much less detailed description of the experiences and feelings of the characters. The ballet

---

[48] Krasovskaya (2008), 66–7. See further Macintosh, this volume.
[49] *Arhiv direkcii Imperatorskih teatrov* (1892), ed. Pogozhev et al.   [50] Valberkh (2010), 126.
[51] Vsevolodski-Gerngross (1918–37).   [52] Krasovskaya (1981), 265–6.
[53] Lepskaya (1996), 126, 134.   [54] Vsevolodski-Gerngross (1918–37).

programme—of a new and 'slightly bizarre' spectacle[55]—helped the viewer to understand what exactly the actors in the pantomime were performing. In the Stuttgart libretto there is a balance between the actors' actions and feelings, expressed by glances, gestures, and poses. In the Russian libretto, the description of action prevailed; in the Stuttgart libretto, by contrast, after Jason finally refuses Medea in scene 8, we learn that Medea:

> […] les yeux fixés vers la terre, paroît immobile; l'arrêt de sa disgrace absorbe, pour ainsi dire, toutes les facultés de son âme; elle est dans l'anéantissement le plus affreux, lorsque tout à coup elle en sort pour se livrer toute entière à sa rage.
>
> [[She] appears motionless with her eyes fixed on the ground. The shock of her humiliation engulfs, so to say, her soul. She is plunged into a terrible abyss, then suddenly gives herself over entirely to rage.]   (*Médée et Jason*, 1763, 81–2)

In the St Petersburg libretto of 1789 this text is missing; instead Medea immediately calls on the forces of hell to help (Programme, 1789, 8–9).

In scene 8, when Medea and her children appear at the celebration of the marriage of Jason and Creusa, the Stuttgart libretto reads:

> Jason est pénétré de honte et de dépit; Créuse est saisie de crainte et n'ose plus lever les yeux. Créon témoigne le plus violent courroux; le peuple consterné attend en frémissant l'issue d'un tel événement.
>
> [Jason is full of shame and frustration; Creusa, gripped by fear, hesitates to lift her eyes. Creon expresses violent fury; the anxious people await with fear the terrifying events to follow.]   (*Médée et Jason*, 1763, 84)

In the St Petersburg libretto of 1789 this description finds only a very faint echo in the phrase: 'La consternation se peint sur tous les visages' [consternation is painted on all their faces] (Programme, 1789, 11).

A more significant difference was the inclusion of two new scenes that delayed the conflict and augmented the themes of passion and doubt. The viewer once again sees Jason's treachery, while Medea pounces on Creusa with a dagger, her first attempt at revenge. This attempt fails but anticipates the scene to come. In the Stuttgart programme, the arrangement between Jason and Creon, who offers Jason his daughter and his throne (scene 2),

---

follows after the holiday scene at Creon's Palace (scene 1). Then Medea appears with the children, begging Jason to remember his vows, asking him to take her life rather than to pursue his love elsewhere (scene 3). A scene of Jason's doubts ensues (scene 3), and finally his feeling for Creusa triumphs (scene 4). In the St Petersburg libretto, between scenes 1 and 2, there are two more scenes. There is a mutual declaration of love between Jason and Creusa and when Jason hugs Creusa, Medea enters (alone, without the children); Jason and Creusa are embarrassed, whilst Medea again, as in the first scene, tries to hide her feelings and pretend that she does not notice anything and simply pretends to be full of friendly feelings towards her rival. Jason joins his wife's and his lover's hands, then *un pas de trois* follows, in which Jason and Creusa reveal their feelings, forgetting about Medea's presence:

> Médée convaincue de leur perfidie, s'élance, un poignard à la main sur Creüse.
>
> [Medea, convinced of their treachery, rushes with the dagger at Creusa]
>
> (Programme, 1789, 6–7)

Only then does the arrangement between Creon and Jason follow, as well as Medea's arrival with the children, before another scene of Jason's hesitation and the appearance of Creusa, who offers Jason a choice between Medea and herself. Jason chooses Creusa (in front of Medea) and demands that Medea leave Corinth.

This prolongation of the narrative in many ways resembles a modern-day melodrama: in several scenes, characters seem to appear at the wrong moment; in others, a short-sighted hero forgets about his wife upon seeing his new girlfriend—he changes his mind every minute. However, all these vicissitudes serve to explain the final act—Medea's revenge.[56]

Unexpectedly, Creon's room turns into a cave of demons and the audience watches Medea surrounded by Hell's powers: Revenge and the Furies give her deadly objects.[57] The collapse of the palace at the end of the ballet is widely mentioned in theatrical critiques of the time. For example, Andrey Bolotov

---

[56] The programme of the tragic ballet *Medea* has also been preserved, and it was published in 1804 in volume 3 of the St Petersburg edition of Noverre's *Lettres sur la danse*. It combines scenes from the Stuttgart version (literally translated without abbreviations) and additional scenes from the St Petersburg version of 1789, doubling the conflict. Here Medea catches Jason kissing Creusa's knees. Medea 'ne pouvant supporter sans mourir l'idée de l'ingratitude et de l'infidélité de son epoux' ['unable to bear the thought of her husband's ingratitude and infidelity']. Noverre (1804), 69. Creusa is leaning over her in an act of pity. When she regains consciousness and sees Creusa above her, Medea pulls out the dagger.

[57] Interestingly, among other eighteenth-century theatre relics, Ostankino Palace's exhibition (in Moscow) used to have a papier-mâché box, decorated with gold lace, and white, green, and blue

wrote of the 1789 premiere: 'I was afraid lest the theatre caught fire, due to the terrible scenery changes.'[58] Ivan Valberkh, who played the role of Jason and staged the ballet in 1808 recalled: 'Yesterday, Kolosova [Creusa] was nearly burnt and I barely avoided smashing my skull. Meanwhile I died well and slipped away from the curtains.'[59]

Longepierre's Tragedy

The transition from male-oriented heroic tragedy to 'She-tragedy'[60] with a suffering woman as the protagonist took place in Russia of the 1780s–1820s, over a hundred years later than in many western European countries, in the context of the emergence of female actresses, female spectators, playwrights, and translators of drama.[61] Acting in this period became more natural, the actor/ actress became a hero/heroine, and theatrical criticism as the evaluation of the art of acting came into being. But the main cultural result of the 'feminization of drama' in Russia at this time was the transition from theatre as court ritual and lifestyle, which was still true as late as the 1790s, to theatre as an aesthetic experience valuable in itself; the transition from theatre as a place of political and social representation, to theatre as a place where the viewer sympathized with the misfortunes and experiences of heroes and heroines.

Innocent, suffering heroines, victims of human injustice, all appeared in Russian theatre in the so-called sentimental drama from the 1760s–1790s. But there were only few suffering heroines from ancient tragedies at this time. Russian playwrights did not adapt ancient dramas directly, but through Racine or contemporary French and German adaptations. The 1819 production of Longepierre's *Médée*, with Ekaterina Semenova in the title role, appeared in this context.[62] At the end of her career Semenova (Figure 3.7) was renowned for her performances in both Racine's *Phèdre* (1823, translated by M. Lobanov) and Longepierre's *Médée*.

---

beads, which was one of the props from the *Medea and Jason* ballet performed in Sheremetev's serf theatre and thought to have been Medea's gift to Creon. Yelizarova (1944), 218.

[58] Bolotov (1873), 700.   [59] Valberkh (2010), 126.

[60] Cf. Hall and Macintosh (2005), 78 on the earlier 'feminization' of British theatre.

[61] Before the 1750s female roles were performed by men on the Russian stage and women appeared only as part of foreign touring troupes. Women dancers appeared in the Russian theatre from the 1750s, female dramatic actresses only after 1757.

[62] Semenova also enjoyed acclaim in the role of Antigone in *Oedipus in Athens* by A. Ozerov (based on Jean-François Ducis' *Oedipe chez Admète* and *Oedipe à Colon*, the libretto for the opera by Sacchini, *Oedipe à Colon*); and she appeared later as Polyxena (1808, in a reworking of Chateaubriand's *The Trojan Women*) and as Clytemnestra (1815, in Racine's version of *Iphigenia in Aulis*, translated by M. Lobanov).

Figure 3.7 Ekaterina Semenova as Amenaida

But from 1808–10, it was a French troupe who performed Longepierre's 1694 tragedy *Médée*, this time in French, starring Marguerite Georges. In 1818, the tragedy was translated into Russian (*Medea*, 1819) and the premiere took place at Semenova's benefit at the Bolshoi Theatre in St Petersburg on 15 May 1819. The play was performed six times during the course of that year and subsequently once in 1823, 1825, and 1829.[63]

The translation of Longepierre's version proved to be a curious example of collaboration: five poets worked together, each one translating one act of the tragedy.[64] Contemporaries criticized the translation and, as A. S. Pushkin pointed out, 'every father renounced his brainchild one by one.'[65] By the time

---

[63] Vsevolodski-Gerngross (1918–37).
[64] Delvig (1959), 233.   [65] Pushkin (1962), 250.

the translation was complete, the play already seemed outdated, especially with its long monologues designed for the French style of declamatory performance. The *Moscow Telegraph* magazine described the play in 1829 as 'a classic tragedy, which the public is very reluctant to visit'.[66] According to Pushkin, the tragedy's success was due solely to Ekaterina Semenova's performances. The audience was especially astonished by two scenes: in the second act, Creon threatens Medea: 'Ma patience enfin commence à se lasser, Et pourrait [...]' ['My patience finally begins to fray, and could do [...]']; Médée: 'Tu le peux; mais, Tyran! Redoute mon courroux. Crains [...]' ['So it may [...] but, Tyrant, dread my wrath [...]'];[67] and in the fifth act, Medea shows a bloody dagger and tells Jason: 'C'est de mon sang, du tien qu'elle est teinte et fumante' ['This is my blood [on this dagger], but it is also yours, red and steaming']. At these ripostes, the audience burst into applause.[68]

Longepierre's *Medea*, written in accordance with the model of neo-classical French tragedy, gives prominence to the political plot. Creon is excused for exiling Medea, as he has to take care of his country's safety. Jason and Medea's marriage is deemed criminal ('this marriage is followed by problems, despised by Hellas and rejected by the gods'[69]), while Jason's marriage to the innocent and impeccable Creusa is his catharsis—and the foundation of Corinthian fortune. Creon is tortured by those who want to avenge Medea and by those who decimate the Corinthian inhabitants. Once, he decided to be noble and hide 'the criminal'; now, he has to obey the requirements of public duty. The motif of Medea's exile, as her well-deserved punishment, appears in the text several times. But despite all this, the public empathized with Medea.

Semenova's Medea touched the audience with 'her sensitivity as powerful as her vengeance'.[70] In the ballet, the spectators sympathized with the innocent victim, Creusa, who is 'decent and humiliated';[71] whereas in the tragedy the innocent victim was Medea herself—'the most gentle mother on the stage', 'a miserable creature'; and on 'Watching her performance, nearly everybody cried throughout the entire fourth act'.[72] According to the remarks in the manuscript, this scene takes place in a dark room with only a table covered by a black cloth. The room serves as both a hall (the children come here, Medea talks to them) and as Hell's cave, where Furius appeals to Tartarus' power (*Medea*, 1819, 18). The focus on the star actress, on her ability to show

---

[66] Vsevolodski-Gerngross (1918–37).
[67] Delvig (1959), 152–3; Longepierre (2000 [1694]), 25–6.
[68] Longepierre (2000 [1694]), 80.   [69] *Medea* (1819), 5.   [70] Pletnyov (1822), 220.
[71] 'Moskovskie zapiski' (1810), 314.   [72] Izmajlov (1819), 329.

emotional transitions between tenderness and fury and make the audience empathize with the tragic heroine is very close to the perception of she-tragedy in the eighteenth-century British theatre.[73]

Different *Medea*s were performed successively on the same stage. In 1808, for example, both a ballet and Longepierre tragedy by a French theatre company featured in the repertoire with actors who knew one another well. The future Russian star of Medea, Ekaterina Semenova, and the best ballet dancer of Noverre's *Medea*, Eugenia Kolosova, lived together; and both had learned from Mlle George's dramatic acting.[74] From November to December of 1819, both the tragedy and the ballet were performed four times in the Moscow Bolshoi Theatre on the same stage. In February 1821 on the same stage, with an interval of two days, there was a Medea melodrama performed by a German company and a ballet on the same subject.[75] But the audience treated the three versions of the tragic Medea differently.

We do not know whether the audience appreciated the complexity of Medea's character in Benda's melodrama, but what is irrefutable is that the ballet was valued more highly for its thrilling plot and scenography. The impression on audiences was one of horror: Nadezhda Kaligraph as Medea in the melodrama was like 'a real Fury, belched by Tartarus, with infernal laughter, hellfire and hellish tears'.[76] 'We felt excitement and horror in our hearts', a reporter wrote of Eugenia Kolosova as Medea in Noverre's ballet.[77]

However, both acting and public tastes were gradually changing. A reviewer in 1810 admired how skilfully the 'dancers' faces' work (referring to Kolosova as Medea and Valberkh as Jason). And he did not forget to mention that without dramatic skill, without the ability to express feelings, 'silent action pantomime ballet turned into a senseless grimacing'.[78] The scene of Medea's and Creusa's fake reconciliation was considered the most impressive part of the ballet (except for the final scene with the palace's destruction). Here Kolosova demonstrated 'the pretensions of an angry witch' and her smiling face masked a horrible threat.[79]

The theme of otherness that remains in Ovid's reception doesn't appear in the tragic Medea,[80] nor does the theme of gender inequality appear at this time. Both do not seem to have been introduced to representations of the

---

[73] Hall and Macintosh (2005), 79–82. See further, Krämer, this volume.
[74] Valberkh (2010), 105, 118.   [75] Vsevolodski-Gerngross (1918–37).
[76] Koni (1840).   [77] Yushkov (1806), 14.
[78] 'Moskovskie zapiski' (1810), 314.   [79] *Vestnik Evropy* (1810), 314.
[80] Longepierre's Jason shouts to Medea in the finale: 'Ah! Barbare [...]'. Longepierre (2000 [1694]), 80. The Russian translator writes: 'Inhumane [...]'. *Medea* (1819), 25. See further Albrektson, this volume.

Russian Medea until the end of the nineteenth and the beginning of the twentieth century, when the first Russian translations of Euripides' tragedy appeared.[81] Before then, as we have heard, reviewers perceived Ekaterina Semenova as the embodiment of the ancient Greek character. Her admirers thought her profile resembled the ancient cameos;[82] and her interpretation of the role seemed to be the perfect embodiment of horror and sympathy, considered by Aristotle as the essential components of tragedy.

The Female Century

There is a gap now between the images of contemporary Medea in love and tragic Medea taking revenge. The story of the Golden Fleece has become the subject of adventure blockbusters—full of battles, exoticism, and wonders; the story of Medea's revenge has become a theme of several art-house performances aimed specifically at psychology and psychoanalysis. In the eighteenth century there were no such divisions and so the theatre was fertile ground for receiving Medea's tragic image—by both sophisticated and general spectators watching the ballet, the tragedy, or the melodrama.

A strong woman's image seems to be significant not only for eighteenth-century Russian art, but also for the art of living and governing. The Russian eighteenth century is often called 'the female century', as five of the seven leaders were women, two of whom ruled long and proudly. Elizabeth Petrovna governed for about twenty years (1742–61), and Catherine the Great ruled for thirty-four years (1762–96). In contrast, the men's (following Peter the Great) reigns were short, and uninspired. Peter II Alexeyevich ascended the throne at the age of twelve and died two-and-a-half years later of smallpox. Peter III reigned for six months and was then overthrown by his wife. Another name for the Russian eighteenth century is 'the century of the palace coups', as the women proved to be stronger and more determined than the men.

The 'female century' ran contrary to the patriarchal traditions of the government, which still went on functioning, despite the modern actuality of women in power. Lady Rondeau wrote a letter from Russia in 1733, in which she mentioned a dialogue between Anna Ioannovna and the Chinese ambassador: 'Her Majesty asked him: from all the things which differed from their own customs, what appeared to him to be the most extraordinary?

---

[81] Malein (1918), 37.   [82] Karatygin (1929), 199–200.

He answered: Seeing a woman on the throne.'[83] Thirty years later, travelling around Russia, Giacomo Casanova said something similar, without any reference to Chinese wisdom: 'Il semble que la Russie soit une terre de confusion pour les sexes: des femmes font de l'administration et de la diplomatie' ['It seems that Russia is a land of confusion regarding the sexes: women deal with administration and diplomacy'].[84]

Women's ability to take up arms results from what Wortman has called 'identity of the sexes and sexual ambivalence' in the scenarios of power of the Russian rulers.[85] He maintains that the Russian empresses managed to fuse together two images—of the conqueror and guard, the power of weapons and the power of mercy. Androgynous images of power manifested themselves in the fact that female empresses demonstrated male qualities and masculine behaviour. The empresses crowned by the Guard troops wore military uniforms, were given the rank of colonel, and liked hunting, which was a substitute for military amusements. Georg Christoph Grooth painted Elizabeth Petrovna as an heir of Peter I riding side-saddle on a horse, with a sheathed sword and a ceremonial baton (1743, The State Tretyakov Gallery). Catherine II in the portrait by Vigilius Eriksen is riding a horse with an unsheathed sword and is wearing male dress and heading the Guard troops. This portrait depicts an episode when Catherine in June 1762 went from St Petersburg to Peterhof to overthrow her husband Peter III (1762, The State Hermitage Museum). In this sense, there was a distinct allegorical likeness between the empresses and Jason, and between receiving the throne and stealing the Golden Fleece. Thus, an androgynous image of the empress was not at all strange.

On the whole, the life of Russian women underwent great changes in the eighteenth century. Instead of women's formerly reclusive way of life, common in aristocratic families of pre-Petrine Russia, public life and celebrations became unimaginable without women's participation. Problems relating to marriage and choosing a groom still belonged to the domain of parents or elderly relatives, but the woman's 'choice of the heart' was now also taken into account. Real fondness was considered the true basis of marriage in memoirs and diaries. Secret weddings and elopements also took place; though, for the most part, they were condemned. Parents and relatives often refused to help women who had married without their approval.[86] In the same vein, in his 'Rhetoric', Mikhail Lomonosov uses Medea's story as a cautionary example:

---

[83] Vigor (1777), 83.   [84] Casanova (1843), 285.
[85] Wortman (2006), 40.   [86] Pushkareva (2012).

'When the end is similar to the beginning: Medea and Jason fornicated illegally, they separated illegally and killed their children while separating.'[87] Thus, Medea's tragic fate could serve as an instructive example for daughters who disobey the will of their fathers.

One of the most illustrative examples of a love marriage and independent will, which was famous in the theatrical world and in court society of the end of the eighteenth century, was the relationship between the married actors Elizaveta and Sila Sandunov (Benda's melodrama *Medea* was staged in 1802 at their benefit performance). The young Elizaveta Uranova, in an attempt to avoid Count Bezborodko's courtship which prevented her from marrying Sandunov, asked Empress Catherine the Great to intercede—literally onstage. She agreed and the extraordinary event took place in 1791.

For a long time, divination remained one of the most important spheres of women's activities and influence. Faith Wigzell points out that the motif of fortune-telling and divination was not only significant in Russian literature, but also in the everyday lives of women. So-called 'home magic' was rather common, even among the westernized nobility. Dream interpretation, faith in signs, and healing with herbs and ointments were all women's activities.[88] Vasily Maykov, author of the first poetic Russian translation of the *Metamorphoses*—an ode where Catherine's patronage of the Russian navy is compared to the magical powers of Jason's assistant—named an old villager Medea in his mock-epic 'Elisey; or, Bacchus Enraged' (1771). She dealt in herbs, roots, beans, dried sparrows, and 'devil's fingers'. She could prevent diseases by chanting incantations; drive away demons; find lost things; and also eliminate the desire to write poems.[89]

Other evidence of women's magical powers includes the appearance of sublime images of priestesses and flying goddesses, which were a part of the visual and theatrical experience of the eighteenth-century audience. Images of goddesses flying through the sky appear copiously on palaces and the domes of public institutions, in the machines of the theatre.

The image of a priestess or goddess was also one of Catherine II's personifications. She proved to be the first and only Russian empress depicted as Minerva (see Stefano Torelli's *Catherine II as Minerva, Patroness of the Arts*, 1770; Jean-Dominique Rachette's *Catherine II as Minerva*, porcelain bust, 1783); as Themis (see M. I. Kozlovsky's *Catherine the Great as Themis*, sculpture, 1796); and as Justice in the image of a priestess at the altar shrouded in clouds of smoke (Dmitry Levitzky's *Catherine II as Legislator in the Temple of*

---

[87] Lomonosov (1952 [1744]).   [88] Wigzell (1998).   [89] Maikov (1867), 347.

the Goddess of Justice, 1783; Ivan Prokofiev's *A sketch of a statue on Derzhavin's ode 'Videniye Murzy'*, 1803). Like an ancient Greek goddess, Catherine is depicted travelling in a chariot to Tauris (see Jean-Dominique Rachette's *Crimean Journey of Catherine the Great*, 1787; Jean-Jacques Avril the Elder's *Catherine II on her Travels in 1787*, 1790). In another piece of art, she embraces two children (Ivan Prokofiev's *Catherine the Great as Tellus Mater*, a sketch of a group sculpture for the Moscow Orphanage, 1790). What is striking is that the Empress's image as a priestess shared the same visual elements as the images used to portray Medea.

In Russian panegyric poetry, the visual arts, and theatrical allegories, Catherine II was portrayed as Minerva, Astrea, Themis, Dido, and Olympia.[90] In the European press, memoirs, travelogues, and historical essays about Russia, she was routinely compared to the figure of Clytemnestra—a 'Northern Clytemnestra', who reigned after killing her own husband.[91] However, such associations were unlikely to have been possible in Russian discourse. Similarly impossible was the comparison with Medea, who killed her children. One could only compare the Empress with Medea, the patroness of heroes, the mighty sorceress, thereby completely eliminating the tragic and bloody parts of the story.

Conclusions

Was the Russian eighteenth century 'silent about Medea', as Claudio Napoli has suggested? Apparently not. But literary sources alone can't give us the full picture because it was in the theatre that the afterlife of Medea in Russia of the long eighteenth century proves key. As we have seen, Medea in Russia at this time was not the result of any advances in classical scholarship; rather, it was the result of cultural transfer. Klein defined one of the features of eighteenth-century Russian art as the principle of the 'reproduction of Western culture'.[92] Medea was in many ways transplanted to Russian soil from other European literatures and dramaturgy.

The history of theatrical productions of Medea in their respective political, aesthetic, and social contexts shows how art was emancipated from state power in the long eighteenth century. The performances concerning the Golden Fleece were a form of political representation, an adaptation of one of

---

[90] For Dido, see Korndorf (2011), 177–254.
[91] For Catherine II as Clytemnestra see, for example, Taylor (2012).   [92] Klein (2005), 319.

the many allegories of imperial power. The plays concerning Medea in Corinth, by contrast, show both an interest in theatrical innovation (especially in Benda's melodrama and Noverre's ballet) and an attempt to stage a genuine tragedy with a great actress in the title role (as with the Russian productions of Longepierre's *Medea*).

These three very different *Medeas* of Russian theatre reached the Russian stage by different routes. But when they converged, they happened to be at the epicentre of transition from a didactic, allegorical, and spectacular theatre to one that prized emotional and aesthetic affect. Medea was not the main driving force behind the 'feminization of drama' that took place on the Russian stage at the turn of the century, but the Medea tragic performances, above all, formed a bridge between a mid-eighteenth-century theatre of action, exciting spectacle, and conventional passion and the new emergent theatre of sincere emotional experience and compassion.

4

An Imperial Medea

Spain, Portugal, the Colonies

Anthony John Lappin

Jason, the Argonauts, Medea, and the Golden Fleece became the key legend taken from Graeco-Roman antiquity to explore and expose the postcolonial situation of Latin America and Brazil, a veritable dramatic and poetic tradition which began in the middle of the twentieth century, involving dramatists from the Caribbean to the southern cone. The playwrights offered reworkings of the Medea myth as a means to understand the Spanish conquest,[1] or to consider the plight of indigenous (or, simply, poor) women through a dramatization of the process of rural–urban drift,[2] or to approach the issues of miscegenation.[3] The former colonial nations, of course, have their own modern traditions, too, forged in opposition to their mid-century dictatorships.[4]

The Medea story seems ideal for appropriation to a colonial situation, or, perhaps, even more readily to a postcolonial and dictatorial situation. As a tale of destruction and dismemberment, it lends itself particularly to the

---

[1] Two Mexican authors, Sotelo Inclán (1957) and Magaña (1967) cast the conquistador Cortés as Jason and, as Medea, La Malinche, the indigenous woman who was his interpreter. Magaña later (1985) changed the work's title from the classicizing *Los argonautas* to *Cortés y la Malinche*. Cypess (1996), 19. The Peruvian Juan Ríos was the first to use the motif, in *La selva* of 1950. Salazar Bondy (1952); Ríos (1961); Miranda Cancela (2020), 146.

[2] Buarque de Holanda and Pontes (1975); Lauriola (2019), 204–6; Salvaneschi (1992); Radrigán (2004); Ramírez Hein (2000); González (2000); Moreno Jashés (1999). Salvaneschi's work is perhaps best described as a modernized translation, and was issued in a limited-edition print. Moreno Jashés' drama recently received a film adaptation, which he directed himself (2019). Stoklos' *Des-Medéia* (1995, first performed 1989) may be grouped with these plays, decrying as it does the 'neo-liberal betrayal of Brazil'. See Damasceno (2003), 177; Sanches (1995). There is a similar resistance to infanticide in the 2019 theatrical production, *Medea va* (see below, n. 67).

[3] Olavo (1961); Nogueira Coelho (2013), 359–60; further, Paiva dos Santos (2015); Santaliz (1992); Miranda Cancela (2002); Triana (1991); Nikoloutsos (2015).

[4] For Spain, see Bergamín (1954); Riaza (2006); Aguirre (2006); Lourenzo (2009); Cano (2012); Paso (2016). There have been a number of dramatic recreations in Portugal, by Dionísio (1992); see Silva (2019b); Cláudio (2008); see Real (2018); Hörster and Silva (2019b), as well as rewritings by Pais Brandão (1998) and Correia (2006); see Hörster and Silva (2019a). The fascist Estado Novo showed a degree of hostility to translations and performances of Euripides: Real (2018), 225. In Brazil, Chico Buarque's *Gota d'água*, an adaptation of Oduvaldo Vianna Filho's own adaptation of Euripides for television, was also subject to censorship by the military dictatorship.

Anthony John Lappin, *An Imperial Medea: Spain, Portugal, the Colonies* In: *Mapping Medea: Revolutions and Transfers 1750–1800*. Edited by: Anna Albrektson and Fiona Macintosh, Oxford University Press.
© Anna Albrektson and Fiona Macintosh 2023. DOI: 10.1093/oso/9780192884190.003.0004

imaginaire of the chaotic politics of dictatorships, brutal oppression, and lost opportunities that the second half of the twentieth century bequeathed to most Latin American countries. Not surprisingly, every decade saw one or more theatrical incarnations of Medea appear on the new-world stage, and this chapter seeks to uncover their colonial forebears of the eighteenth century.

Any attempt to force all of this material into a single 'argument', however elegant and satisfying, would seriously belie its complexity and the various intellectual currents in which each evocation of Medea was situated. Thus the fundamental violence of Medea's murder of her children may draw attention not because of its unnaturalness or its implications for postcolonial theory, but because it focuses vivid concerns about verisimilitude (and the purpose of dramatic performance), together with fundamental questions about representation which could signal a range of allegiances within a much wider cultural crusade.

This chapter will progress on roughly chronological lines. Nevertheless, it does not begin as the bells counted down the last seconds of 1749 to accompany the revels of the mostly drunken denizens of Madrid in the Puerta del Sol. One of the features of the Medea story (or, rather, stories) is the persistence, into the late eighteenth century, of previous, even canonical, tellings of the tale from the seventeenth century. Thus any consideration of Medea 1750–1800 has to consider how earlier Medeas were still being evoked, performed, and printed. Unlike some other national literatures, Iberian and American writers and audiences at this time were not faced with a *tabula rasa* when it came to Medea, but an accumulation of strata of previous well-known and still current versions.

Early Modern Spanish Medeas

Sixteenth-century playwrights were quick to seize on Medea as a theme,[5] but it was in the seventeenth century that the choice elements became vehicles for moral reflection and imperial self-projection. Perhaps the earliest was an *auto sacramental* (an allegorical mystery play), which equated the Golden Fleece with the lost sheep, Medea with sinful humanity, the Argonauts with the

---

[5] Lope de Rueda (1567); Alonso de La Vega (1566). For Medea in the hands of poets, see Rocha Pereira (1963–4); Martínez Cabezón (2014). For a 1590 Corpus procession which may have mixed the story of Medea with that of Psyche, see Agulló (1972), 56–7.

Apostles, and Jason with Christ; and was therefore called *El divino Jasón*.[6] Its attribution to Calderón de la Barca in its sole printing ensured it would be copied into the 1770s,[7] almost as a form of historical contraband in the face of the 1765 royal order banning performance of these types of plays.[8] This prohibition would go on to have a deep significance for the popularity of the Medea story, as we shall see.

Medea also attracted the attention of three of the leading Spanish dramatists of the seventeenth century, whose shadows fell far into the eighteenth. Lope de Vega's *El vellocino de oro* was explicitly designed for royal summer entertainment—although a raging fire destroyed the scenery during its first performance on 17 May 1622. Here the myth of Medea was linked to a number of elements: the Spanish empire, and its bounteous supplies of gold;[9] the chivalric motif of the Order of the Golden Fleece,[10] whose master, Felipe IV, had just turned seventeen, and in whose honour the entertainments were being staged;[11] the conversion of Jason and the Argonauts into Catholic Crusaders (a trope beloved of Charles V),[12] who sought to unite Europe beneath Spanish dominion, and who fought against Troy (i.e., their geographical successors, the Ottomans).[13] And it was written for an elite group of ladies-in-waiting who were taking part in a dramatic competition that added an extra interest to the festivities.[14]

Lope's play was not revived. This was not the case as regards Calderón's own use of the Medea story, which formed one act of his monumental and multi-staged entertainment for another lavish court celebration of midsummer 1636, *Los tres mayores prodigios*. The work continued to be in the public eye well into the second half of the eighteenth century. Published in Madrid as part of his collected works of 1726 and 1760–3, it generated enough interest to be published singly in Barcelona during the 1760s or 1770s, and to be further performed in the capital in the early 1780s:[15] no mean feat, given the

---

[6] See Calderón de la Barca (1664). The work was printed in a collection whose authority cannot be relied upon. Arellano and Cilveti (1992), 57–8. On the play, see Río Torres-Murciano (2010).

[7] Early eighteenth century: Madrid, Biblioteca Nacional de España [BnE], mss/16279, fols. 3r–26v (a miscellaneous collection); mid-eighteenth century: mss/16882 (single copy); mss/22565, fols. 98r–126r (originally fourteen volumes dedicated to Calderón, from the 1770s).

[8] Sala Valldaura (2010), 106; Esquer Torres (1965).   [9] Sánchez Jiménez (2002), 287.

[10] Although the order is mainly referred to as *el Orden del Toisón de Oro*, it was called, in the early modern period, *el Orden del Vellocino dorado*, as can be seen in the statutes (cf. Madrid, BnE, mss/71945 and mss/13756).

[11] Botello (2014), 161; Díez Borque (1995), 173.   [12] Tanner (1993), 156.

[13] Botello (2014), 166; the Order of the Fleece is explicitly understood as a crusading organization in Gómez de Ciudad Real (1546).

[14] Ferrer Valls (1993), 183–5.   [15] Calderón de la Barca (1760), (1785).

outlandish staging required, involving separate stages and three distinct theatrical companies.[16] Calderón concentrates on the seduction of Medea and, consequently, her magic that enables Jason to defeat the monsters, take the Fleece, and then escape with her after she hexes her vengeful father's army so that his soldiers fight against each other. Other parts of the narrative are not mentioned.

A much fuller account of Medea's story is found in another mid-seventeenth-century play whose popularity also stretched well into the eighteenth: Francisco de Rojas Zorilla's (†1648) *Los encantos de Medea*, published perhaps eight times after 1700.[17] The final scene has Jason drawing back a curtain to an inner room, revealing the two children killed by Medea. The debt to Seneca is clear, as might be anticipated, since translations of his works had been made on the peninsula since the Middle Ages.[18] But whilst Seneca's *Tragoediae* were certainly available to a specialized readership, they did not find favour with Iberian publishers.[19] Nor, for that matter, did Euripides, although Buchanan may well have had his Latin translation performed after he had been recruited to satisfy João III's desire to modernize studies at the University of Coimbra.[20] The Senecan translation into Italian by Lodovico Dolce (1560) made its way, in manuscript, to the papers of Juan de Argaiz Bretón, inquisitor general of Córdoba and the Navarre in the early eighteenth century.[21] Nevertheless, there was nothing in Spain or Portugal to match the steady rhythm of translations of the classical tragedians being produced in northern Europe.[22]

Yet the popularity of Zorilla's play was not simply a laudable enthusiasm for classical material: *Los encantos de Medea* advertised the play's charms in the title and the play would have used 'magic' on stage, and this 'magic' allowed full rein to the baroque fascination with the machinery of illusion. Although

---

[16] Pociña Pérez (1996).

[17] Rojas Zorilla (1645), (1651), (1680), (1704), (c. 1705), (1742), (c. 1750), (c. 1760), (1792), (c. 1799a), (c. 1799b).

[18] Seneca, perhaps due to his Cordoban origin, was well-represented in translation on the peninsula: Round (1974–7); Blüher (1983); Lucía Megías (1997), 363. A manuscript translation into Castilian of the early eighteenth century is preserved at Madrid, BnE, mss/14244/8.

[19] Commentaries abounded: beside Nicholas Trevet's thirteenth-century commentary to the Tragedies, see Rader in Seneca (1631); Farnaby in Seneca (1713), (1748), (1785); Gronovius and Grotius in Seneca (1728).

[20] Gomes dos Santos (1963–4). The translation was published that year: Euripides (1543) to accompany Erasmus' Latin translations of *Hecuba* and *Iphigenia in Aulide*: Euripides (1506), (1507); it was then excerpted to accompany other texts, e.g., Aeschylus, Sophocles, and Euripides (1567).

[21] Madrid, BnE, mss/17533. *Medea* begins the collection, but is acephalous (fols. 34r–60v), and so the current Biblioteca nacional catalogue fails to identify this text.

[22] See Seneca (1795); Morelly (1778); Euripides (1747), (1778), (1781–3), (1782).

(at least initially) the more refined awareness of *desengaño* (the knowledge that the world of the senses and the self was but a tissue of deceit) could jostle with the plebeians' gaping wonder and transported delight, over time the theatre came to rely more and more on the special effects of staging in a search for paying customers.[23]

Between Portugal and Brazil

Zorilla's title was taken over into Portuguese by António José da Silva, who was born in Brazil but was eventually executed in Lisbon by the Portuguese Inquisition for crypto-Judaism. His gory end has, regrettably, infused his own surefooted and ironic writing with a retrospective gloom of tragedy. *Os encantos de Medéa* had its first performance in 1735; it had been composed for, and was performed by, puppets, in a dedicated and highly popular theatre, in the Lisboetan Bairro Alto. Portuguese theatre had been almost totally displaced by foreign (particularly Italian and Spanish) companies.[24] Nevertheless, the *teatro de marionetas* allowed a recognizably Portuguese tradition to take shape—without the inconvenience, for example, of having to worry over what the ecclesiastical authorities would make of any questionable reputations of local actresses.

The performances were melodramas in the etymological sense, providing a mixture of spoken word and sung arias, and the puppetry allowed a low-cost solution to the contemporary thirst for wonders and *coups de scène*: thus one character is vomited out of a dragon's mouth. The lyricism and the classical focus of the plays da Silva wrote for the theatre (all but one has an antique subject) were directly influenced by the new winds sweeping the Portuguese court, where Italian musical entertainment (sung by Italian singers from the Royal Chapel) was becoming, after the accession of João V, and the arrival of Domenico Scarlatti in 1719, a *recherché* entertainment for the upper nobility, particularly during Carnival. Of note was the resetting by the Portuguese composer Francisco António de Almeida (1733), of the half-a-century old comic libretto first set to music for Carnival in Prague by Antonio Draghi (1680). The tale offers a classical setting, a polygamous storyline (the original title was *La pazienza di Socrate con due mogli*), explained as being due to an Athenian decree to increase the birth-rate after losing so many men in

---

[23] Andioc (1976), 35.   [24] Brito (1996), 178.

warfare, and supported by a sub-plot in which an aristocratic love triangle is formed.[25]

The Bairro Alto marionettes were perhaps the poor-man's castrati (the latter, at great expense, performed in the Royal Chapel); the music, too, was the local version of Italianate composition, written by the cantor of Lisbon Cathedral, António Teixeira (1707–74), recently returned from fourteen years of studies in Rome. Yet *Os encantos de Medéa* did not follow its predecessors' dependence upon the established contours of the myth: da Silva compressed the action, producing a love triangle between Jason–Medéa (co-regent with her father)–Creúsa (Medéa's cousin), in which Jason manipulates Medéa's passion for him to gain the Fleece whilst angling for Creúsa's affections. Medéa's father, however, has kept a watchful eye on proceedings, and rather than siding with Medéa in seeking to destroy Jason and Creúsa as they flee, acknowledges their relationship, grants them permission to marry, and even presents the Golden Fleece as their wedding present, thus welcoming them back to the court. Eta's attitude to his elder daughter, Medéa, however, is much sterner: because of her treachery, she is condemned to die immured in a tower (from which fate she escapes, at the end of the drama, flying off on a cloud).

Numerous traditions converge in the reorganization of the elements of the myth that the play represents: the *capa y espada comedia*, where the father is often the gull of his cunning daughter, determined to get her man; the long-term effects of the romances of chivalry, via whose cultural and homogeniz-ing blending Medéa became just another fearsome but ultimately frustrated witch—like Morgana, like Urgana—who provided opposition to the knightly hero.[26] The rather ironic liberties taken with the Medea story, though, may have been due to yet another part of the classical inheritance being brought to bear upon the telling of the tale—namely the broader question surrounding the suitable objects of mimesis.

The more neo-classically inclined theoreticians opined that verisimilitude in a drama was essential, and inevitably Horace's dicta concerning Medea in his *Ars Poetica* were invoked:

---

[25] Draghi (1680): fol. A2v, 'Si finge, che, a riguardo del Decreto di douer pilgare due Mogli, alcuni Padri hauessero introdotto di dare a' loro Figli vna Moglie secondo il loro volere, e l'altra lasciare, che la prendessero i Figli à lor gusto. Che perciò Melito, vn Prencipe Ateniese, amato da due Precipesse, Rodisette, & Edronica, douendo pigliar per Moglie vna, destinatili dal Padre, e l'altra elegersi per sua volontà, si troui in graue intrico nell'elettione d'una delle due, che lo amauano.'

[26] Campos García Rojas (2011); Martínez Cabezón (2014), 400. The trope continued into the eight-eenth century, with the 1774 verse-translation of Giovanni Carlo Passeroni's *Il Cicerone* by the Jesuit José Francisco de Isla: canto XV, stanza lxix: 'No hai Furia, no hai Medusa, no hai Medea / comparable con ella' ('No Fury, no Medusa, no Medea is there / who may be compared to her').

> Nec pueros coram populo Medea trucidet
> Aut humana palam coquat exta nefarius Atreus;
> Aut in avem Progne vertatur, Cadmus in anguem.
> Quodcumque ostendis mihi sic, incredulus odi.

[Let not Medea butcher her Sons in Presence of the Spectators; or impious Atreus openly prepare his Banquet of human entrails; nor let Progne be transformed into a Bird, Cadmus into a Serpent. Whatever of this kind you set before me, shocks Belief and raises Abhorrence.][27]

The Spanish scholar and critic Ignacio de Luzán (1702–54), in his unflagging attempts to make Spanish audiences more like the sophisticated French, was at pains to specify just what Horace meant by this condemnation, indicating that there was a significant groundswell of opinion which condemned Medea's infanticide as 'mythical' (in the modern sense), 'fantastic' (in the unbelievable sense), and, potentially, ridiculous (and not only in the Horatian sense):

> De suerte que aquí Horacio sólo encarga que no se ejecuten en público ciertas muertes cuyo modo trae consigo mucha barbarie e inhumanidad, y esto no porque sea de parecer que nunca se hayan de ejecutar en presencia del auditorio las muertes y demás acciones trágicas comprendidas en la turbación, sino porque tales muertes, por ser demasiadamente horribles, bárbaras y extraordinarias en el modo, serían increíbles. Y que ésta sea la *mente de* Horacio se prueba evidentemente con lo que él mismo añade: Quaecumque ostendis mihi sic, incredulus odi.

> [Such that here Horace only charges that certain deaths should not be shown before the public; such deaths as are intrinsically extremely barbarous and most cruel; and this not because he thinks that deaths and other tragic actions sprung from anguish should never be performed, but rather because such deaths, due to their being too terrible, too uncivilized, too out-of-the-ordinary in the manner in which they were carried out, would be unbelievable. And that this is what Horace intended is show clearly when he himself adds 'Quaecumque ostendis mihi sic, incredulosus odi'.][28]

Further, Horace links Medea's magical assistance of Jason with her wish to harm Creúsa in Epode III.10–15:

---

[27] Horace, *Ars poetica*, ll. 185–8; text and translation from Horace (1753), II, 384–5.
[28] Unless otherwise indicated, translations are my own. For Luzán's enthusiasm for Racine (translations of whose works had very limited success), see Sala Valldaura (2010), 99.

> Ut Argonautas praeter omnes candidum
> Medea mirata est ducem,
> Ignota tauris illigaturum juga,
> Perunxit hoc Iasonem:
> Hoc delibutis ulta donis pellicem,
> Serpente fugit alite.

[When Medea admired their handsome captain more than the other Argonauts, she bedaubed Jason with this, as he was going to fasten the unknown yoke to the bulls: and having revenged herself on his mistress, Creusa, by her gifts, prepared with this, she fled on her winged serpent.][29]

Within this refocusing of the story, then, Medea, Jason, and Creusa are thus conjoined, without any inconvenient reminiscence of infanticide.[30]

In *Os encantos de Medéa*, da Silva follows Luzán and other neo-classical critics in seeking to combine credibility and verisimilitude: of all the major characters, it is only the sorceress, Medea, who refuses to deceive, refuses to cast a spell to force Jason to love her, whilst all around her others spin their webs of self-serving deceit.[31] And this Jason is hardly heroic, despite his flaunting of his good looks.[32]

Theatre in Portugal, whether with strings or without, was soon cut short. Da Silva's death in 1737 was followed by the closure of all theatres in 1742 as the terrors of divine judgement began to weigh upon João V's ageing conscience. Undoubtedly as a reaction, da Silva's plays were published anonymously by the director of the puppet theatre, Antonio José de Oliveira, in 1744, in a volume itself dedicated to the only nobility that counted, the allegorical *Senhora Pecunia Argentina*, in an attempt to recoup at least some profit.[33] Actual members of the nobility, to whom it would have been worth dedicating the publication, were unlikely to associate themselves with anything quite so low-brow. Oliveira's efforts were a success, and the volume was reprinted in 1746, and in 1787, possibly from the manuscript written out by Oliveira himself between 1782 and 1784 (Figure 4.1).

Both printings made their way to Brazil.[34] *Os encantos de Medéa* thus lived on, being revived for a week during August 1757 in one of the most important cities of the empire, São Paulo, which was beginning to position itself as a

---

[29] Smart (1757), II, 158–9.
[30] A similar solution is found later, in Vogel's (1786) *La toison d'or*, although in this Medea does stab and kill her love-rival.
[31] Santos Simões (2002).   [32] Silva (2019a).
[33] *Teatro cómico* (1744).   [34] Borba de Moraes (1969), I, 381; II, 856.

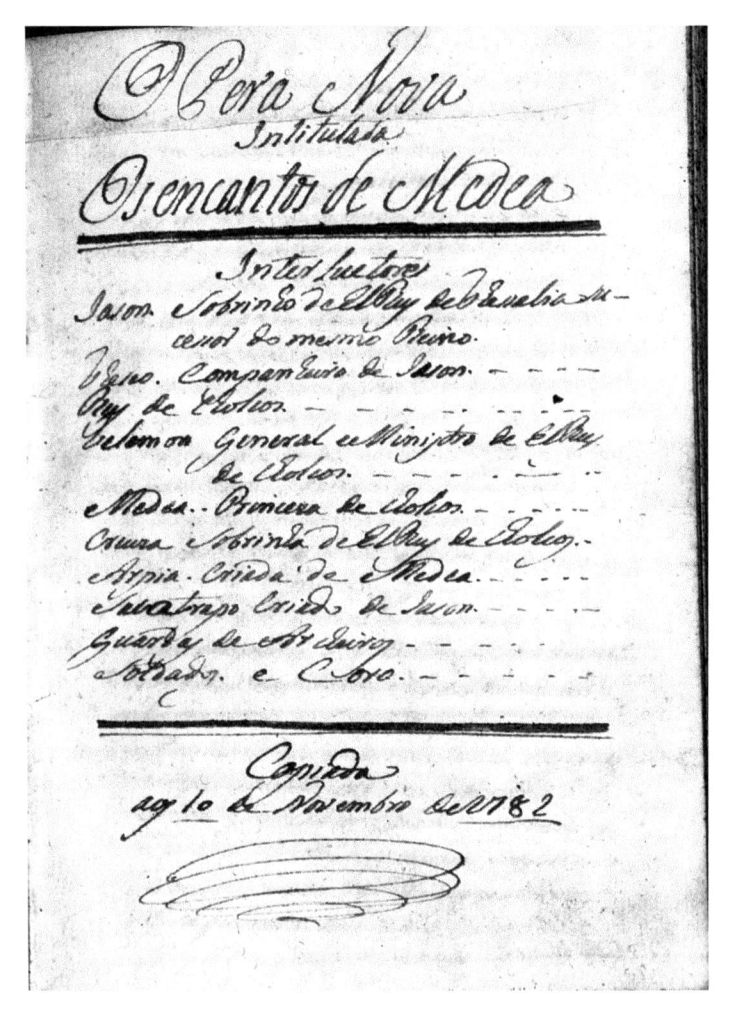

Figure 4.1 Frontispiece of manuscript, 'Opera nova intitulada Os encantos de Medea' by António José da Silva

mercantile alternative to the capital in Portugal.[35] The melodrama was again performed, this time in Rio de Janeiro, in 1770, and repeatedly thereafter, and also in Ouro Preto and Cuiabá, over the following twenty-five years.[36] No doubt due to the fireworks used for the magic thunderbolts, the Rio opera house hosting *Medéa* burnt down during a performance in the 1770s,[37] recalling Lope's own misfortune over a century earlier, and providing a memorable evening's entertainment for the *cariocas* in attendance.

[35] Nery (2008); Budasz (2008), 77.
[36] Lange (1964), 8. Interest raised by the performances might explain the Brazilian publication of *Fábula de Jazaõ e Medea* in 1786.
[37] Moreira de Azevedo (1877), II, 140.

The recreation of the play in Brazil—partly to be explained by nationalist sentiment over the author's birth—also focuses attention upon the crucial aspect in the play, that of gold, and its corrupting influence. New gold deposits discovered in Ouro Preto had been used by João V to fund a lavishly expansive imperial project (including the employment of those reassuringly expensive Italian castrati), and to keep his court in standards not seen since the early sixteenth century. That court, however, read through the lens of Colchis, was a place of deceit and a lack of decency. Thus, beneath the mythological comedy, as Castro Filho has argued, lies a satire of the obsession for gold and social competition in the centre of Brazilian gold production, Ouro Preto, and a criticism of the political and commercial relations between the colony (Brazil) and the metropolis (Lisbon).[38] Such a reading of the opera is perhaps inevitable: as Verena Dolle has stated, the myth of Medea has constantly provided a lens through which to see indigenous–colonial relations.[39] And rather than the triumph of empire which was a significant element in seventeenth-century dramas, the recreation of da Silva's *Medéa* allows a colonial problematization of empire to be represented through the very European cultural form of opera (Figure 4.2). The original form of the drama, puppet theatre, is still vibrant in Portugal, and *Os encantos de Medéa* has been revived into the twenty-first century.

Figure 4.2 The eighteenth-century Opera House in Ouro Preto, Brazil

---

[38] Castro Filho (2016), 33; Silveira (2015), 115, even sees a criticism of the Inquisition. For drama in Brazil, see Morreco Brescia (2010).

[39] Dolle (2014), xii.

Medea in Opera and Popular Musical Entertainments

Opera for the Portuguese royal court featured Medea twice. Gaetano Martinelli's *Teséo* (1783) depicts Medea in exile, abandoned by Jason, falling love with Teseo, being rebuffed, swearing vengeance, and flying (literally) into a murderous fury, only to be interrupted by the appearance of Minerva, who halts the action to wish the prince in attendance a happy birthday. Ten years later, a manuscript copy of Gaetano Andreozzi's *Giasone e Medea* made its way to Lisbon, presumably from Madrid, where the composer was then working, although a printed version also appeared in Naples during the same year.[40] Giandomenico Boggio's *La conquista del vello d'oro* (1791), with music by Gaetano Isola, would also seem to have been performed, with some of Medea's arias preserved in manuscript.[41]

The traditional Spanish form of melodrama, the *zarzuela* (so named after the royal palace in which its mix of spoken verse, arias, and dance had originally provided entertainment) had fallen out of favour in the early seventeenth century, only surviving through imitation of the Italianate forms which, as we have seen, also dominated Portugal; it enjoyed, however, a brief revival in the 1760s.[42] The year 1768 saw the performance of *Jason, o la conquista del vellocino: zarzuela heroica*,[43] composed by the indefatigable imitator of French and Italian theatre Ramón de la Cruz, with music composed by an Italian in royal service.[44] The cast was all-female, and Jason was played by a popular singer, Francisca Ladvenant.[45] The work was subsequently taken up by a second company during the same year.[46]

---

[40] Andreozzi (1793a), (1793b). The year 1749 saw Giovanni Battista Mele's *opera seria*, *El vellón de oro conquistado* performed before Fernando VI in the Retiro Palace in 1749 (Menéndez y Pelayo, 1896, lxiii, n. 1).

[41] Lisbon, Biblioteca Nacional de Portugal [BnP], ms. M.M 142//2, 3, 9.

[42] Chase (1939).   [43] Brunetti (1768); Le Duc (2013), 11.

[44] *Jasón, o la conquista del vellocino* was an attempt to cash in on the success of his successful 'zarzuela heroica' earlier in the year, *Briseida*, which dramatized the story of Briseis, with music by Antonio Rodríguez de Hita. The reluctance to treat the matter any earlier may have been due to a degree of uncertainty over the status of the Order of the Golden Fleece, since a diplomatic spat had rumbled on from 1740 when the Habsburgs continued to style themselves masters of the Order, against, as the Bourbons maintained, what had been agreed previously. The spirit of the piece is perhaps directly attributable to Cavalli's *Giasone, dramma per musica*, Cicognini (1649), or its updated version, *Il novella Giasone dramma per musica*, Cicognini and Apolloni (1671 and 1676). See also Minato (1678), (1717).

[45] See Cotarelo y Mori (1896) for a biography; Francisca was very much eclipsed by her sister, María, who had died a year earlier; Francisca died in 1770.

[46] Angulo Díaz (2020); the score has been partly preserved in Madrid, Biblioteca Histórica Municipal, Mus 54–2.

Jason twice saves the life of Eetas, king of Colchis, and asks directly for the Fleece—no subterfuge is involved; Eetas, at the end of the drama, grants Jason the Fleece out of gratitude. Nevertheless, the plot is enlivened by an inflexion of love triangles, in which Hypsipile, queen of Lemnos (and Jason's repudiated wife), and Estiro, king of Albania (and Medea's rejected suitor), plot together to have their revenge. The motif of the burning palace (usually attributed to Medea as one of the ways in which it was explained how she killed her own love rival, Creusa) is here attributed to Hypsipile and Estiro, although no harm comes of it; indeed, Jason intercedes for their pardon as a further sign of his noble heroism.

In line with censorious critics emboldened by the Age of Reason, and despite a clearly popular audience, the *zarzuela* maintains an even, distinguished tone. In the *zarzuela*, there is none of the comic knockabout found in the *comedia* or the comic opera; rather the influence of Metastasio had taken deep root.[47] Yet the marvellous is not abandoned: at the culmination of the drama, Medea and her choir of nymphs sing to encourage Jason and his men to seize the Fleece:

> Mientras canta el coro, Jasòn con los Argonautas sujeta los Toros, ara el campo, y siembra los huesos de Dragon, y acabado de cantar salen por los escotillones Soldados armados que se forman, y al son de una sinfornia dan la batalla en que los vencen los Argonautas, matando à todos: Despues se vuelve à repetir el coro, y mientras èl, Jasòn adormece la Serpiente y corta el árbol en que està el Vellocino, del que saldrán al tiempo de cortarle llamas, y se oirá un trueno.

> [Whilst the choir sings, Jason with the Argonauts tie down the Bulls, plough the field, and sow the Dragon bones, and once they have finished singing, Soldiers with weapons come out through the trap-doors, and to the music of a symphony they start to fight; the Argonauts overcome them, killing them all. Afterwards, the choir returns to its refrain, and whilst he, Jason, sends the Serpent to sleep and cuts down the tree (on which the Fleece is placed), from which, at the same time as it is cut down, flames jump out, and thunder is heard.]

---

[47] Sala Valldaura (2010), 118.

Yet *Jasón, o la conquista del vellocino* did not return to the stage; it was a casualty of the collapse of popularity of the *zarzuela*, which disappeared from the boards of Madrid by 1776, and the form remained abandoned for a further six decades.

Tastes, despite longstanding impatience with neo-classical precepts, were slowly changing in Spain. For some, such as the Scottish travel writer Alexander Jardine,[48] these changes were coming far too slowly in comparison to other parts of Europe. Still, sentimental drama was, from the 1780s, becoming much more accepted and acceptable for the greater part of the theatre-going public.[49] Yet other changes were afoot, as well. The structured entertainments of the first half of the century (dances, card games, musical pieces) had developed into multi-faceted public spectacles, responding to a growing public demand for concerts and musical spectaculars.[50]

Medea thus appears in this new context as part of the balletic final act of a fourfold dramatic performance in Madrid arranged by the immensely productive Luciano Francisco Comella (1793): an opening musical drama, followed by a short tragedy focusing on an indomitable former lady-in-waiting to Mary Queen of Scots, sent to her death by Elizabeth I of England.[51] This tear-jerker is then followed by a jocose sketch (with expressive symphonic accompaniment), in which a schoolboy laments his coming punishment at the hands of his teacher.

Medea y Jason is the fourth and final part of the evening's performance. Divided into two scenes, a detailed description is provided of Medea's actions throughout. The first scene presents Jason's repudiation of Medea in favour of Creusa, and the former's banishment: Medea requests one last interview with Jason from the messenger that brought her Jason's decree sending her into exile, and, when he has left the stage, summons the furies and swears vengeance. The second scene is set in Creon's court, where Jason's marriage to Creusa is announced; Medea barges in, but pretends to seek to offer a peace-offering—a bunch of flowers to Creusa. The latter, poisoned by the flowers, faints; she is carried off by the guards; Medea confronts Jason, recalls their past together, and, when this has no effect, kills both children in front of

---

[48] Jardine (1788), 163–4: 'The Spanish theatre is still, perhaps, nearly the same as in the time of Lopez de Vega [sic] [...]. Nothing sentimental or pathetic; much high-flown figure and bombast; endless strings of metaphors; much incident and intrigue, but little or nothing natural. Yet the beautiful flowery language of Lopez [sic] is charming. They have lately attempted some translated pieces, and some tolerable imitations of the passions, for the first time perhaps since Cervantes. I have just seen one of them acted, our Gamester. I observed, that the audience generally laughed in ridicule at the places where I wept; at the most pathetic parts; for it was tolerably acted by some of Olavide's disciples.'

[49] García Garrosa (1990), 59–63.   [50] Martínez Redondo (2017).

[51] Comella's manuscript libretto of the musical drama *El puerto de Flandes* has survived: Seville, Biblioteca Universitaria, Fondo Antiguo, ms. A 250/109(3bis). On Comella, see Anguio Egea (2006).

him. He summons help, and all appear on stage only for Medea to invoke the chthonic powers, there is a thunder-clap, and all are frozen in their tracks for a moment; Creusa recovers with the others, and runs about as if on fire; Medea invokes the furies, disappears under the stage, and the scene suddenly changes to an infernal cavern, with Medea high above them on a chariot, rejoicing in her vengeance; the furies pursue the mortals, and the curtain falls.[52]

The taste for magic and the spectacular is quite clearly alive and well, and the popular appeal of breath-taking transformations and stylized but impressive actions is deployed effectively as a rousing conclusion to a series of tableaux in which each dramatic segment focuses upon a certain type of punishment, taken to excess: María Lambrum is executed for possessing a portrait of Mary Queen of Scots—the depiction of tyrannical royal power just after the French Revolution was of something more than just academic interest; Perico the schoolboy is punished for his carelessness in breaking something by accident; and Jason for his infidelity (although the children here are clearly innocent).

Classicizing Medea

As the century drew to a close, Medea was granted two diverse, but classicizing, poetic depictions. In Portugal, Manoel de Bocage, during his imprisonment (for debauchery) in the notorious Lisboetan prison, O Limoeiro, underwent spiritual reform through the guidance of the Brazilian Franciscan, Frei José Mariano da Conceição Veloso. During this period of rehabilitation, Bocage produced a series of well-turned classical translations. Italianate opera was still the starting point for any treatment of Medea, and in Bocage's poem entitled *Cantata*, Medea is one of three in a sequence about women unlucky in love.[53] The tone brilliantly captures the histrionic style of opera, built around the twin poles of love–vengeance and monstrosity–nature.[54] Bocage was also

---

[52] Comella (1793), 17–19. The subject may well have been inspired by Noverre's remarkably popular *Médée et Jason* (see further chapters by Dotlačilová and Macintosh, this volume). A particular similarity is found with Gaetano Vestris' version, *Médée et Jason* of 1771 (see the contemporary descriptions of the performances of the ballet during the 1770s from the *Mercure de France* in Foster, 1996, 84–5). Other danced versions of the story were by Clerico (1792) and Foppa (1793).

[53] Guedes Ferreira (2013); Bocage (1802), 150–4.

[54] Possibly inspired by Marinelli's *La vendetta di Medea* (1791); cf. Balsamo (1798). Other Italian treatments at the time were by Palazzi (1726, 1749), Rasetti (1745), and Sografi (1789, 1793). The importance of Mestastasio cannot be underestimated: a translation of his dramas was published by João Carneiro da Silva (1782), and Portuguese translations and original libretti began to be published from 1736 and 1737 respectively; see, further, Costa Miranda (1984), 224. In Spain, an enthusiasm for Mestastasio can be traced from mid-century. Sala Valldaura (2010), 118.

drawing upon his own past as a tormented and jealous *roué*; yet it was the present which was exercising him rather more: the sequence looks with growing alarm at the chaos spreading through the *ancien régime*. Like Francisco de Goya, Bocage mused on the escape of demons and the chthonic powers as *liberté, fraternité, égalité* were sucking the life out of the moderate reforming impulses (and near-unanimous support for absolute monarchy) of the Enlightenment.[55]

A direct contrast to Bocage's proto-gothic appalled delight in invoking the infernal deities and endless darkness, Benito Rubio y Ortega's *Medea cruel* (1797), a somewhat painfully Aristotelian take on the story of Medea's vengeance, advertised itself as a *tragedia nueva*. The author, a lawyer by initial training, had subsequently studied in the newly established vehicle for Enlightenment values, the Reales Estudios de San Isidoro, and had presented a thesis there in 1791: 'Reflexiones filosóficas sobre la causa de haber escrito en verso todos los primeros escritores de Grecia, y una noticia de los poetas griegos que han llegado a nuestros días' ('Philosophical reflexions on the cause of all the earliest writers of Greece having used verse, and an *elenchum* of the Greek poets who have come down to the present').

Rubio y Ortega's prologue to *Medea cruel* makes clear why he had chosen the subject matter. First, and foremost, it was possible for him to apply the three unities of time, space, and action in verse-form to the story of Medea's vengeance against Jason, her children, and Creusa: in Corinth, in a period of twenty-four hours, and in hendecasyllables. And second, he avers, he can thereby shun the '*comedias que llaman mágicas*' ('plays which use special effects to represent magic') that serve to distract the watching public from good writing, since they focus merely on the stage design.[56] A search for a classicizing authenticity is everywhere apparent: even Medea's long diatribe reproaching Jason is a straightforward and direct translation of Ovid's relevant *epistola*.[57]

In complete contrast to all of the preceding versions of the Medea myth, Rubio y Ortega's version eschews altogether any hint of magic or anything out of the ordinary. In line with the very best classical precepts, Jason narrates Medea's filicide to the distressingly sententious chorus at the end of the play. The death of Creusa is brought about not by spells, by an enchanted dress or

---

[55] Beales (1990).

[56] Rubio y Ortega (1797), vi–vii; for the great popularity of the 'magic' plays, Calderone (1983).

[57] Which had been translated in hendecasyllables somewhat earlier by the ferocious opponent of neo-Classicism, García de la Huerta (1779), 301–19. This 1779 volume also contained an Italian translation of the same in terza rima by Ignazio Cinisselli (260–85) and a further version by Ignacio de Luzán (286–301).

the cursing of the palace with fire; no, Medea's brother is hidden in a trunk of clothes she sends to Creusa, and, once he has gained entry to the palace, sets the building ablaze. Jason, in cowardly fashion, saves his own skin despite Creusa's plaintive cries.

The determinedly euhemerizing approach to Medea's story had been felt for many years already in Spain. Boccaccio, of course, had suggested that Medea had fomented a rebellion in Colchis to aid Jason,[58] but the real breakthrough had come with one of Thomas Erpenius' most gifted students, Samuel Bochart (1599–1667), whose knowledge of many of the languages of the ancient eastern Mediterranean led him to provide a key to decipher the 'true' (i.e., non-marvellous) meaning behind the figures of the myth.[59]

The great Benedictine, Jerónimo Benito Feijoo, was the first to make use of the linguistic observations supplied by Bochart:

> Las quiméricas hazañas de Jasón, y robo de el vellocino de oro, explica históricamente el célebre Samuel Bochart, por medio de la inteligencia que tenía de la lengua phenicia, descubriendo, que algunas vozes equívocas de aquel idioma dieron ocasión a la fábrica de esta portentosa fábula. La voz syriaca gaza, en la lengua phenicia, significa igualmente un tesoro que un vellocino; la voz saur, que significa una muralla, designa también un toro; y la voz nachas es común para significar dragón y hierro. Assí, en vez de decir que Jasón, rompiendo, o abanzando una muralla, defendida con gente armada, havía robado el tesoro de el rey de la Cólquida, se suposo haver domado los toros, que respiraban fuego, y el espantoso dragón, que era guarda de el vellocino, para apoderarse de él. Ni el amor de Medea y fuga con Jasón tienen nada de extraordinario, para que Juno y Minerva intervin-iesen en esta aventura, bastando para ella una pasión tan natural, acom-pañada de alguna resolución.[60]

> [Jason's chimerical deeds, and the theft of the Golden Fleece is explained in historical terms by the famous Samuel Bochart, via his knowledge of Phoenician, showing that some equivocal words in that language gave rise

---

[58] Río Torres-Murciano (2010), 48; Morse (1996), 198–202.

[59] Bochart (1651), 528CD; for the de-confessionalized reception of his work in the eighteenth century, infused with interest generated by contemporary expeditions to the Middle East, see Shalev (2011), 202. His method of interpretation should be distinguished from allegorical readings of the story, which asserted that the tale encoded some form of gnosis: Pérez de Moya (1599), fol. 365v, where—based on etymology—Jason's flight with Medea is a search for moral betterment; or the wide-spread (and much mocked) connection of the legend with alchemy; for example, Bluteau (1721), VIII.590; (1736), 367. Cf. Krämer, this volume.

[60] Feijoo (1742–60), 360.

to this portentous tale. The Syriac *gaza*, in Phoenician, means as much *a treasure* as it does *a fleece*; the word *saur*, which indicates *a wall*, also means *a bull*; and the word *nachas* can be used for both *dragon* and *iron*. And so, instead of saying that Jason, by breaking or throwing down a defensive wall, which was defended by men at arms, had stolen the king of Colchis' treasure, he was supposed to have tamed the bulls which breathed fire, and the frightful dragon, which was the guardian of the fleece, in order to take possession of it. Nor are Medea's love and escape with Jason at all extraordinary such that Juno and Minerva should have become involved in this adventure, since all that was needed was a most natural passion, accompanied by a certain degree of determination.]

Bochart's linguistic euhemerism found further echo in Manuel Lanz de Casafonda's ruminations on the origins of idolatry,[61] wherein he blames the quid pro quo on the conscious machinations of Phoenician idol-priests. The rationalized story could thus be accepted as fact, and thereby given a date, as we see in Miravel y Casadevante's historical dictionary:

> [...] y después de haber muerto los hijos que ella había tenido de Jason, se escapó á Athenas sobre los dragones alados, ó por mejor decir en un baxel llamado los Dragones alados. Esta expedición de Jason y de sus compañeros llamados Argonautas, á fin de robar los tesoros de Eetas, rey de Colchida, figurados por el Toyson de oro, debe colocarse en el año del mundo 2273, y 1262 antes de Jesu Christo; 69 antes que principiasse la guerra de Troya.[62]

> [[...] and after murdering the boys that she had had with Jason, she escaped Athens on winged dragons, or, rather, on a boat called 'The Winged Dragons'. This expedition of Jason's, and his companions, called Argonauts, with the purpose of stealing the treasures of Eetas, king of Colchis, which are depicted through the Golden Fleece, should be placed in *anno mundi* 2273, 1262 BC, 69 years before the war of Troy began.]

Rubio y Ortega, then, in stripping the story of anything even remotely marvellous was providing a plausible account of events as they might actually have occurred. The play aims at a high style yet a profound emotional impact: it is, essentially, awash with hendecasyllabic weeping. Here, for example, is the representation (with the original punctuation) of a short speech by one of Medea's bairns:[63]

---

[61] Aguilar Piñal (1972), 41–2.   [62] Miravel y Casadevante (1753), V.45.
[63] Act II, scene V; Rubio y Ortega (1797), 43.

> ¡Ay ::: Madre ::: que este llanto ::: no me dexa
> Decir ::: lo que tenia ::: que deciros:::!
> ¡Qué tormento ::: yo muero de congojas :::
> Desmaya el corazón ::: para decirlo ::::!
>   [Alas!…Mother!…my tears…won't let me
> Say…what I had…to tell you…!
> What torment!…I die from sorrow….
> My heart faints…just to say it…!]

It would seem that Rubio y Ortega's *Medea cruel* was never inflicted upon a paying audience.[64] And, in a sense, its lack of dramatic prospects from the moment of its publication pointed to the limits of the neo-classical project in Spain, which, in literature at least, set itself against the last vestiges of Habsburgian baroque with an emphasis upon the verisimilitudinous, the rational, and, of course, the undelightingly didactic. Banning saints' plays with their miracles and demons had simply led to an increased emphasis upon magic, with its wonders and demons and hence Medea, in her various incarnations. But Rubio y Ortega's determination to present Medea without any of the accoutrements that made her popular sealed his failure. Well might the neo-classical poet/playwright Leandro Fernández de Moratín complain bitterly about the opera *Giasone e Medea* (which he saw in Naples at the beginning of the 1790s) for its numerous defects in his eyes, but the classicizing tragedies were limited in appeal to a very restricted circle, which, despite the labour of translation, adaptation, and the occasional performance, remained stubbornly narrow during the period.[65]

Conclusion

The figure of Medea by the end of the eighteenth century was a composite, an inheritance of still-read sixteenth- and seventeenth-century drama, highbrow evocation of the classics through translation or citation,[66] or in various forms of popular entertainment—melodramas, the ephemera of dance-routines, and Italianate operas adapted to Iberian tastes. Indeed, it was

---

[64] Which was also true of the first of the neo-classical tragic experiments, Agustín de Montiano's *Virginia* and *Ataúlfo* (1750, 1753), defined by Lafarga (2010), 118, as a 'bienintencionado experimento de salón' (a well-meaning thought experiment).

[65] Fernández de Moratín (1991), 282–9; Lafarga (2010), 121; Tolivar Alas (1988).

[66] For instance, Medea's self-description in Ovid, 'Video meliora probaque, deteriora sequor' ('I see and approve what is better; I follow the worse') could be dropped into a letter with proverbial force by Manuel de Rodán at the very end of 1769. Azara (1846), I.379.

probably the sheer multiplicity of the baroque Medea—whose glories were fading but were still appreciated and defended—which meant more northern, more modern conceptions of her role and symbolism failed to take root in the eighteenth century.

There is, nonetheless, a distinct change in the use of the figure of Medea between 1750 and 1800. The primary interest (indeed, the commercial interest) of the figure was, as in the late twentieth century, as a means of representing empire, of providing a cipher for the relations of metropolis and periphery. But the eighteenth-century Medea changes, in response to new ideas of classicism and politeness, marking a division between a high-brow appreciation of austere Senecanism against a popular enjoyment of the pantomime (which nevertheless has its own cultural cachet) or the *zarzuela*.

Something similar happened with the Latin American Medeas with which this chapter began: although canonized as the metaphor for the act and process of colonization, recent adaptations have taken a more individualist and neo-bourgeois line towards the myth: both Ana López Montaner's *Medea o la desesperada conquista del fraude* (2006) and the Puerto Rican film director Alexandra Latishev Salazar's *Medea* (2017) present the protagonist in a pro-choice key. Mariana Percovich's monologue *Medea de Olimar* (2009) relates the myth to a real-life crime (Olivo, 2010),[67] and Fermani's *El escorpión blanco* (2012), also a short monologue, presents an existentialist rejection of suffering.[68] Given the overwhelming postcolonial tradition established in the twentieth century, these productions self-consciously advocate a neo-bourgeois individualism, and an embrace of the western, middle-class, liberal concerns of those who consume the artworks.

This refocus, as we have seen, has always been part of the protean process of shaping Medea's story, and the shifting of emphases and details are often a personal choice of authors who seek to place themselves within traditions of

---

[67] Both López Montaner and Percovich's works are, as yet, unpublished. Similarly the Brazilian psychoanalyst and poet Clara de Góes has also not yet published her *Medea en promenade* (2012), which continues the long Brazilian tradition of adaptations of Euripides (see Silva, 2016). Brazilian translations of the classical texts into Portuguese have never ceased, e.g., Gouvêia Júnior (2014); Euripides (1988a), (1988b), (1991), (2005), (2010); Seneca (1993). Some of Euripides' text (with macaronic additions of English, Italian, German, and Portuguese) became the disjointed libretto for Jocy de Oliveira's sixth opera, *Kseni—a estrangeira* (2006), mixing European instruments with those drawn from the Brazilian tradition; Franco Perpetuo (2006). The dramatic gestures were read as an appeal for individual liberty regardless of the constraints of culture from the first performance; Staff Writer (2006); see further Lauriola (2019), 106. The same holds for the time-travelling Medea in *Medea va* by the Argentine theatre company La Rueda Teatro; Brea (2019); Fleitas (2019).

[68] Silventi (2010).

representation and criticism. Indeed, Stoklos (1995) was not the first author to dispense with filicide, as we have seen. Yet with her long continuities over time in the Hispanic and Lusophone world, and her deep cultural roots, Medea has proved to be an excellent resource for authors seeking to navigate dominant cultural currents, through their enthusiastic developments of some parts of the story-complex, but also through their silences.

5

Inverting the Barbarian

Estrangement and Excess in the Eighteenth-Century Medea

Anna Albrektson

In Ovid's *Heroides* XII, the verse epistle 'From Medea to Jason', Medea laments her present situation in Corinth. She reflects on the past in her native Colchis on the Black Sea coast, and how her 'maidenly innocence' led her to trust the Greek hero Jason, the man who has now betrayed her:

> I, the maiden who am now at last become a barbarian in your eyes, who now am poor, who now seem baneful – I closed the lids of the flame-like eyes in slumber wrought by my drug, and gave into your hand the fleece to steal away unharmed.[1]

The contrast between the situation in Colchis, where Medea helped Jason seize the Golden Fleece by putting the dragon to sleep, and her present situation in Corinth, where she is humiliated and betrayed by her husband's perjury, is explicit. Medea, once the helper maiden of the enemy, has now been transformed into a new being, a barbarian.

It is important to turn back to Euripides for a moment, in order to trace the vicissitudes of the barbarian in the various Medeas of antiquity. In an exchange between Medea and Jason in the second episode of Euripides' tragedy, Medea is clearly defined as a barbarian by her husband. She is described as a woman from the non-Greek areas of the Black Sea, a woman who is lucky to live in a Greek society. According to Jason, she should be thankful since Greece has brought her both renown and the blessings of the rule of law. At line 591, in a bitter exchange with Jason, Medea refers to herself as 'a barbarian

---

[1] Ovid (1977), ll. 105–8. All translations from Latin and Greek are taken from the Loeb editions.

Anna Albrektson, *Inverting the Barbarian: Estrangement and Excess in the Eighteenth-Century Medea* In: *Mapping Medea: Revolutions and Transfers 1750–1800*. Edited by: Anna Albrektson and Fiona Macintosh, Oxford University Press.
© Anna Albrektson and Fiona Macintosh 2023. DOI: 10.1093/oso/9780192884190.003.0005

wife' who 'would discredit' him.[2] Hall points out that the alleged lawlessness of barbarians was a way of constructing 'Hellenic ethnicity', a shared 'culture' with specific focus on Athenian democracy.[3] Fifth-century tragedy established a new language, inscribing the identity of the barbarian into well-known characters: 'To an archaic Greek [...] Medea [was] a sorceress; to the fifth-century theatre-goer an essential aspect of such figures' identities was that they were barbarians.'[4]

Euripides' use of the term 'barbarian' is much more clear-cut than Ovid's. This 'vocabulary of barbarism' was, as Hall argues, central to Athenian tragedy, and called for contrasts between man and woman, democracy and tyranny, Olympian gods and the chthonic powers.[5] In Ovid's verse epistle, Medea's predicament is not simply an ethnic label, situating her as a foreign woman from a lawless land. On the contrary, she has *become* a barbarian, and perhaps not even to all. Ovid suggests that Medea has become a barbarian in the eyes of the Greek hero Jason. It is, in fact, Jason who has changed.[6]

This chapter argues that it is discussion of the barbarian between 1750 and 1800 that becomes a major driving force in the transformations of the protagonist Medea. First, in the sentimental renderings during the 1770s and the 1780s, 'barbarian' replaces the baroque 'witch'; and, secondly, from the 1790s onwards, 'barbarian' acquires the additional focus on ethnicity.

European Identity Formation and the Barbarian

Throughout the century, authors, philosophers, historians, artists, and travellers debated human diversity and whether human nature could be defined as stable in space and over time. Medea plays of the late eighteenth century function prismatically, and the eponymous figure is often employed to address the most pressing issues of the period, not least those concerning the limits of the human.[7] In eighteenth-century Europe, encounters with remote peoples

---

[2] Euripides (2001), 335. Hall connects this to a law restricting Athenian citizenship only to the offspring of two Athenian parents. See also Winkler (2009), 29–30.

[3] Hall (1989), 190–200.   [4] Hall (1989), 54.   [5] Hall (1989), 205; Winkler (2009), 31–2.

[6] On the definitions of the barbarian in Euripides' tragedy and Ovid's epistle, see Winkler (2009), 28–32, 42–3. The Medea of Ovid's *Metamorphoses* VII is a dangerous witch, and the designation barbarian does not, according to Winkler, indicate the antithetical pattern of Greek and barbarian. Neither Apollonius of Rhodes, nor Seneca, pursues the ethnic division of barbarian and Greek in their representations of Medea.

[7] This study is part of the project 'Moving Medea: The Transcultural Stage in the Eighteenth Century', supported by the Riksbankens Jubileumsfond (granted under my former surname Cullhed). See Cullhed (2017).

in the wake of colonial and scientific enterprises put the question of universality and the significance of difference on the agenda. References to the barbarian, as we will see, evoke questions about human identity and diversity, and, inevitably, reflect on extreme behaviour and violence.[8] Euripides and Ovid function as intertexts in this process, highlighting two versions of the barbarian: either as an ethnic characteristic, as in Euripides' polarity between Greeks and barbarians, or as an Ovidian ethical principle, according to the changeable evaluation of certain actions.

It is indeed surprising that the quintessential barbarian of western culture—Medea—has met with so little interest within this surging scholarly field of the barbarian as cultural concept. Medea is exemplary not only to the study of the barbarian in cultural history, but specifically to the flux of identity formation during the revolutionary period of the late eighteenth century. In recent years, the barbarian has been defined as 'a key-word of European and Western identity formation', and the historical study of the concept has been the focus for a number of ambitious studies.[9] The 'structural instability of the opposition between civilization and barbarism' has been broadly identified and there is a general consensus that 'Barbarism challenges the very principle of binarism upon which the difference between civilization and barbarism is founded.'[10]

Inevitably, research on Medea and the barbarian gestures towards postcolonial theory, and the concept of hybridity plays a major role in Markus Winkler's study of Medea in the late eighteenth and early nineteenth centuries.[11] Even more importantly, Moser, Boletsi, and Winkler argue for the need to incorporate literary texts into discussions of the barbarian. These new approaches focus on 'the performativity of *barbarism* through the rhetoric of texts'; and it is claimed that it is equally important to place literary texts alongside the dictionaries, encyclopaedias, and other common sources from the period.[12]

If Euripides and Ovid provide early examples of the commonplace of the barbarian within western culture, the binary opposition between Greeks and barbarians was transferred into new constellations over time: Romans were

---

[8] See for example Brown (1993); Outram (1995); Wheeler (2000); Nussbaum (2003); Wahrman (2004); Harvey (2012); Stuurman (2017). For a nuanced discussion of both the Enlightenment and the role of postcolonial theory, see Carey and Festa (2009).

[9] Winkler et al. (2018), 2. See also Moser and Boletsi (2015a).

[10] Moser and Boletsi (2015b), 16, 18. See also Winkler (2009), 32, on the incoherence of the concept barbarian.

[11] Winkler (2009). Winkler refers to Said (6). See also Carey and Festa (2009).

[12] Moser and Boletsi (2015b), 21. See also Boletsi (2013); Winkler (2018), 32. Winkler defines his own approach as close to Foucault's genealogical point of view, in its avoidance of the search for an origin, or an essence of the barbarian. Winkler (2018), 23.

opposed to all barbarians who did not accept Roman rule, and Christians during the Middle Ages were defined in relation to barbaric pagans, not least Muslims. With European expansion into the New World, a new opposition was created, 'between "civilized" Europeans and "barbarous" indigenous populations'.[13]

In the eighteenth century, the barbarian was far removed from the primarily linguistic and political otherness delineated in the Greek sources, while the categories of transgression and, not least, of excess were very much in evidence. The 'enemy-concept'—to use Koselleck's term—in the eighteenth century was superseded by a temporal concept, in a standard outline of the history of humankind.[14] In the *Encyclopédie* and in dictionaries in various European languages, philosophers of Europe identified a three- or four-stage historicity: a first, savage stage of hunters was followed by a second pastoral stage of barbarism, which was distinguished by a more developed society and sense of community; the third phase consisted of a civilized society, based on agriculture, which was followed by the fourth phase of trade and political institutions.[15]

However, the tendency to criticize civilization also led to a 'positive revaluation of barbarism' in the eighteenth century.[16] Barbarians became 'symbols of humanity unburdened by law' in paintings and other visual representations.[17] In poetry, so-called primitive poetry came into vogue: Hebrew verse came to be regarded as the oldest extant example of 'authentic' and passionate original poetry; and it was veneration for the primitive that triggered one of the most famous literary frauds, with the publication in 1760 of James Macpherson's supposedly ancient poems of Ossian. It would seem that the concept of the barbarian both harboured the traditional aspects of an 'enemy-concept', as the counterpart of humanity, and the very core of this presupposed humanity, defined in sentimental terms.

Although theoretically diverse, current research often points to the changeability and malleability of concepts such as humanity, race, and gender in the eighteenth century. The shorthand for femininity in the second half of the eighteenth century—'the domestic code'—identified the ideal woman as

---

[13] Winkler (2018), 21; Moser and Boletsi (2015b), 18.

[14] Moser (2018), 47; Koselleck (1985). Moser describes the eighteenth-century concept of barbarism as 'one of the genealogical taproots of the modern concept of culture'. Moser (2018), 48.

[15] Moser (2018), 46–7. Moser includes Montesquieu, Rousseau, Adam Smith, and Herder. See Koselleck (2002), 169 on temporalization. See also Wheeler (2000), 7, *passim*; Wahrman (2004), 92, 103, 118; Stuurman (2017), 289–90.

[16] Moser (2018), 128. On 'Barbarian Art: Herder and Goethe', see Moser (2018), 128–34.

[17] Pinault Sørensen (2001), 161.

'modest, chaste, pious, compassionate, and virtuous', and radically played down previous notions of lustful women.[18] There is a general agreement about decisive changes in the 1790s, when both racial characteristics and gender divisions were assigned a stronger classificatory and normative function, which laid the path for the so-called scientific racial theories of the nineteenth century.[19] As we will see, the concept of the barbarian—central to the Euripidean and Ovidian representations of Medea—intertwines during the revolutionary period with current discourses of femininity, ethnicity and ethics, humanity, and race.

Ethics, Ethnicity, and Sensibility

The terms 'ethics' and 'ethnicity' are employed in this chapter to signify the two extremes in accounts of the barbarian in the late eighteenth century. Calling Jason a barbarian would imply an ethical understanding of barbarism, since it applies to a Greek. While the ethical aspect of the barbarian signifies a moral condition without temporal or spatial boundaries, a malleable condition with fluid relations to gender and racial categories, the ethnic barbarian is subjected to specific conditions in space and time. However, in the eighteenth century the identity of a social group in relation to others was not necessarily a stable category, a fact which complicates a simple binary between the ethical and the ethnic barbarian. Barbarian ethnicity could thus be described either as being based on culture/climate and thus changeable according to eighteenth-century views, or as being based on innate and unchangeable factors, parallel and intertwined with the emerging definitions of race and gender towards the end of the eighteenth century.[20] Actions can be classified as barbaric according to the ethical definition, while the ethnic barbarian concerns not actions but a condition—being a barbarian—based on the cultural confines of a certain group in a specific historical moment.

In line with recent studies, the concept of ethnicity is often defined in terms of 'flux' and 'process', also stressing the complex interrelationship between

---

[18] Francus (2012), 2; Dabhoiwala (2012).

[19] Wahrman (2004), 86 insists on using race as a descriptive term. Wheeler (2000), 300 concludes: 'Distinguishing more carefully among historical constellations of race, racism, and ethnocentrism is key to analyzing the past.' See also Kidd (1999), 5; Nussbaum (2003), 59, 254–6; Carey and Festa (2009); Stuurman (2017), 344–5. On gender and domesticity, see Francus (2012), 8–12. On race and gender, also Outram (1995), 63–95.

[20] Winkler (2018), 19 describes the barbarian in terms of an 'ethnocentric enemy- and identity-concept'.

ethnicity, race, and gender. Ethnicity concerns relationship, the 'between' and not the 'inside' of a group; and it mainly concerns social identity, and has both a political and symbolic meaning. Hall's concept of ethnicity, as a subjective definition identifying a group in relation to the others—the barbarians— functions in a similar way.[21] By coupling barbarism with both ethics and ethnicity, my readings of eighteenth-century Medea plays place the protagonist not only in relation to antiquity, but also in relation to broader eighteenth-century discourses.

A further aim here is to establish how particular modes of representation relate to the barbarian, such as the sentimental focus on interiority, the belief in shared emotions, and the ideal of compassionate femininity. During the eighteenth century, sentimentalism was an ideal that at times covered all aspects of civic life, as William Reddy argues in his study of the French Revolution in the history of emotions.[22] Current scholarship on literary sentimentality and sensibility—the terms are often used interchangeably— approaches the very same issues of ethics and ethnicity within the discourse of the barbarian. Sensibility is at times hailed as 'the mother of humanity', at other times kept at a distance, keeping the other as an object of compassion at 'a proper distance'.[23] Furthermore, sentimentality blends with displacement as an aesthetic strategy. The negotiations between the idea of human universality and the identification of barbaric others is parallel to ambiguities in relation to spatiality and temporality. Well-known strategies, such as placing stories with disturbing content in a distant era and a remote geography, were common during the eighteenth century.[24] In the case of Medea, sentimentalism, as well as the strategy of displacement, becomes an important mode of representing the ambiguities of eighteenth-century ethnicity, gender, and race, converging in the figure of the barbarian.

Barbaric Exchanges in the 1770s and 1780s

In Jean-Marie-Bernard Clément's 1779 *Médée*, a tragedy performed in Paris without much success, but printed and circulated in the decade before the

---

[21] Hylland Eriksen (2010), 1, 5–9, 13, 16, 211–15. I rely on Hylland Eriksen's definition of ethnicity as a concept concerning the classification of people and group relationships. Hall (1989), 3 on an 'objective' definition of ethnicity seems outdated. See also Kidd (1999), 5.
[22] Reddy (2001), 210.   [23] See Festa (2006), 55–66, on sentimentality and empire.
[24] Dobie (2010), 11. The same strategy of displacement is essential to Athenian tragedy.

Revolution, the protagonists take turns in being identified with the barbarian.[25] Clément's tragedy is emblematic of the way that violence is suppressed on stage in eighteenth-century Medeas.[26] He describes his 1779 tragedy *Médée* as an attempt to represent 'the development of the passions' on stage, and he uses the word barbarian in a number of senses.[27] First, he criticizes the Senecan tradition in his preface, and more specifically Longepierre's *Médée* from 1697, performed frequently during the eighteenth century.[28] Medea dramas focusing on the supernatural, *le merveilleux*, and the taste for horror, have made Medea 'a monster of barbarity', '*un monstre du barbarie*', Clément concludes.[29] He declares that his version of Medea follows in the footsteps of Euripides, and he sets the stage for 'a woman led by love alone into crime; she is unhappy and to be pitied because she has been abandoned'.[30]

Clément's criticism here undoubtedly refers to the opulence of the baroque stage, and presumably extends to the vogue for incantation scenes common in Medea operas.[31] A Medea placed in a grotto, summoning furies, producing earthquakes and thunderstorms with a stroke of her wand suggests a typical Medea in the tradition of baroque opera.[32] The pagan rites of the Medea story connoted barbarity, not least when displayed with the alluring machinery of the theatre stage. It becomes absolutely clear that Clément criticizes the representation of Medea as a witch, defined as a barbarian, and with this reinterpretation of the protagonist we see a decisive eighteenth-century change in relation to the preceding baroque era.[33]

The preface suggests that the question of excess, the main characteristic of the barbarian, is qualified—Clément rejects excess in terms of the supernatural, but he advocates emotional excess, in terms of the representation of human suffering on stage. The supernatural connects to the pagan, and Medea's barbarity in Clément's version suggests an otherness based on faith, one of the central categories of difference in the eighteenth century.[34] However, the French author's enactment of the discourse of the barbarian is primarily based

---

[25] Clément (1779). On Clément, see Wygant (2007), 163–74; Wygant (2010); Schweitzer (2007).

[26] See Schweitzer, this volume.   [27] Clément (1779), [iii].

[28] See Figure 6.2 of Mlle Clairon in an eighteenth-century revival in Macintosh, this volume.

[29] Clément (1779), ix. References to all Medea dramas will be given within brackets in the main text. Unless otherwise indicated, all translations are my own.

[30] Translation by Wygant (2007), 165; Clément (1779), [iii].

[31] Leopold (1998), 131.

[32] On costumes and stage aspects, see Dotlačilová, this volume; on Medea and the baroque, see Macintosh, this volume.

[33] On Medea as a witch in French literature, see Wygant (2007). Cf. Hall (1989), 54.

[34] As Wheeler points out, religion and clothing were considered primary factors of difference in the eighteenth century. Wheeler (2000), 14. Also Wahrman (2004), 93.

on the opposition between the feeling heart and the callousness of the barbarian, and not as a straightforward rejection of excessive passions. I suggest that the concept of the barbarian serves a structural function in the tragedy: Clément's decision to let the protagonists take turns in the role of the barbarian serves the purpose of intensifying the tragic development, and highlights the changing relationship between the main characters. The exchange involves a reflection upon barbarity, and its function as a category signifying ethical choices or an ethnic condition.

In the first act, Jason informs Médée that he has decided to keep the children and send Médée away. The eighteenth-century versions on this point rely more heavily on Seneca than Euripides, and the specific focus on the separation of mother and children is crucial to the period's focus on sentimental motherhood. Not surprisingly, the very idea of separating a mother from her children invokes the eighteenth-century notion of callous barbarity. In the opening scenes of eighteenth-century Medea plays, this display of Jason's glaring cruelty had every possibility of moving the audience to sympathize with the mother Medea. Clément's Médée reacts with surprise and horror, and depicts the fate of the children at a foreign court, forgotten by their unfaithful father, and finally 'sacrificed to the sons of their stepmother' (33). Médée concludes (33):

> Et je le souffrirois! Dis, le crois-tu, barbare?
> Le crois-tu?
> [And I would suffer this! Tell me, do you believe that, barbarian?
> Do you believe that?]

That Médée should accept Jason's decision is out of the question, and Jason's act proves him to be the barbarian, the cruel and inhuman husband and father. Médée's use of '*tu*' is a sign of her emotional strain, and it is the well-versed barbarian Jason who retains the formal '*vous*' in the exchange.[35] Clément's tragedy positions Médée firmly as a mother figure, in line with the ideal of domesticity in the eighteenth century.[36] Médée's focus on her role as a mother moves her close to the notion of 'natural' morality, and of universalism, in contrast to the '*un*-naturalness of civilisation'.[37]

---

[35] I wish to extend my thanks to Professor Marie-Christine Skuncke for this observation.
[36] I use Francus' term 'domesticity' as a definition of femininity relevant for all language areas in question here.
[37] Outram (1995), 83–4.

Clément tends to reserve the designation barbarian for particular actions, that is, in the ethical sense of the concept. This means that the protagonists can take turns in being barbarians. In the second act, Médée explains to her confidante that her love for Jason has made her heart barbarous (42):

> Depuis qu'un triste amour me possede & m'égare,
> Tu sais combien ce cœur est devenu barbare.
> [Since an unhappy love possesses me and leads me astray,
> You know to what extent this heart has become barbarous.]

Clément's Médée locates barbarity in her heart and this is in line with one of the definitions, 'cœur barbare', in the dictionary of the French Academy from 1799.[38] The barbarian is heartless—and the barbarous heart is unfeeling, empty, closed to compassion. However, Médée tells the story of becoming the barbarian herself as the result of her love for Jason. Clément's tragedy turns out to suggest that, on this point, excess is, after all, the problem—too much love can transform into its opposite, the horrifying barbarous heart. That love transforms into revenge is one of the main features of the story, and Médée stabs her two sons to death. After killing her two sons, Médée asks the furies in a soliloquy to exercise their barbarity on her heart (45): 'Exercez sur mon cœur toute vos barbaries'—the furies are not seen on stage, they solely exist as her inner vision.[39]

In the final scene, Jason calls Médée's heart barbarous—'ton barbare cœur' (50)—and on this point they finally agree. But Medea explains that her 'inhuman' and 'bloodstained' heart would never have become cruel, but for her love for Jason.[40] To her confidante she argues that her deeds were involuntary (*involontaire*) and she enumerates the 'auteurs des crimes de Médée' (48): a cowardly husband, her own 'fire', his perjury, his marriage, and 'les transports dont je suis obsédée' ('the raptures I have become obsessed with'). In this very rational exchange, Médée denies responsibility for her horrific infanticide, and she systematically explains that it is primarily Jason who is to blame. While Jason is responsible for acts such as cowardice, perjury, and a remarriage, her own acts concern the passions: the fire of love remains the source of Médée's revenge, as do the 'transports', or raptures, which, according to Clément, have become an 'obsession'. Médée, speaking about herself in the

---

[38] This 'barbarousness of heart' is present in Euripides' *Helen* (l. 501), as Hall (1989), 205 points out.
[39] See also Schweitzer, this volume.
[40] 'Ce cœur, qui, pour toi seul au crime accoutumé, / N'est devenu cruel que pour t'avoir aimé' (50).

third person, analyses her own obsession with the ecstasy of passion, and this admission brings back into the tragedy the emotional excess of the ethnic barbarian. While most of the play has exchanged ethnicity for ethics, in the sense discussed earlier, this last admission by Médée retains a tint of the otherness of barbaric societies, removed from the normality of western culture.

However, the definition of the barbarian sways in Clément's tragedy. It is noteworthy that Jason's failings, his effeminacy shown by cowardice, reflect Medea's allegations in Euripides' tragedy, that of *anandria*, unmanliness.[41] And in her defence of her role as a mother, Médée adapts to the ideal of a universal and natural femininity of the eighteenth century, presenting a moral imperative to a society based on artificiality. By claiming the role of a senti- mental mother, Médée is able to turn Jason into an ethical barbarian.

The inversions of emotions—love into vengefulness, passion into despair and jealousy—and the inversion of intimate relations—father to barbarian in the first act, and mother to barbarian in the third—define the tragic core of Clément's *Médée*. Anyone, not least family members, can take up the position of the barbarian for short or long periods, a characteristic of the ethical barbarian. The contrast between male and female barbarity depends on cause—excessive callousness on the one hand, and excessive passion on the other—and functions as a basic definition of late eighteenth-century gender difference.[42] Both versions of the barbarian—passionate excess as well as inhuman insensitivity—inevitably lead to disaster. The barbarian is both the most, and the least, passionate protagonist in the tragedy, and this dialectic between the gendered kinds of barbarity enables Clément to construct a tragedy with turning points as well as with passages underscoring sympathy for the unhappy protagonist.

In many Athenian tragedies, 'the unfettered passions of barbarians come to be closely associated with their ethnicity'.[43] In Clément's representation of Médée, the ethical and the ethnic barbarian are, at times, difficult to distin- guish from each other, and the question of race does not seem to be addressed in the tragedy. The excess of passions could indeed be attributed to barbarity as an ethnic characteristic, but does not seem to have any bearings on skin colour or cultural customs. Finally, Médée cannot live on in her role as the cruel barbarian. As a consequence, Clément contributes a new ending: instead of placing a triumphant Médée on the dragon chariot, defining herself as the vengeful demi-goddess, Clément's protagonist stays within the limits of her

---

[41]   Hall (1989), 208 on courage/manliness 'as one of the cardinal Hellenic virtues'.
[42]   See Outram (1995), 80–95.   [43]   Hall (1989), 125.

Figure 5.1 Bengt Lidner

human identity—her passions underscore her humanity, her adherence to a universal ideal of tender femininity—and this enables the audience to sympathize with the character. To fulfil the dramatic structure, the tragedy ends with Médée's suicide, her barbarous heart the focal point as she plunges a dagger to her breast.

There are obvious points of comparison between Clément's tragedy and the lesser known opera libretto *Medea* from 1784 by the Swedish author Bengt Lidner (Figure 5.1), which was never set to music or performed in the eighteenth century.

This printed libretto is of considerable importance to my argument on account of its focus on Jason's oath.[44] Lidner studied Greek in Göttingen with Professor Christian Gottlob Heyne, and stayed in Paris in the early 1780s, and was well read in both French and German literature. Lidner's libretto, with the

---

[44] Lidner, *Medea* (1936–7). On Lidner, see Lysell (2004); Cullhed (2006), (2011), (2013).

collapsing 'enemy concept', is exemplary here. However in Lidner's libretto, there is clear hope for change: a character can decide to turn back from barbarity and change his or her identity. Lidner uses the designation barbarian in the very first scene of his libretto, when Medea watches the preparations for Jason's wedding to Creusa, with her confidante, and admits that she still loves Jason (289):

> Jag älskar ännu - - - ännu - - - O, Barbar!
> En ångerfull blick; och Medea förlåter.
> [I still love - - - still - - - O, Barbarian!
> A repentant glance; and Medea forgives.]

Jason's barbarity concerns his actions—he has abandoned his spouse Medea, and broken his vow of fidelity. While Medea's feelings are unchanged, she still hopes that Jason will return to her. To her it is still possible to forgive the barbarous acts, and consequently Jason would shed his identity as the cruel barbarian. In the second act, Lidner explores the shifting identities of Jason even further. Medea claims that Jason was not born a barbarian—he once loved, and therefore he cannot become heartless (305). To add to the outrage of Jason's inhumanity, Medea expresses her astonishment at the fact that a father, Jason, could act in this way, and betray a mother, herself (321).

Lidner's definition of fatherhood and motherhood within an intimate family presupposes love and tenderness. The key structure in Lidner's libretto is the contrast between love and barbarity—love invokes the fullness of passion, while barbarity marks its opposite, the 'marble heart', a lack of humanity, emotional coldness. Lidner to some extent exonerates Medea, on the grounds of her passions—any passion seems preferable to the callousness of the barbarian. As Krämer remarks, the aesthetics of compassion and affect was explored on stage, as a means to secure 'the emotional participation of the audience'.[45] In comparison to Clément, Lidner brings this argument a step further. This particular sentimental interpretation of the word advocates strong feelings, from love and compassion to the understandable feelings of anger and despair when confronted with callousness, tyranny, or oppression. However, Lidner's victimized and sensitive Medea towards the end of the opera is transformed into a highly Senecan avenger; and the murder of the two sons takes place on stage, in spite of Horace's well-known objection.[46] Indeed, the actions of the

---

[45] See Krämer, this volume, 149.   [46] See Schweitzer, this volume.

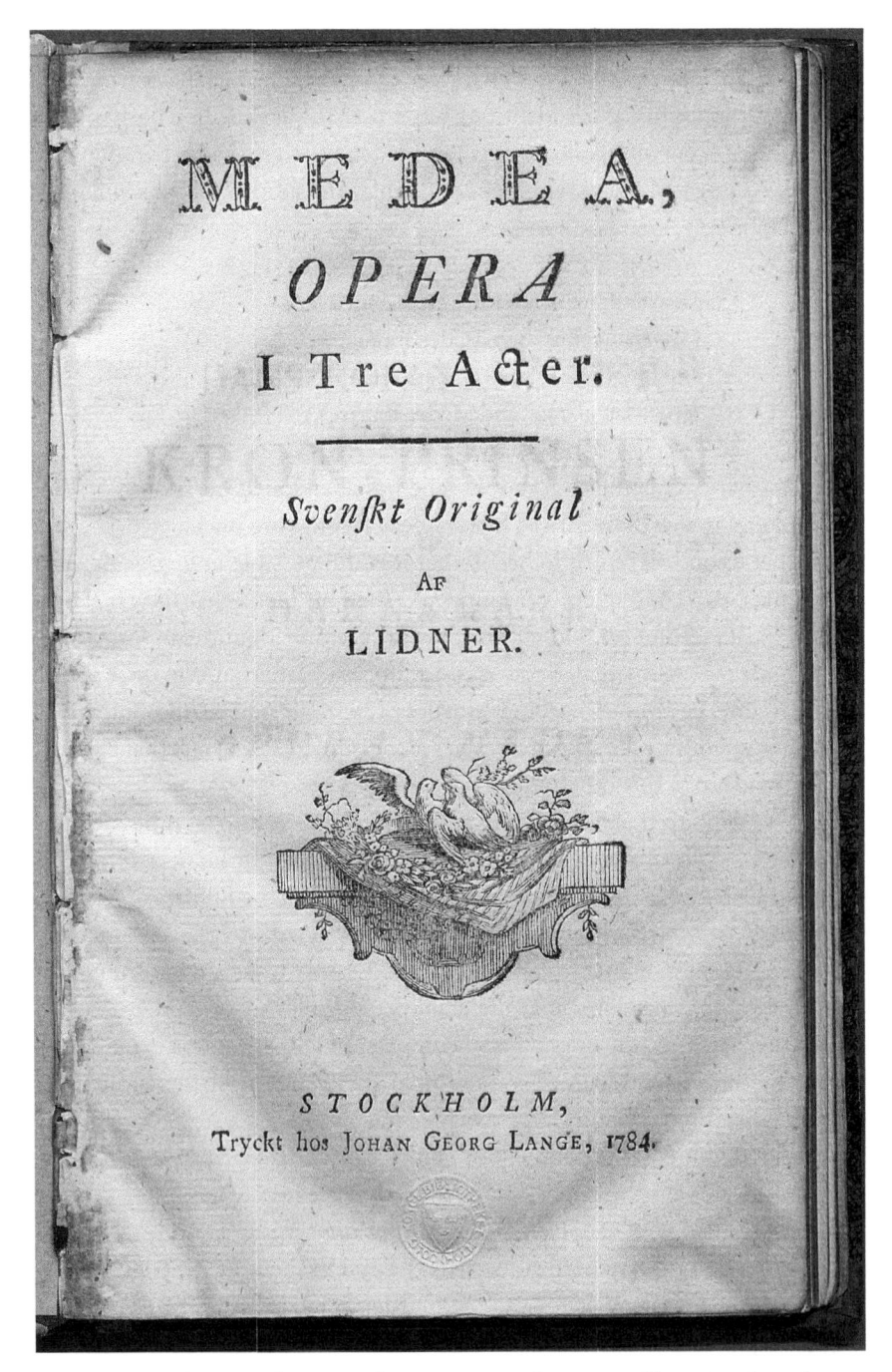

Figure 5.2 Title page of Bengt Lidner, *MEDEA, OPERA in Three Acts* (1784)

betrayed woman are barbarous, even by sentimental standards, but the blame is pushed even further towards the often male barbarians, the perjurers, the inconstant rakes. This version of the barbarian shows the resonance not only of eighteenth-century domestic ideals of femininity, but of the sentimental ideal of sincerity and natural morality inherent in this emotional regime, to adopt Reddy's term.[47] As Outram points out, these qualities were specifically identified as feminine in the eighteenth century.[48] It is telling that Lidner uses the designation 'barbarian' ten times in the libretto (Figure 5.2), every single time indicating Jason.

Ethics and the Barbaric Tyrant of the 1770s and 1780s

In the historical dictionary of the Swedish language, the definition of the barbarian as a heartless and inhuman person is specifically explained as having no ethnic bearings.[49] The editor points out that this particular usage is common in the works by Swedish poets of the late eighteenth century. One of the examples from the Swedish corpus contrasts the hero and the barbarian, and thus genders the use of the concept.[50] The example shows a telling parallel to Lidner, where Jason's reversal from hero to barbarian is in evidence from the opening scene.

The main turn from ethnicity to ethics, that is, from what I have described as cultural or innate characteristics of a certain group, defining itself in relation to others, to a moral conception concerning all humans, is evident in other languages too. The *Eighteenth Century Collections Online* (ECCO) demonstrate that the use of ethnic characteristics for the barbarian from 1750 to 1800 is found with reference to uncivilized and wild people, remote both in time and space, that are described as barbarian. As Hall points out, orientalism, defining barbarians, not least Persians, as cruel is evident in Greek tragedy.[51] In fiction of the eighteenth century, barbarity is generally not combined with

---

[47] Reddy (2001).   [48] Outram (1995), 83–4.

[49] The Swedish dictionary *Svenska Akademiens ordbok* (SAOB) is an ongoing project, a historical dictionary based on extensive excerpts from historical sources from the sixteenth century and onwards. See https://www.saob.se/ [last accessed 15 February 2023].

[50] 'Nej, du ej Hjelte är – du är barbar, om vana / Dig nöjet söka lärt i dina bröders blod' ('No, you are not a hero – you are a barbarian, since habit / has taught you to seek pleasure in your brothers' blood'). Stenhammar (1793), [295]. Further examples indicate that the barbarian cannot be touched by tears, he is heartless. SAOB, vol. 2 (1903), col. B 298. https://www.saob.se/artikel/?unik=B_0161-0148. bo4C&pz=5 [last accessed 15 February 2023].

[51] Hall (1989), 99, with reference to Said's *Orientalism* and his discussion of Aeschylus, *Persians*.

traits concerned with ethnicity, in the meaning of specific cultural practices of a particular society.

Dictionaries tend, instead, to highlight what I have termed the ethical pole of the concept. If we turn to the word 'barbarity', the synonyms given are 'inhumanity' and 'cruelty' both in English and in French.[52] Eighteenth-century writers such as John Cleland, Henry Fielding, and Samuel Richardson offer examples of this particular kind of emotional cruelty. A line by Fielding (*The Grub Street Opera*) summarizes the main characteristics of this use: 'Away, false perjur'd barbarous wretch'.[53] An anonymous novel from the early eighteenth century bears the title *The dreadful Tragedy; or, the Barbarous Lover* (1715).[54] The cruelty of love defines this version of the eighteenth-century barbarian and its connection to emotional perjury is of particular interest to the Medea story. In this context, the French translation of Horace's *Ars poetica* by Le Bel in 1769 is noteworthy: 'que rien ne puisse abbattre le cœur barbare de Médée', 'so that nothing can appease Medea's barbarous heart'.[55] Compare a very different, literal English translation of Horace's remark: 'Let Medea be fierce and unyielding'.[56] The insertion of the barbarous heart (*le cœur barbare*) in the French translation signals its late eighteenth-century French ideological and poetical context.[57] In the widely used German dictionary by Adelung from the 1790s, we find similar definitions. The barbarian denotes 'a hard and cruel human being'; '*einen harten, grausamen Menschen*'.[58] One of the sample sentences marks the temporal aspect we saw in Ovid's verse epistle. In the German case it is Cato who 'became a barbarian'. Sample sentences and expressions in English, German, French, and Swedish highlight the intimate relations between family members or lovers. Both a barbarian father and a barbarous heart are among the recurring examples.[59]

The barbarian is each one of us; each of us can act barbarously, not least as a reaction to cruelty. It comes as no surprise that Lidner not only uses 'Barbarian!' as his favourite exclamation, but combines the words 'Barbarian' and 'Tyrant' frequently. A barbarian is also a tyrant, and both are rejected by Lidner in his mission for a world order based on sentimental grounds. On a more general level, the discussion of the barbarian fits well into an overarching

---

[52] See for example Boyer (1764); Deletanville (1794), in ECCO. See also Feraud, *Dictionnaire critique de la langue française* (1787), http://catalogue.bnf.fr/ark:/12148/cb351538037 [last accessed 3 July 2023]; *Dictionnaire de l'Académie française* (1798), http://catalogue.bnf.fr/ark:/12148/cb35474154c [last accessed 3 July 2023].

[53] Fielding (1755), vol. 2, 24.

[54] See also Worldcat: https://www.worldcat.org/search?qt=worldcat_org_all&q=the+dreadful+tragedy+or+the+barbarous+lover [last accessed 15 February 2023].

[55] Schweitzer, this volume, n. 22, with references.   [56] Horace (1929), 461 (l. 123).

[57] Schweitzer, n. 22, this volume.   [58] Adelung (1793–1801).

[59] Adelung (1793–1801), 'Ein barbarischer Vater'; *Dictionnaire de l'Académie française* (1798), 'Cœur barbare'.

Enlightenment context. Cruelty and inhumanity were exercised by rulers of different kinds. James Thomson, author of the famous long poem *The Seasons*, mentions 'the barbarity of courts', indicating a political inversion of the barbarian, very much in line with the *Sturm und Drang* movement in the German-speaking areas.[60]

The contrast in space, between the court and the city on the one hand, and the peaceful countryside on the other, is laden with political implications in poetry, not least since the days of Augustus. The contrast was extended in spatial terms, when comparing Europe with the unspoiled nature of the New World. In the great French *Encyclopédie*, in the entry 'Esclavage', the word turns up in a description of how slavery affects the slave owner. He becomes a barbarian in the very sense discussed here, 'il devient fier, prompt, colère, dur, voluptueux, barbare', combining typical barbaric traits such as pride, fits of anger, hard-heartedness, and voluptuousness.[61] The point of departure in the entry is that every man is born free, and every slave owner is transformed into a tyrant by the very system of slavery.[62]

This discourse is present in a variety of media and contexts. Eighteenth-century artists visualized the 'natural' affections of humankind, and represented the barbaric stage in the history of humankind as an ideal and as a contrast to the tyrant-barbarian. The French artist Jean-Jacques-François Le Barbier was one of the contributors, choosing his themes from abbé Raynal's famous work on the two Indies.[63] His depiction of native Americans celebrating maternal and paternal devotion at the tomb of their dead child is a striking example of this sentimental view of 'natural' family bonds.[64] In fact, in a dictionary from 1773, the *Dictionnaire des mœurs* by Jean-François de Bastide (Paris, 1773), the entry '*Civilisé*' is understood in a negative sense, and contrasted to an earlier stage when humankind was '*libre & barbare*', 'free and barbarous'.[65] A civilized people is, according to de Bastide, '*soumis & corrompu*', that is, 'subjugated and corrupt'. This contrast is explored in the many versions of the very popular Inkle and Yarico story, which parallels in multiple ways Medea's fate.[66] The discourse of the barbarian connects to the emotional ideal of sentimentality as a considerable force extending beyond literature

---

[60] Thomson (1744), l. 1522.

[61] Jaucourt (1751), 937, https://gallica.bnf.fr/ark:/12148/bpt6k50537q/f972.item.r=esclavage [last accessed 3 July 2023].

[62] This section from the *Encyclopédie* is noted by Rohner (2016), 56 discussing *Inkle and Yariko*. Felsenstein (1999), 32 refers to English sources describing slave owners 'hardened in barbarity'.

[63] On Le Barbier's painting, see Standen (1989), 257–8; Smith (1990).

[64] Pinault Sørensen (2001), 161.

[65] Bastide (1773), 35, https://www.google.co.uk/books/edition/_/-kdaAAAAcAAJ?gbpv=1 [last accessed 3 July 2023].

[66] See introductory chapter to this volume.

and the arts, and also to the gender ideals connecting femininity with sincerity and an elevated morality based on universalist premises.[67] Further, the question of skin colour becomes apparent in the depictions of the white male as a barbarian, and the people of colour as sentimental ideals of humanity. The barbarian becomes a container for the rejected aspects of contemporary western society.

The Barbaric Oath in the 1770s and 1780s

Within the late eighteenth-century sentimental context, it is logical to focus on the notion of the universality of mankind.[68] Lidner's poetics certainly included this ethical universalism, expressed in the never-ending possibilities of shedding tears on behalf of, and together with, wretched fellow human beings from the entire globe. In the case of Medea, this view transformed the story in several ways. Medea took on the identity of the seduced innocent in several of the eighteenth-century versions, as in Gotter's 1775 melodrama, and in Clément's tragedy, a role that called for a transformation of Jason into a barbarian, in the terms of a libertine rake, characterized by his inconstancy, and his cunning use of false promises as a means of seduction.[69] Thus, the Medea story was adapted to eighteenth-century dramatic conventions, with a focus on predatory male sexuality associated with aristocratic amorality, and its victim, the innocent, gullible, and modest virgin of bourgeois and domestic values. It is obvious that Jason's oath of fidelity to Medea—carried out in a sacred grove in Colchis in order to guarantee the Greek hero the assistance of Medea in his quest for the Golden Fleece—is of vital importance to the story.[70] Ovid's verse letter 'Medea to Jason' suggests that Jason was not sincere even in Colchis.[71]

The oath on the one hand serves as a sign of Jason's perjury, his status as an emotional barbarian, but, on the other, it can serve as a sign of Medea's barbaric origins, if we turn to eighteenth-century views on barbaric customs.[72] For Adam Smith, the oath was characteristic of the barbaric pastoral stage of human development, and regarded as a primitive version of the contract. It relied on the idea of oral language as being transparent, on the emergence

---

[67] Cf. Reddy (2001); Outram (1995).   [68] Reddy (2001), 154–61.

[69] This line of argument is developed in Cullhed (2017), 93–6.

[70] On the importance of the oath in the fifth century BCE, see Scodel (2010), 122.

[71] Cullhed (2017), 94–5. 'I saw also tears—they, too, played their part in the deception. Thus quickly was I ensnared, girl that I was, by your words.' Ovid (1977), ll. 91–2.

[72] Moser (2018), 114–44.

of 'an intralinguistic public', and was associated with ritual and solemnity.[73] And it also carried the threat of fear and terror, since it was often inscribed into the body, as well as into memory. In fact, Seneca's Medea slashes her arms when she summons Hecate and poisons Creusa's robe, a display of the role of blood and ritual in pagan rites.[74] To Rousseau, the oath represented an extraordinary binding force. Moser remarks that 'the exchange between contracting parties obeys an economy of excess'.[75] Excess, being one of the most stable characteristics of the barbarian, is shown to be closely connected with the oath, or, perhaps more accurately, with the consequences of breaking an oath. Medea's revenge is fundamentally barbarian, as it is envisaged by Rousseau and Smith (and, indeed, Seneca), not least in its recourse to violence and terror.

With the notion of the oath as a barbarian trait within the three- or four-stage history of humankind, it is obvious that the eighteenth-century audience had several possibilities for interpreting Jason's oath and Medea's revenge. On the one hand, Jason could be adapted into a typical eighteenth-century stage libertine, preying on a modest young woman with false promises of matrimony. This version is common in several poetical genres as well as in the novel of the eighteenth century, and underscores the ethical aspect of barbarity. On the other hand, Jason could be understood as a Greek, unaccustomed to the meaning of an oath in barbaric Colchis, thus separating Greek civilization from the more primitive society of the Black Sea coast, in accordance with eighteenth-century discussions of the history of humankind. With this second interpretation, Medea's revenge fits into the idea of barbaric excess, and indicates that she becomes a temporal barbarian, representing a society with barbarian customs in the ethnic sense, a past that is dependent upon affectivity and an economy of excess.

This intervention by the eighteenth-century poets is notable and an important key to the interpretation of Medea in intertextual terms. The print audience, as well as parts of the theatre audience, were generally familiar with the ancient versions. The inversion of the barbarian invoked the presence of Euripides' tragedy, and highlighted the overarching change of perspective—from Medea being the ethnic barbarian to Jason being the emotional barbarian. I suggest that this particular choice of words—Medea calling Jason a barbarian ten times in Lidner's libretto—forms a sentimental and universalist argument for Medea's point of view. In fact, contemporary reactions to

[73] Moser (2018), 118–19.
[74] Seneca (2018), 386–7 (ll. 807–11). The scene does not depict an oath in a strict sense, but a ritual ensuring Medea the aid of the chthonic forces for her revenge.
[75] Moser (2018), 123.

Gotter's melodrama underline her appeal not only as a human being but as 'one of us'. Krämer quotes Johann Friedrich Schink, who expands on Medea's ability to 'affect our hearts'. She is 'not a monster alien to our society, but a human woman'.[76] The fact that she is identified as part of 'our society' rules out an ethnic othering of the protagonist. However, the question of Medea's ethnicity returns, since her understanding of the oath suggests that she, in spite of her conformity to a domestic gender ideal, belongs to a barbarian society, spatially and temporally remote from the staged Corinth.

By highlighting loving motherhood and marital fidelity as feminine qualities, the eighteenth-century authors attempt to redeem Medea from her otherness, while Jason turns into the barbarous other. As a case of displacement, the Medea story is indeed ambiguous, in its negotiation of a classical geography in relation to the eighteenth-century world of the transatlantic slave trade and empire. What is evident is that the wider space is replaced by the domestic scenery, a confined space indicating specific versions of masculinity and femininity, while remaining a space with rather porous walls. Ethnicity is played down in this vision of universal compassion with the victims of inhumanity and cruelty being gendered female. However, the oath as a barbaric custom tends to let barbarity in by the back door, not least with Yarico of Moquet's travelogue as an intertext.[77] Medea's revenge turns her into a temporal and spatial barbarian by her recourse to excess and terror.

Ostracizing the Barbarian in the 1790s

The last decade of the eighteenth century, after the French Revolution of 1789, marks a shift in the representation of the barbarian in European Medea plays. As I have mentioned, there is a general agreement in recent scholarship about an increasing separation of genders and races at the turn of the nineteenth century, and Reddy argues that the collapse of sentimentality as a model for society led to a decisive turning point in the 1790s.[78] These cultural changes posed challenges to the notion of universality, and consequently to the idea of the barbarian as a purely ethical term.

Although several aspects recur, the Medeas from the very end of the eighteenth century invert many of the sentimental claims of those of the 1770s and 1780s. The adjustments can be traced in Hoffmann's and Cherubini's

---

[76] See Krämer, this volume, the section on Gotter.
[77] Cf. the introductory chapter to this volume.   [78] Reddy (2001).

Médée, and more radically in the German versions by Klinger from 1787 and 1791. The focus on Jason as a barbarian wanes, and the question of ethnic otherness becomes more explicitly paired with the question of gender, by placing Medea and her rival Kreusa (or Glauce, or Dircé) on stage. The two women represent opposite versions of femininity, and the question of Medea's divine origins also becomes a focal point in Klinger's *Medea in Korinth* (Figure 5.3).[79]

The question of the barbarian is also transferred to new geographical areas, as in Klinger's *Medea auf dem Kaukasos* (1791). The belief in the blessings of barbarity as a temporal stage wanes, and ethnicity and space become categories of renewed interest. In his second Medea tragedy, Klinger confronts his protagonist with a group of incorrigible barbarians in a critique of Goethe's enlightened *Iphigenie auf Tauris*.[80]

Hoffmann's libretto from 1797 positions both Médée and Jason as barbarians, much in line with Clément's earlier work.[81] However, the similarities are played down by the tendency to redefine the barbarian both spatially and emotionally, pushing the concept towards an ethnic definition. The position of the innocent young maiden is to an increasing degree transferred from Medea to Jason's new bride. In Euripides' tragedy, she never enters the stage, but her presence is prominent in the works from the 1790s and in the early nineteenth century. In the opening scene of Hoffmann's and Cherubini's opera, a troubled Dircé sings an air to Hymen, wishing for the '*barbare étrangère*', the foreign barbarian, to be removed from her presence (3). Medea's foreignness once more turns out to be a defining characteristic. The characteristics of Medea as an ethnic barbarian follow the standard outline—her excessive '*colère*' and her supernatural powers threaten the union between Jason and his new bride Dircé. While excess was an ambiguous characteristic in Clément's tragedy, and embraced fully by Lidner, Hoffmann takes further steps towards establishing emotional excess as a sign of the ethnic barbarian.

At the end of the first act, a conversation between Jason and Médée turns into an open conflict. Créon has just banned Médée from Corinth, and Médée pleads with Jason. Her husband proves deaf to her entreaty, and Médée cries out (16): 'choisis, choisis, barbare / Ou l'amour le plus tendre, ou mon inimitié'. ['choose, choose, barbarian / Either the most tender love, or my enmity.'] Relapsing into the passionate '*tu*' form, as in Clément's tragedy, Médée points out the inhumanity and cruelty of Jason's behaviour. However, she also states that all her emotions are extreme; both her love and her enmity are

[79] See Lysell, this volume.   [80] On Iphigenia, see further Hall, this volume.
[81] Hoffmann and Cherubini (1797); Wygant (2010), 136–7, *passim*.

Figure 5.3 Frontispiece to Klinger's *Medea in Korinth* (1787)

boundless. Later on, in preparing her revenge, Médée appeals to the powers of her barbarian origins, in order to steel her heart. She is fully aware of her own transformation into a barbarian. And at the very end, in the final encounter between Jason and Médée, it is Jason who cries out to the murderous mother: 'Barbare, ou sont mes fils?' (47). While retaining much of the dual aspect of barbarity we saw in Clément, Hoffmann pushes the concept of the barbarian back to questions of ethnicity and of ominous excess. Even though Jason's cruelty can be described as ethically barbarous, it is evident that Medea's pagan and foreign origin marks her out. As an ethnic outsider and barbarian, her revenge is horrifying. With the inclusion of Dircé as an acting and singing character, Medea's emotional range is also diminished. She has less opportunity to expand on her own passions, from motherly tenderness to the full-blown rage of the woman scorned. By the expansion of the cast, the sentimental means of displaying Medea's troubled interiority through soliloquy are exchanged for a bifurcation of two opposing female characters. The Enlightenment understanding of the oath, as part of a specific stage in the history of humankind, has been replaced by an otherness based on Medea's place of origin, and on her beliefs in menacing powers (Figure 5.4).

Klinger's first Medea tragedy emphasizes the juxtaposition and conflict between Medea and Kreusa even more than in Hoffmann's libretto. This is the point where Medea's otherness is positioned primarily as a gender problem: Jason feels belittled by his larger-than-life spouse, and he prefers the innocent Kreusa. In an initial exchange with Kreon he admits to his relationship with Medea: 'ihr Geschöpf bin ich, und möcht' als Mensch und Mann das meyne sein', 'I am her creature, and I wish to be my own, as a human being and as a man' (12). Kreusa, on the other hand, is described as shy, mild, innocent, and gentle, the very opposite of Medea (12).[82] Further, this young woman has befriended Medea's sons, she is submissive to her father, and she promises to obey Jason. She even admits that her love is not as ardent as Medea's: it feels like a gentle shimmer in her bosom.[83] In fact, Medea is a general threat to Jason's masculinity, his role as a Greek hero, while the submissive child-bride is said to awaken his ambition.[84] Kreon and Jason agree on expelling Medea, who is a threat to both of them as heroes and rulers, and together they decide on Jason's union with Kreusa.

---

[82] Klinger uses the words 'schüchtern', 'sanft', 'weich' (16).
[83] Klinger (2012), 30: 'Sanft schimmerts in meinem Busen.'
[84] '[…] die jungfräuliche Braut öffnet mein Aug' den Strahlen, die auf der Bahn des Ruhms uns leuchten!', 'the maidenly bride opens my eyes to the rays that for us enlighten the road of glory!', Klinger (2012), 17.

Figure 5.4 Title page of Hoffmann and Cherubini, *Médée* (1797)

It would seem that Klinger articulates the Athenian view of connecting barbarity with matriarchal rule, 'a reversal of the Hellenic norm'.[85] Medea's predicament is her failure to lead the life of a woman, and not let her divinity become an obstacle in relation to both her husband and other human beings.

[85] Hall (1989), 202.

She even comments on the position of women in Greece, in a subtle rewriting of Euripides' 'Women of Corinth' speech (41): 'Auch weiß ich, daß ihr Griechen, dem Weibe sehr beschränkte Grenzen setzt. Mein Geist kennt keine [...]' ('I know well, that you Greeks set very confined limits to womanhood. My mind knows no limits [...]'). In marked contrast to her Euripidean counterpart who appeals to female solidarity per se, Klinger's Medea proclaims that she is not like a Greek woman at all. She is certainly a barbarian, but mainly in terms of a divine woman of barbarian excess.

In the fourth act, Medea kills her two sons as a retribution not only for the brother she killed when fleeing Colchis, but also for an infant brother, neglected by Hecate as a consequence of Medea's betrayal. It is certainly noteworthy that the revenge in Klinger's version is not motivated by her, but a sacrifice demanded by Hecate, who Klinger makes her mother. During the day, the influence of her paternal ancestor, the Sun, guides her, but at nightfall she is subjected to the dark powers of Hecate. The conflicting deities are ostensibly gendered, and defined in terms of a schematic binary between day and night, indicating a moral split between the positive aspects of light and the 'blackness' of darkness. The sacrifice is demanded by Hecate and in the act, Medea is forced to embrace her own divinity, though unwillingly.[86] The primeval forces of pagan matrilineal revenge are present, and they are not replaced by enlightened rules of law, as in the final part of Aeschylus' *Oresteia*. The infanticide functions here as 'a re-integration into barbaric prehistory'.[87] In this context, Medea's actions are primarily the sign of the barbarian and chthonic feminine divine sphere to which she both belongs and succumbs. Her choice is the choice of darkness and the underworld in contrast to the enlightened possibilities under the sun.[88] She also accepts matriarchal rule by recognizing the power of her mother Hecate. Thus, Klinger reinforces the dichotomies of the Greek concept of the barbarian.

Klinger's second Medea tragedy, *Medea in Kaukasos* (1791) is even more radical in terms of the barbarian. It marks a complete break with the sentimental view of the barbarian discussed earlier. In this tragedy, it is no longer a question of whether Medea is a barbarian or not, but about the possibility of civilizing a barbaric 'horde' from the Caucasus. Medea's final quest is to shed her divine identity and to accept the limits of humankind. She utters an oath to relinquish her divine powers, and to subject herself to Destiny (*das Schiksal* [*sic*]), a recurring protagonist in Klinger's two Medea tragedies. Her aim is to enlighten the local tribe: 'Ich will diesem Volke Licht und Recht aufdecken' (109),

---

[86] Cf. Lysell, this volume.   [87] Krämer, this volume.
[88] Hall (1989), 204–5, with reference to Zeitlin's interpretation of the *Oresteia*.

'I will reveal light and law to this people'. Both her oath and her ambition to bring the blessings of the law to the Caucasus function as mirror images of Euripides' version of Jason's oath in Colchis, and of his remark on how Medea was granted the benefit of a life under Greek law. In fact, Medea also breaks her oath: in order to save the young Roxane from being sacrificed by the Druids, she uses her magic power and splits the altar stone in two. After this last performance of power, she willingly takes the consequences of her own perjury. She tries to convince the horde to accept her happy message, her knowledge about agriculture, and a rather Christianized version of father Zeus, but fails completely.

As Lü points out, Klinger raises a question about the limits of enlightenment: is it viable to force enlightenment upon someone, or is the use of force in itself a betrayal of enlightenment ideals? The tragedy addresses issues of acute relevance during the early 1790s, and Lü reads Klinger's tragedy as a direct response to the outbreak of the French Revolution.[89] Medea asks herself whether she must 'shroud [herself] in fear' in order to 'force' the trembling horde 'to good' (124). Her final answer is in the negative, and Klinger thus points to the failure of her 'civilising mission'.[90] In fact, her display of power impresses the Druids, but as soon as she communicates her decision to live as a human being, they decide on sacrificing her: the power relations are turned around. Medea finds her peace—she accepts her identity as a human, and she willingly accepts death by her own hand as a kind of retribution for her own deeds. It is a humanized Medea who falls to the ground, a Medea who has finally come to terms with her own actions, and who welcomes even the eternal punishment awaiting her. In a sense, she accepts her own otherness, and pays the price. Her failure as a divine woman leads to her death, while Medea as a representative of a humbled version of femininity is embraced by means of suicide.

As several scholars have suggested, Klinger's tragedy can be read together with Goethe's *Iphigenie auf Tauris*.[91] Goethe's enlightened optimism, according to which the barbarians of Tauris are humanized and civilized by Iphigenie's message of love, is mirrored by Klinger's complete disbelief in universal understanding between humans. To Lü, the horde 'manifests the whole barbarity of the mob in the French Revolution'.[92] Klinger's tragedy thus needs to be read through the lens of a very specific moment in history and is

---

[89] Lü (2009), 77.   [90] Lü (2009), 78.
[91] See Lü (2009), 74–85; Winkler (2009); Lü (2010); Poeplau (2012), 251–8.
[92] Lü (2010), 157.

consequently separated from previous versions of Medea. Klinger critiques the possibility of combining the principles of humanity and truth with the use of force. Further, Klinger questions the humanizing principle of sentimental femininity, present in Goethe's *Iphigenie auf Tauris*, as well as in the *Medea* plays of the 1770s and 1780s.

In the tragedy, the horde insists on human sacrifice, the Druids rule by fear, their god is the great Destroyer. The contextual importance of a travelogue by George Keate and the philosopher and encyclopaedist Nicolas-Antoine Boulanger's work on the origins of religion has been noted.[93] Keate's report from a 1783 shipwreck at the Pelew islands (modern Palau) described the inhabitants as noble savages and their society as showing traits of 'the ideal of an enlightened European bourgeois society'; and Boulanger traced the destructive power of early religion and the priesthood to the traumatic experiences of natural disasters, such as the deluge.[94] Klinger was also in correspondence with the philosopher Friedrich Schleiermacher when working on his second Medea tragedy, and stressed the obvious contrast between these two descriptions of humankind. Again he suggests the possibility of accepting the positive representation of the noble savage, while also being aware of the more sordid power relations of a society based on the fear of (super)natural forces, human sacrifice, despotism, and the authority of priesthood. Klinger's youthful support of Rousseau was superseded by Boulanger's influence, but as the letter to Schleiermacher suggests, the very contrast became productive in his dramatic work.[95]

Klinger does not use the term barbarian in his tragedy. Medea refers to the members of the so-called horde (*die Horde*) as 'children of raw nature' (*Kinder der rohen Natur*) (104). The description of the Caucasians is similar to the reports of travelogues, and they fit into the system of historical development of human societies discussed earlier in this chapter. The *Horde* represent the pastoral stage of barbarism, and Medea's plan is to speed up history and transform their society by introducing agriculture. It is noteworthy that the rule of the Druids, based on Boulanger's criticism of ancient priesthood, fits so well into the eighteenth-century criticism of civilized customs. The accusation of dissimulation, articulated not least during the Terror, and of tyranny, echo both Rousseau's perspective and Boulanger's views.[96] Dissimulation was one of the main charges against civilization, from a

---

[93] By the editors Hartmann et al. in Klinger (2012).
[94] Klinger (2012), xxviii.   [95] Poeplau (2012), 253; Lü (2009), 74–5; Lü (2010), 157.
[96] On the sentimental emotional regime of the terror, see Reddy (2001), esp. 173–210.

primitivist view hailing the natural stage, while according to Boulanger it also characterized early religious rule.

In their critiques of dissimulation, it would seem that Rousseau and Boulanger agree, despite the contrast in their evaluation of the early stages of human history. Their broadly opposing views were uttered simultaneously, and side by side, during the eighteenth century, and both were products of the Enlightenment investigation into humankind and its historicity. Klinger's answer to Goethe is another contribution to the debate about humanity and the barbarian, but it also marks a decisive change in the representation of Medea and the barbarian. From this point on, the optimism wanes, and Medea's inability to behave like an ideal woman is connected to the discourse of the barbarian. In Klinger's Caucasian tragedy, both Medea and the *Horde* could be described as barbarians—Medea as a being estranged both in Greece and in the Caucasus, and the *Horde* by their cruel customs and spatial remoteness. The representation of the barbarians has relapsed into a question of ethnicity in the essentialist version, and into a fundamental disbelief in universalism. The language of sentimentalism is no longer viable for the protagonist Medea.

The focus on the Caucasus, however, would fit into the pattern of displacement. If we rely on Lü and her reading of the *Horde* as a parallel to the revolutionary mob in France, Klinger certainly resorts to a kind of displacement in time and space. The Druid frames his world view as a defence of cyclical time, when rejecting the promise of perfectibility of enlightenment linear time (157): 'We are fine the way we are, and we do not want to be better than our fathers.'[97] By this statement, Klinger crushes the idea of the natural morality of the barbarian, an idea cherished during the previous decades. It leaves not only Medea, but all barbarians, in a grim and never-ending state of society, and ostracizes them from the new definition of the civilized world. In fact, the Austrian playwright Grillparzer takes the cue from Klinger, and in his Medea trilogy *Das goldene Vließ* (*The Golden Fleece*) from 1821, the question of miscegenation is introduced to identify Medea's barbaric otherness as an ethnic trait. With Grillparzer, the turning point of the 1790s is imparted to the new century.

Conclusion

The inverted barbarian—the cruel and inhuman father, lover, or ex-hero, sometimes Jason, often Inkle of the Inkle and Yarico story—occupies a

---

[97] 'Wir sind gut so wie wir sind, und wollen nicht besser als unsre Väter sein.' Klinger (2012), 157.

position on the late eighteenth-century stage for a very short period from the 1770s to the 1780s. He is the double of the aristocratic libertine, of the tyrant and the slave owner, and his function is to act as foil to Medea as a humanized and victimized mother and spouse. The insistence on the happy stage of barbarity in human history is on the one hand used as a model for revealing European cruelty and barbarity, on the other for revealing the disastrous consequences of cultural encounters. Medea is both victim of the callous Jason *and* barbarous other through her excessive passion. Her sentimental appeal is also an aesthetic choice, with an insistence on naturalness, authenticity, and an exploration of subjectivity, not least inspired by Ovid's epistolary Medea. If we adopt Festa's view of sensibility as an aesthetic means to both erase and uphold difference between groups, Medea seems to be both universally similar and the permanent outsider. Indeed, the sentimental language of drama from the 1770s and 1780s at times succeeded in representing Medea as a member of a universal humankind, displaying the desired qualities of domestic femininity. As a protagonist from a tragedy within the admired classical canon, Medea is for most of the eighteenth century, primarily viewed as participant within a shared culture, within which explorations of so-called universal passions from antiquity onwards were not just possible but understood to be essential.

Even within a postcolonial reading of these texts, race is seldom an overt category within the eighteenth-century discourse about the barbarian. When skin colour appears in the texts, it tends to be in parallel to the barbarian as a moral and malleable concept—blackness is a property of hearts, as shown in the introductory chapter to this volume. Otherness is primarily ethical, and difference in ethnic terms is considered changeable. Further, it is obvious that cultural differences are often suppressed. On stage, it would seem that all characters tend to share an enlightened, Christian, and bourgeois ideology, apart from one or two male European barbarians. Medea is represented by white actresses, and her costume is often adapted to that of any western princess of serious drama.[98] However, barbarian ethnicity tends to seep into the story, as it invokes tales of colonial encounters and with its focus on the barbaric oath. Barbarity may well concern actions but not the character's essence.

By the turn of the century, gender increasingly becomes the dominant focus. With Klinger and the 1790s, the inversion is reversed, and the barbarian moves from the intimate sphere of sentimentality to the otherness of the Caucasus. The new Medea versions can be interpreted in relation to both the

---

[98] See further Dotlačilová, this volume.

horrors of the Revolution and the failure of sentimental universality after the Terror. Medea's part as the loving and tender woman is taken over by her rival, combining childlike innocence with motherly tenderness, and finally it is Medea herself who is expelled from the realm of femininity. She loses her complex subjectivity, as it had been expressed in the language of sentimentality, and her motherly tenderness, and is, once more, defined in terms of her connection to the barbarity of the feminine chthonic powers. Medea is, anew, a barbarian in ethnic terms, and barbarity thus becomes her very essence, her being.

Hall concludes her study of the Greek barbarians of Athenian tragedy with a reflection on the inversion of the barbarian: 'The barbaric Greeks and noble barbarians of Euripides therefore *presupposed* the invented ethnocentric world of tragedy.'[99] The same tendency is certainly evident in eighteenth-century Medea, but the Enlightenment of the eighteenth century did take further steps in probing into the possibilities of universalism. However, this window was firmly closed with the erasure of sentimentalism as a political choice, as Reddy argues. With the 1790s, the new and primarily ethnic focus on the barbarian moved Medea away from humankind, and positioned her as a terrifying demi-goddess. Now Kreusa becomes the main object of identification and compassion, while Medea explores the realms of exile and the forces controlling human existence. Medea had come a long way: from the witch of the sixteenth and seventeenth centuries, via the unique sentimental and universal woman of the 1770s and 1780s, to the ethnic barbarian of the 1790s. As a being expelled from the domestic sphere, Medea of the nineteenth century could voice the predicament of ethnic otherness.

---

[99] Hall (1989), 222.

PART II

LOCAL INTERPRETATIONS AND GLOBAL ISSUES: ONTOLOGY AND FORM

6

From Hearth to Hades

Breaking Boundaries with Medea and *ballet d'action*

Fiona Macintosh

In her pioneering study, *Medea, Magic, and Modernity in France: Stages and Histories, 1553–1797*, Amy Wygant draws attention to two markedly different French dictionary definitions of Medea: Chompré's *Dictionnaire abrégé de la fable* (1766), where Médée is '*grande magicienne*' *tout court*; and Noël's *Dictionnaire de la fable* (1810), where there is no mention of Medea's infanticide, merely a statement that the Corinthians paid off Euripides to make her responsible for the killing of her children. According to Noël's 1810 entry, Medea's magical powers serve to assist humankind rather than simply effect revenge.

Clearly something happened to the French popular perception of Medea between 1766 and 1810 for this humanization and, more importantly, for the exoneration of Medea to happen. For Wygant, it is Cherubini's opera *Médée* of 1797, where Medea's infanticide is mitigated, that explains the transformation; and Wygant is no doubt correct that Cherubini's adoption of the ancient detail regarding the Corinthian crowd's fury is a decisive detail in the changing reception of Medea's story at this time.[1] In the two most influential nineteenth-century versions, Grillparzer's *Das goldene Vließ* (1821) and Legouvé's *Médée* (1854), it is again the fury of the Corinthians that forces Medea to commit altruistic filicide.

However, it is important to recall that Cherubini was by no means the first to mitigate the infanticide. As early as 1698, Charles Gildon's *Phaeton* had reverted to the pre-Euripidean version to exonerate Medea: here it is the Corinthians who kill the children in fury on learning that Medea has murdered both their king and his daughter; and it is their slaughter of the children that leads in turn to Medea's madness and subsequent suicide. In Charles Johnson's *The Tragedy of Medæa* (1731), the children are not killed at all but

---

[1] Wygant (2007), 163–8.

Fiona Macintosh, *From Hearth to Hades: Breaking Boundaries with Medea and* ballet d'action In: *Mapping Medea: Revolutions and Transfers 1750–1800*. Edited by: Anna Albrektson and Fiona Macintosh, Oxford University Press.
© Anna Albrektson and Fiona Macintosh 2023. DOI: 10.1093/oso/9780192884190.003.0006

sent by their mother into exile; and it is Jason's consequent emotional collapse that prompts Medea's remorse and subsequent suicide.[2]

Cherubini's version alone, therefore, fails to explain Noël's 1810 humanized Medea—there were numerous other modern antecedents that provided an alternative to Medea, the Senecan *grande magicienne*. But the immediate foundations for Cherubini's operatic version were undoubtedly laid in the 1760s, in what was to become the most influential version of Medea in the last part of the eighteenth century, Jean-Georges Noverre's *ballet d'action*, *Médée et Jason* (1763), and especially in its expanded version (from 1776), which was performed across Europe. Here in Noverre's dance narrative, Médée is no *magicienne* pure and simple; on the contrary, she is clearly a woman wronged by a thoroughly ignoble, ingrate of a husband. Noverre's Médée is truly Euripidean as solicitous mother, spurned wife, *and* woman with supranormal powers. But Noverre's treatment of Medea, in turn, didn't come *ex nihilo*: it too is rooted in previous dramatic and, especially, operatic versions of Medea's narrative from at least the end of the seventeenth century.

This chapter takes as its focus Noverre's *ballet d'action* and probes the verity of the choreographer's claims in his treatise *Lettres sur la danse* (1760) that:

> [...] there are undoubtedly, a great many things that pantomime can only indicate, but in regard to the passions there is a degree of expression to which words cannot attain or, rather, there are passions for which no words exist. Then dancing allied with action triumphs.[3]

From the late seventeenth century, it became apparent that Medea's 'passions' could not be contained within, nor indeed confined to, serious spoken drama. Medea could no longer be given full rein within the dramatic playhouse. As a crosser of boundaries—geographical, social, and political—both in antiquity and especially during this period, Medea also posed considerable threat to the eighteenth-century institutional boundaries for the performance arts.

According to Voltaire in a preface to the new edition of Pierre Corneille's *Médée* in 1764, Medea is no longer a fit subject for tragedy: the dragon-drawn chariot is implausible, and an infanticidal Medea who is not magician is merely monstrous and repellent.[4] Indeed, in many ways, Medea embodies the excesses associated with the baroque rather than conforming to any strict, neo-classically prescribed notion of decorum. In this respect, she both resembles and was dependent upon the innovations of the great Italian stage

---

[2] Hall and Macintosh (2005), 84–93.   [3] Noverre (1930).   [4] Corneille (1764).

designer Giacomo Torelli, whose famous machines for the stage had marvelled theatre-goers across Europe in the previous century and who was also referred to as '*sorcière*'.

The onstage presence of spectators in Paris from 1637 had put an end to elaborate scenic effects; but with Voltaire's stage reforms from 1759 onwards, which included the removal of the onstage audience, the possibility of plays with large crowd scenes and elaborate stage machinery arose once more. By the 1760s, there were also new challenges to the dominance of bourgeois realism in the playhouse. And with the reproduction of Torelli's drawings in an article on 'Machines du Théâtre' in Diderot and d'Alembert's *Encyclopédie* (1759), the baroque designer's scenic innovations began to enjoy a revival. Despite Voltaire's evident scepticism as to the value of elaborate stage machinery to serious spoken theatre, Torelli's technological powers were once more back in vogue. This stage sorcerer was admired both for his capacity to create the illusion of infinity and for his perfect control over both the horizontal and vertical spaces in the playhouse.

Medea had much in common with the baroque artist in her command of space and her ability to create the illusion of infinite potential, and she was not surprisingly regularly linked to the eighteenth-century conception of the sublime. In the commentary on Ps. Longinus' treatise that accompanied the first French translation in 1674, Boileau had singled out the combination of rhetorical economy and emotional immensity in the Senecan and Corneillean versions of *Medea* as examples of the sublime.[5] Some eighty years later, Medea conforms absolutely to Edmund Burke's sublime and tragic figure: a social outcast, who is politically dangerous because of an apparent ability to wield infinite power; and one for whom the stage of life is simply too narrow a space in which to operate.[6]

According to Noverre, his *Médée et Jason* (1763) was his most 'sublime' ballet. And there is a very real sense in which the leap that Medea makes from hearth to Hades and finally upwards into the sky can only take place within the hyper-real spaces of Europe's eighteenth-century opera houses. When Voltaire excludes Medea from tragedy's realm, he adds: 'Aujourd'hui nous le [= le sujet de Médée] reléguons à l'Opéra, qui est parmi nous l'empire des fables [...]'.[7] However, what Voltaire did not anticipate was the power of Noverre's *ballet d'action*, which showed how the opera house in turn could

---

[5] Boileau Despréaux (1674).   [6] Burke (1757).
[7] Voltaire in Corneille (1764): 'Today, we relegate the subject of Medea to opera, which is for us the realm of myth [...]'.

provide new models for serious spoken theatre. Noverre had spent time with Garrick in London in the 1750s, where he had watched at first hand the tragic actor's embodiment of the Shakespearean sublime. Noverre's *Médée et Jason* was in many ways seminal, not simply because it was staged throughout Europe in the last decades of the eighteenth century,[8] but also because it provided a radically different model for tragedy. This new kind of tragedy, informed no less by Euripides than it was by the late eighteenth-century theatrical sublime, was able to accommodate Medea in all her complexity and enabled her return to the playhouses of Europe and the Americas in the following century.

Pierre Corneille and the 'Narrowing' of Theatrical Spaces

It is necessary to go back to Pierre Corneille's commentary on his 1635 *Médée* to understand how Medea began to be constrained by theatrical theory and convention at this time. Corneille's commentary appeared in the first published edition of the play in 1639, two years after the controversy surrounding *Le Cid* and in a real sense written in response to the newly codified strictures of neo-classical theory. Medea may well have found a voice in Corneille's spoken drama in 1635 but in many ways this was her last chance before neo-classical theory would determine that all that Medea represented lay beyond the bounds of what was dramatically permissible.

According to the most prominent of those theorists, Jean Chapelain, *le merveilleux* (Aristotle's *to thaumaston*) had to be held in check by the probable or else it became 'monstrous', as was the case in Corneille's tragicomic *Le Cid*. Chapelain had argued that the gods alone can render the *invraisemblable* acceptable because they can usher in the miraculous; *le merveilleux* is therefore everything that is contrary to the ordinary course of nature.[9] Medea, with her resort to the marvellous through her magical powers and in her encroachment upon the divine sphere in her final exit in Corneille's version, is in Chapelain's terms a clear embodiment of the 'monstrous'.

In his *Discours* of 1639, Corneille's response to Chapelain and the Academicians is that his play depicts not Medea's monstrosity—indeed at the end of Corneille's tragedy, there is no Senecan onstage killing of one of the children. Instead, Corneille responds, on display in his version is Medea's

---

[8] Noverre's *Médée et Jason* premiered in Stuttgart in 1763; it was then performed in 1770 and 1771 in Paris, 1767 and 1776 in Vienna, 1771 in Venice, 1781 in London, 1789 and 1791 in St Petersburg.
[9] Chapelain (1638).

humanity as abandoned wife, whose claims to justice inform her terrible revenge. And, Corneille continues, the pleasure for the audience here lies in the insights he has offered into human nature *in extremis*. Drawing on both Seneca and Euripides in his play—Seneca in his portrait of Medea as sorcerer, whose wand can fell her enemies with the faintest touch; Euripides in his sympathetic portrait of her as abandoned wife—Corneille adds not only the character of Créuse as an onstage character, but also his own damning portrait of a thoroughly ruthless and unprincipled ruler, Creon, whose venality receives blistering critique from Medea (Act II, ii, 393–5).

However powerful a riposte to Chapelain and his fellow Academicians, Corneille's attempt to resist their increasingly narrow definition of the real, which is based on notions of political and social propriety alone, turned out to be in vain. Hostility to the marvellous in the eighteenth century, for those seeking to re-forge tragedy in the neo-classical mould, is clearly bound up with the rise of theatrical naturalism and its ally, philosophical rationalism. In a world in which Nicholas Rowe's maxim in *The Fair Penitent* (1703), 'We n'er can pity what we n'er can share', holds sway, the realm of the marvellous is excluded from the dramatic stage because it militates against the requisite identification with individuals like 'us'. And whilst Chapelain might feel that the gods can make the marvellous *vraisemblable*, by the mid-eighteenth century, in an age of growing religious scepticism, *le merveilleux* and the supernatural were increasingly considered anachronisms. 'Le merveilleux', argued one prominent Enlightenment critic, only fell within the provenance of the epic poet, 'who paints in black and white, not for our eyes but our imagination' ('qui peint sans couleur, non pas par nos yeux, mais pour notre imagination').[10]

Voltaire's dismissal of Medea's suitability is not simply on the grounds of her infanticide; he also objects to her claims to self-sufficiency: 'Moi, dis-je, et c'est assez' (166), she proclaims at the beginning of the play echoing the Senecan Medea superest; and 'Moi je suis Médée', she utters at the end echoing Seneca's *Medea nunc sum* and signalling her status within a theatrical tradition (910). Eighteenth-century Medeas on the dramatic stage have to be radically refashioned to avoid any trace of the 'marvellous'—of her magical powers/her divine ancestry. Richard Glover's *Medea* (1767) conforms absolutely to this new, constrained, and eventually tamed Medea because her infanticide occurs in an act of 'phrenzy'; and arguably the 'tamed' Medea risks losing all that Medea represents as a mythological figure.[11]

---

[10] Grimm (1754) cited in Russell (1946), 89. See further, Macintosh (2018).
[11] See Hall and Macintosh (2005).

But where does *le merveilleux* go after it is forced from the dramatic stage? As Rameau's librettist, Louis de Cahusac argues in *Lettres sur la danse ancienne et moderne* (1754), '*le merveilleux*' is the distinct function of the '*tragédie lyrique*', which transports the mind by visual and auditory enchantment in awe-inspiring performances.[12] Dance, in Cahusac's terms, is fundamental to defining this different level of reality because it does so with bodily force. In this sense, *le merveilleux* is not incompatible with *le vraisemblable*; there are, as Charles Batteux argues in *Les beaux arts réduits à un même principe* (1746), two kinds of tragedy with different levels of reality—one heroic, called 'tragedy' pure and simple without the marvellous because it is human-focused; the other '*merveilleuse*' on account of the gods, called '*Spectacle Lyrique*' or opera. In short, according to Batteux, opera is the representation of marvellous action, or more precisely, the result of the divine element of epic transposed to the stage ('le divin de L'Epopée mis en spectacle').[13]

Marc-Antoine Charpentier/Thomas Corneille's *Médée* (1693)

We need to look to the Medea of opera—especially to the collaboration in 1693 of Pierre Corneille's brother Thomas, the librettist with Marc-Antoine Charpentier, the composer—for any forerunner to Noverre's danced version. According to Yixu Lü, Charpentier/Corneille's astonishingly powerful and prescient version of Medea had no influence in Germany.[14] It only had twelve performances in 1693 and one failed attempt at a revival in 1711 in Lille. According to Graham Sadler, the Lully *claque* at the Académie Royale de musique had problems with both its Italianate musical harmonies and Charpentier's use of dissonance upon dissonance in the last part of the opera, where the music mirrors the protagonist's mental state.[15] Given its limited performance history, it may well be tenuous to claim that Noverre had any knowledge of Charpentier's opera at all. However, in this psychologically complex and harmonically rich and complicated version of 1693, we find a Médée with many similarities to Noverre's humiliated and rejected lover of 1763; and for various reasons Charpentier's opera merits serious attention. The recent stage premiere by English National Opera, directed by David McVicar, with Sarah Connolly in the title role, was a revelation and has clearly

---

[12] For the links between *le merveilleux* and the sublime, see Cronk (2002); for Cahusac, Van Oostveldt and Bussels (2012), 157–8.
[13] Batteux (1746), 218–20.   [14] Lü (2010).   [15] Sadler and Thompson (2015).

contributed to bringing this forgotten masterpiece back into the repertoire.[16] And in the history of the reception of Medea, the opera is clearly prescient in its handling of the figure of Medea herself.

As in Pierre Corneille's version, Charpentier/Thomas Corneille's Creon is a political operator—telling Jason that he can marry his daughter once the temporary political alliance with her fiancé Orontes is no longer necessary. But for Creon, political and libidinous urges to power are inextricably linked, and his desire for his daughter is barely sublimated. Unlike Pierre Corneille's version, in the Thomas/Charpentier opera Jason cedes ground (as in Euripides and Seneca) to Medea, who comes centre stage.

This Medea is for almost the first three acts subject to doubts about her husband's fidelity—which given the princess' engagement to Orontes might even seem logically unfounded. She is not given ocular proof until the third act when she stumbles upon Jason and Créuse by accident. So for over half the opera we have witnessed not Medea the magician at all but Medea as vulnerable woman, whose misgivings about her husband are conveyed at first through her conversations with her confidante, Nérine. We have also witnessed her having to contemplate the prospect of handing over her children to Créuse, allegedly to guarantee their safety; and finally, this possibly philandering husband still finds his wife attractive—and at the end of Act 2 Jason cannot resist Medea's declaration of love and falls into her arms, until they are summarily interrupted by the arrival of Orontes.

In Act 3 Charpentier/T. Corneille's Medea is finally confronted with the truth she surmised. She tells Orontes about his fiancée and Jason's liaison and so enlists his support. It is only then that the baroque Medea proper begins to emerge as she calls up the furies and the demons to assist her in revenge. In Act 4 as the plot begins to unfold, Medea's magical powers extend to invoking a group of beautiful female spirits who seduce and torment Creon by turns so that he begins to rave; and in a fit of frenzy, he mistakenly kills Orontes and then himself offstage. At this point, Créuse ceases to be the demure daughter of a doting father: she furiously threatens her rival, and Medea, in response, fatally touches the arm of the beautiful golden dress that Jason had earlier urged her to offer up as marriage gift to Créuse. The Corinthian princess dies an agonizing death in Jason's arms, as the poison corrodes her body.

Jason grabs a weapon to take revenge on his wife but is confronted by Medea aloft on a dragon, the mythical gift to baroque stage designers such as

---

[16] It premiered at the London Coliseum in 2013 and was revived at the Grand Théâtre de Genève in 2019 with Anna Caterina in the title role.

Figure 6.1 Final scene of Charpentier's *Médée* (1693)

Torelli and his successors, pronouncing the death of their sons and pointing to the flames that engulf the palace collapsing before their eyes. Demons appear with braziers setting the building ablaze—and there is a strong sense that what the audience is witnessing are the objective correlatives of Medea's disintegrating mind. The demons disappear, night falls on the ruins and the monsters, and a hail of fire descends as the curtain falls (Figure 6.1).

Noverre, Garrick, and the Shakespearean Sublime

The eighteenth-century dance reformers sought to overturn an essentially monarchical version of modern ballet designed for virtuosic display and elaborate scenic effects. To underpin their reforms, they turned to the legitimizing authority of both Aristotle and the ancient dance commentators, Lucian and (less frequently) Libanius.[17] Although there were modern performance influences behind these reforms—notably *commedia dell'arte*, the Venetian *intermezzi*, and the mime artists of the theatres of the French *foires*—Roman pantomime (a direct descendant of Greek tragedy) was the most commonly invoked model. It is also significant that both the novel and *ballet d'action* emerged in the same century:[18] Aristotelian teleological narrative provided the subject matter of both genres and the choreographer's role was often compared to that of novelist. Just as the ancient pantomime dancers, such as the superstars of the Graeco-Roman world, Pylades and Bathyllus, had spoken with the body in their solo performances of multiple roles successively, so now the dancers of *ballet d'action* used corporeal language to tell their versions of the same Graeco-Roman stories. And they did so 'fortified with the vigour of eighteenth-century *sensibilité*.'[19]

The actor David Garrick was attracting considerable attention in serious drama in London and across Europe with his expressive movement patterns on stage. Garrick brought a new degree of naturalness to his performances but 'his success lay paradoxically in suppressing the natural voice of feeling, as he channelled passion into rhythm, and into his torso.'[20] It was the actor's ability to shift fleetingly and bodily from one passion to the next that led to his fascination with one of the leading dance reformers of his generation,

---

[17] For full accounts of the use of ancient material, see Hall (2008) and Lada-Richards (2010). On modern pantomime in general, see Guest (1996) and Nye (2011).
[18] Foster (1996).   [19] Lada-Richards (2010).   [20] Wiles (2020), 248.

Jean-Georges Noverre.[21] Ballet pantomime, like its ancient forebear, was also characterized by patterns of rapid transition punctuated by moments of arrest.[22] When Garrick invited Noverre to join him in London at Drury Lane Theatre for the 1755–6 season, their shared ambition to transform and to individuate performance was hugely advanced.[23] Even if Noverre's stay in London was cut short because of general hostility to foreign, and especially French, performers against the background of the Seven Years War, what the choreographer learned at first hand from Garrick undoubtedly informed his development of *ballet d'action.*

Noverre had been educated by the Jesuits at the Collège Louis le Grand in Paris, where performing in ancient plays was an essential part of the curriculum. Dancers in the period are often called actors,[24] and now Noverre had the opportunity to learn from the leading actor of his generation. Furthermore, since Garrick's wife, Eva Weigel, had studied dance in Vienna with Franz Hilverding, the actor/manager was fully aware of the exciting developments in danced drama and of just how much the actor in turn could learn from the dancer's corporeality. However, the principal mediating figure in this especially fruitful relationship was neither dancer nor actor: it was the emergent 'genius' of the second half of the eighteenth century, William Shakespeare, whose ascendancy was initiated primarily through Garrick's performances, which went on to afford new understandings of tragedy in performance.[25]

Noverre was especially struck by Garrick's performances as Macbeth; and Garrick returned the compliment by calling Noverre the 'Shakespeare of the dance'.[26] More significantly, it was Garrick's celebrated interpretation of *Macbeth*, above all, that proved crucial in shaping not just Noverre's *Médée et Jason* but also new understandings of the figure of Medea, in general, in the last part of the century. Just before Noverre's arrival in London in 1755, Garrick had sent his leading lady, Hannah Pritchard, to Paris to work with Noverre's company. It is clear from Thomas Davies' 1780 account of Pritchard's farewell performance as Lady Macbeth in 1768 just how much the actor had

[21] Wiles (2020), 367, citing Murphy (1801).

[22] See Lada Richards (2010), who also points out the complex confluence of ideas that contribute to 'the aesthetic of bodily eloquence': earlier in the century, in the bodily expressive performances of the French actor LeKain and the castrato opera singer Nicolini Grimaldi; and later, in the visual arts (notably Jacques-Louis David's celebration of the body as bearer of character and passion), which more broadly influenced Emma Hamilton's Attitudes.

[23] On the anti-French feeling in London at this time, which led to Noverre having to cut short his stay in London, see Taylor (2000); on Noverre's return immediately after the Revolution in 1791–3, see Chazin-Bennahum (1983), (1988).

[24] Nye (2011), 139.   [25] Bate (1997).   [26] McIntyre (1999), 258, 248.

learned from watching the expressive corporeality of the dancers of ballet pantomime:

> Mrs Pritchard's action, before and after the commission of the horrid deed was strongly characteristical; it presented an image of a mind insensible to compunction, and inflexibly bent to cruelty [...] When she seized the instruments of death, and cried, 'GIVE ME THE DAGGERS!' her look and action cannot be described, and will not soon be forgotten by the surviving spectators.[27]

When Davies goes on to praise Pritchard for her performance in the sleep-walking scene, where her 'acting resembled those sudden flashes of lightning, which more accurately discover the horrors of surrounding darkness', it is clear that she is ushering in other realms of experience for the onlookers.[28]

What Garrick and Pritchard were both able to bring to Shakespeare's tragedy were moments of the theatrical sublime—the supervention of a realm beyond language, in which marked disjunctions of high and low provided the actor with the potential for psychological insights as they teetered on the brink of the supranormal.[29] Edmund Burke had earlier in 1757 identified Shakespeare as the source of pathos rather than the sublime in *A Philosophical Enquiry into the Origin of our Ideas of the Sublime and Beautiful*. But in the wake of the French Revolution, Lady Macbeth becomes for him a major point of reference. He discovers, for example, the inrush of the demonic in 'unsex me here / and fill me, from the crown to the toe, top-full / of direst cruelty' (I, v.16), with the verb 'unsex' having particularly anti-revolutionary topicality as it was used to denigrate the female revolutionary sympathizers in France and in Britain.[30] Burke was a close friend of Garrick and behind the philosopher's invocations of *Macbeth* undoubtedly lies Garrick's staging of the play at Drury Lane.

From 1785 the definitive Lady Macbeth was no longer Hannah Pritchard but Sarah Siddons, who according to Horace Walpole, had originally turned down the parts of both Lady Macbeth and Medea because 'she did not look on them as female characters'.[31] Years later in her memoirs, however, after Siddons had made Lady Macbeth her signature role, she describes Lady Macbeth as a 'feminine, nay, perhaps even fragile'.[32] Like Pritchard, whose performances had plumbed and illuminated the 'darkness' in Lady Macbeth,

[27] Davies (1780), 2: 182–3.   [28] Davies (1780), 2: 183–4.
[29] Stabler (2005) on Thomas Warton (1781).   [30] Burke (1968 [1790]); Burdett (2016), 87–8.
[31] Parsons (1909), 79. For comment, see Noble (2006), 51.   [32] Brown (2005), 119.

Siddons was understood to have additionally brought a fragility to the 'darkness', which in combination permitted the spectator to apprehend a sense of the infinite. According to Burke, this particular blend induced in the onlooker 'that sort of delightful horror, which is the most genuine effect, and truest test of the sublime'.[33] And some years later, commenting on Siddons' final performance in the role in 1812 some years after her retirement, Hazlitt echoes Burke as Siddons is considered to transport the spectator into the realm of the marvellous:

> [...] regarded less with admiration than with wonder, as if a being of a superior order had dropped from another sphere to awe the world with the majesty of her appearance. She raised tragedy to the skies, or brought it down from thence. It was something above nature. We can conceive of nothing grander. She embodied to our imagination the fables of mythology, of the heroic and deified mortals of elder time. She was not less than a goddess, or than a prophetess inspired by the gods. Power was seated on her brow, passion emanated from her breast as from a shrine. She was Tragedy personified.[34]

Siddons' performances in the role of Lady Macbeth explicitly informed William Beechey's famous portrait *Mrs Siddons with the Emblems of Tragedy* (1793), where she carries a dagger in one hand and the mask of tragedy in another. It was, perhaps, inevitable that Siddons would also become associated with the other great female tragic role at this time, Medea. Hazlitt's account of Siddons as Lady Macbeth in the sleepwalking scene could equally well provide a commentary on Medea's actions in the final scenes of Euripides' tragedy. The associations between the two tragic characters had long been noted, especially in Lady Macbeth's agonizingly protracted, graphic account of threatened violence against her child, whose hammer blow is felt all the harder on account of its delay: 'I have given suck, and know, / How tender 'tis to love the babe that milks me. / I would, while it was smiling in my face, / Have plucked my nipple from his boneless gums / And dashed the brains out, had I so sworn / As you have done to this' (I.vii.54–9).[35]

In his report on the Salon of 1759, Diderot had criticized Carle van Loo for his painting of Mlle Clairon in the role of Medea in a revival of Longepierre's *Médée* (Figure 6.2). Diderot may well be correct to criticize the painting *qua* theatrical representation since the protagonist appears so detached from the action, it is as if she were in another play. But Diderot finds her implausible

---

[33] Burke (1757).   [34] Hazlitt (1816).   [35] Purkiss (2000), 43–7.

MLLE CLAIRON DANS LE RÔLE DE MÉDÉE, D'APRÈS CARLE VAN LOO

Figure 6.2 Carle Van Loo's engraving of Mlle Clairon in Longepierre's *Médée*

for different reasons: '[…] a little Medea, short, stiff, constrained, overloaded with fabric […] not a drop of blood falling from the tip of her dagger or dripping onto her hand: no disorder; no terror'.

For Diderot, having read Burke's *A Philosophical Enquiry into the Origin of our Ideas of the Sublime and Beautiful* (1757), the tamed Medea of neo-classical theatre is a travesty. Now terror is identified as a precondition of the sublime and worthy of admiration and emulation rather than something to be confined to the margins of fantasy alone. As Diderot well knew, Garrick had been instrumental in demonstrating how tragedy and the sublime might find fruitful partnership in expressive corporeal performance.

Whilst there is no evidence that Siddons changed her mind about performing Medea, there were clearly some who felt that they had seen her in the role. Mary Ann Yates had played Medea in Glover's version from its premiere in 1767 until her retirement in 1783 to considerable acclaim. But the illustration

Figure 6.3 Mrs Yates as Medea, by William Dickinson (1771)

Act III.   Medea.   *Scene I.*

Thornthwaite sculp.

Mrs SIDDONS as MEDEA.

I once had Parents — Ye endearing names!
How my torn heart with recollection bleeds!

London. Printed for J. Bell, British Library. Strand Feb.ʸ 18. 1792.

Figure 6.4 Sarah Siddons as Medea in Richard Glover's *Medea*

to John Bell's Acting Edition of the play in 1792 has an engraving not of Yates but of Siddons as Medea. This is clearly the 1771 portrait of Yates as Medea by William Dickinson, upon which Siddons' head has been superimposed. The inference is that even if Siddons didn't play Medea, in the view of many she should have done since Lady Macbeth and Medea in the last part of the eighteenth century have become conjoined in the public imaginary. And when Adelaide Simonet danced the role of Medea in London in 1781, in a version of Noverre's *ballet d'action* by Gaëtan Vestris (who now took the role of Jason and had danced the role in the original production), she was compared to Siddons (even though Siddons had yet to take up the role of Lady Macbeth) (Figures 6.3 and 6.4).

Noverre's *Médée et Jason*

By the last quarter of the eighteenth century, ballet had acquired sufficient status to become a high cultural art form *sui generis*; and it had done so through its participation in, and its major contribution to, the radical reforms introduced by Garrick into the theatre and by Gluck into opera. Noverre repaid his benefactor's hospitality during his time in London by devoting over eight pages of his *Lettres sur la danse* (1760) to the tragedian's mimetic powers. One of the many things that Noverre had learnt from watching Garrick in performance was that profile rather than frontal performance was essential. Instead of the symmetrical lines of courtly dancing, Noverre's dancers 'speak' bodily to each other: feeling rather than abstract ideas provide the subject matter for *ballet d'action*, as the inclusion of Medea's poignard in a famous engraving of the scene between Jason, Medea, and Creuse, in anticipation of the ballet's fatal outcome, seeks to capture.[36]

Much of the 'authority' accorded to *ballet d'action* at this time comes from the fact that it encompasses the fundaments of ancient tragedy—a fully participating chorus (one of the actors, as Aristotle had advocated) and a streamlined plot based on ancient epic tales. Now dance was deemed to follow the ancients in having something important to say. Each ballet, moreover, was accompanied by a detailed programme, which provided a running commentary on the action (even the 'unspoken' words of the dialogues), and on the

---

[36] See the sepia image of *Médée et Jason* at the King's Theatre, London (1781) in the British Museum collection at: https://commons.wikimedia.org/wiki/File:Jason_et_Med%C3%A9e_Ballet_tragique_ (BM_1849,1003.100).jpg) [last accessed 15 February 2023]. For the symmetrical lines of the *ballet de court*, see Weickmann (2007).

music, dance, and scenery. It may well be that had *ballet d'action* employed some spoken words, it would have been less controversial: its claims for bodily movement as a veritable language made it problematic, especially when the programmes contained details that could only be decoded from the performance with some difficulty and/or with detailed foreknowledge of the story.[37] For this reason, the stories had to be well known to the audience, or at the very least made available to the audience well in advance of the performance.[38] In the case of Medea in Europe in the last decade of the eighteenth century, this was not a problem.

The most controversial of all the claims made by the dance reformers was that dance could outperform the other fine arts. Frequently quoted at this time was Lucian's anecdote about the philosopher who sees the pantomime without music/voice but 'hears' because the dancer talks with his hands (*On Dance*). If the ancient pantomime artists demonstrated that the body, especially the hands, merited equal status with the spoken/sung word, the advocates of *ballet d'action* now claimed that dance could speak even more eloquently and more fully than speech—dance could dance the ineffable. What is striking here is the way in which the regions beyond language are linked to sublimity, 'the regions that only become visible when linguistic discourse breaks down'.[39]

The climax of *Médée et Jason*—in the run up to the Revolution and during the revolutionary period itself—demonstrates just how effectively feminine *furor* against male treachery could be conveyed with the help of a surging crowd of Furies on stage brandishing flaming torches. In the final scene of the ballet, Medea enters a realm beyond language as she appears in her chariot drawn by winged dragons who belch out fire; the corpse of one child at her feet, the other on the verge of death. She emits maniacal laughter at Jason's threats; he implores her on bended knee but she is unstoppable. In the age of the Enlightenment, she is suprahuman and in complete control of her own stage machinery. In the opera house alone can this blend of infinite possibility and the sublime outsider be represented onstage. Furies and demons flood the scene; she throws a poignard at Jason. The Furies disarm him to prolong his agony, then they chase him, enchain him, and chase and enchain him again—foreshadowing the dangerous dancing choruses of women in numerous *ballets d'action* to come (think, Pierre Gardel's *Télémaque*) but also in the *ballet des nonnes* of Meyerbeer's *Robert Le Diable* and the chorus of Wilis of

---

[37] Nye (2011), 37.
[38] Programmes were often circulated in advance of the performance, see Foster (1996), 216.
[39] Lada-Richards (2010).

Giselle.[40] Medea here orders one of the Fates to hand Jason the dagger; he grabs it and kills himself near the body of his betrothed. Then Medea flies off leaving the palace ablaze while the earth rumbles as the lightning and thunder roar. As with Charpentier, the rain of fire descends as the palace collapses. The livret comments: '*Médée triomphe et disparoit*'.

However, although Medea departs triumphant and as a suprahuman force, surrounded by other suprahuman/demonic female forces, for most of Noverre's *ballet d'action*, as with Charpentier's opera, she is intensely human. Indeed, in many ways, the final scene does not let the spectator forget her human status: scenically both her suprahuman self and her status as mortal woman are clearly signalled. For Medea significantly takes her exit in the ballet (and in the iconographic tradition of the eighteenth century) in a chariot set on the diagonal axis—the axis reserved for the humans in the baroque theatre—in marked contrast to the gods, who arrive and depart on the vertical axis (Figure 6.5).[41]

Figure 6.5 Final scene with Gaëtan Vestris and Mme Simonet (*c*. 1781)

---

[40] Macintosh (2013).

[41] I learned of this important distinction during a tour of the eighteenth-century Drottningholm Theatre, Stockholm.

Noverre's ballet with music by Jean-Joseph Rodolphe, which opened in Stuttgart at the Court of the Duke of Württemberg as part of his birthday celebrations and as an entr'acte between the acts of Pierre Laujon/Niccolò Jomelli's *Didone abbandonata*, was the first sympathetic treatment of Medea in the German-speaking world.[42] From the outset of Noverre's ballet, Medea as with Charpentier's protagonist, has only hunches and not proof about Jason's infidelity. As with Pierre Corneille's Créon, Noverre's Creon is Machiavellian—from the first scene, when festivities are being conducted to welcome Jason and Medea to Corinth, Creon distracts Medea in order to promote an alliance between Jason and his daughter; and then (Polonius-like) he hides behind the arras to spy on his daughter and her new lover. Medea's jealousy is registered from the beginning but her suspicions are only confirmed when she walks in on the lovers in Part 2 of the ballet: she now lunges at her rival and tries to kill her. Jason intervenes, bizarrely threatening revenge on Medea. The livret is revealing: '*La magicienne frappé de ce nouveau langage, tombe évanouie*.'[43]

It is Jason here who is responsible for the transformation of this Medea; and as if to add insult to injury, it is her rival who catches her as she faints so that when Medea comes round, she discovers the full extent of her humiliated state. She rages, fumes, and now utters threats herself. But even in the first shorter version, which only lasted twenty minutes, there is a particularly moving scene between Medea and her children, which culminates in Medea threatening suicide. When Jason, deeply moved himself, reassures her of his love for her, she falls into his arms. In the longer, thirty-five-minute version after the 1776 performance at the Paris Opéra, Jason lifts his son up proudly and promises to renounce his ambitions for the crown. Jason may well be politically ambitious in a world of *Realpolitik*, but he is also morally weak.

However, as with Charpentier's opera, the tender scene of reaffirmation is rudely interrupted—in Charpentier, it was the entrance of Orontes that effected the fatal *peripeteia* in the action; in Noverre's *ballet d'action*, it is Créuse herself. With her entry, Jason forgets all duty and tenderness towards Medea and continues his public humiliation of her:

> [...] il pousse la cruauté jusqu'à lui ordonner impérieusement d'éviter sa présence: c'est en vain que Médée le suit, et l'implore: il la repousse avec dédain et lui renouvelle l'ordre de fuir et de quitter promptement ses états.
>
> (1804, 15)

---

[42] Lü (2010).   [43] Noverre (1804).

> [[…] he pushes cruelty so far as imperiously to avoid her presence. Medea
> vainly follows and implores him; he pushes her away with disdain and he
> renews the order for her to flee and to leave the land promptly.]

His absolute disregard for their history together and for her feelings finally
brings about Medea's transformation into a witch. Even though this
derogatory label has been applied to Medea since the first scene, it is
only here, over halfway through the ballet, that she begins to display her
suprahuman powers. In the next scene, we watch her immobile, eyes fixed
to the ground before her transition is registered not just bodily (as in
Garrick's theatrical sublime) but also spatially as the set is transformed into
a demonic otherworld:

> […] elle est dans l'anéantissement le plus affreux, mais tout-à-coup elle en
> sort pour se livrer à sa rage. Elle éloigne ses enfants; évoque les enfers, elle
> agite sa baguette magique. Les lieux changent et représentent un autre épou-
> vantable. (1804, 15)
>
> [[…] she is in the most terrible state of abjectivity, but suddenly she pulls
> herself together and succumbs to rage. She moves away from the children,
> calls upon the underworld, waves her magic wand. The scene changes to
> another unbearable place.]

In Noverre's ballet the Euripidean vacillating speech is translated bodily. One
spectator, Joseph Uriot, wrote in 1763 that spectators found Medea and the
children harrowing to witness—it was a heart-wrenching scene that brought
tears to the audience's eyes as they anticipated the imminent infanticide
before their eyes. But Noverre's Medea thinks better—and, on this occasion at
least, the children are saved as she dispatches them with the gifts for the bride
and groom.

    We may have no dance notation for Noverre's ballets but we do have Jean-
Joseph Rodolphe's music. We also have the poetic prose of the ballet programme, which provides a novel-like commentary on the action and often
syntactically enacts the movement patterns onstage. Noverre, as we have
already heard, writes in his treatise on dancing that 'there are undoubtedly, a
great many things that pantomime can only indicate, but in regard to the passions there is a degree of expression to which words cannot attain or, rather,
there are passions for which no words exist. Then dancing allied with action
triumphs.' Dance, together with stage action made possible by the elaborate

baroque stage machinery, render this sublime Medea with her extraordinary emotional range not just possible but also plausible. And it was this new kind of tragedy, informed no less by Euripides than it was by ideas of the theatrical sublime, that enabled Medea's return to serious spoken drama in the playhouses of Europe and the Americas in the following century.

7

Shaping Complexity

Medea in the German-Language Theatre of the Eighteenth Century

Jörg Krämer

Few figures from ancient mythology exhibit such a high degree of contradictory qualities and attributes as Medea. The most striking ambivalence of the figure is the opposition of mother and child murderer, of a life-giving and life-destroying woman. But this is only the most elementary of numerous contradictions and contrasts that intersect in this figure: mighty princess and helpless servant; loving wife and avenging fury; both demi-goddess and omnipotent magician and at the same time powerless woman; victim and perpetrator; traitor to her ancestral family, who herself is betrayed again. All other characters in this myth, even Jason, appear in comparison to Medea as remarkably flat figures.

This high complexity of the mythological figure of Medea, as well as her unparalleled harshness, has presented a challenge, even a provocation for all subsequent cultures. Since Euripides and Apollonius Rhodius' *Argonautica*, with every artistic recreation of this mythical figure came the question of its evaluation. Which aspects of the traditional figure did the respective culture find problematic? What did each re-figuration focus on, how did it deal with the ambivalences and contradictions of the mythical figure? Which features of the figure did it pick up, which ones were reinforced or erased? Did the artistic reworking aim to reduce her ambivalence and complexity? Did it simplify or unify her contradictions? Or did it use the complex, contradictory figure as a gift for creating new kinds of questions?

This chapter examines only a short excerpt from the eminent history of the Medea myth: the representation of the figure on the stages of the German-speaking countries between 1692 and 1790. While the dominant focus of this volume is 1750 to 1800, it is essential to include the preceding half-century in an outline of the specific changes to the German Medea at the end of the

Jörg Krämer, *Shaping Complexity: Medea in the German-Language Theatre of the Eighteenth Century* In: *Mapping Medea: Revolutions and Transfers 1750--1800*. Edited by: Anna Albrektson and Fiona Macintosh, Oxford University Press.
© Anna Albrektson and Fiona Macintosh 2023. DOI: 10.1093/oso/9780192884190.003.0007

eighteenth century. A cross-section of different performance media of the time (musical theatre, drama, ballet, melodrama) will be examined. This chapter concentrates on the scandalous subject of infanticide; and the focus here is more broadly upon Medea's stay in Corinth and dispenses with other parts of the myth (which were certainly also of significance in the eighteenth century).

The central question in this chapter is: How is the complexity of the figure found in ancient mythological accounts reshaped according to the conditions of the eighteenth-century theatre? It is evident that Medea's complexity presented a clear challenge to the norms and systems of thought of eighteenth-century German culture; in order to make the Medea figure publicly acceptable, her complexity therefore had to be fundamentally reduced or reconfigured. Previous research into *Medea* plays of the eighteenth century has often concentrated on the historical development of motifs or on the question of femininity.[1] However, my focus here is on systems of thought and ethical norms, relating, for example, to love, sexuality, marriage, family, parenthood, individuality, subjectivity, and affect, but also to fidelity, justice, and the legitimacy of revenge. Contemporary conceptions also shaped the form of these plays as well as their content. Thus, every artistic recreation of the Medea figure in eighteenth-century theatre had to cope with certain fundamental problems conditioned by the societal norms of the period and by the formal limits of contemporary theatre.[2] The myth, however, could also be used to challenge or further develop existing conventions. For newly emerging theatrical genres such as the melodrama of the late eighteenth century, the Medea figure in particular could offer a perfect test case: the new medium also enabled a new way of shaping the character's ambivalences and of rethinking traditional role patterns.

The Changing Face of Medea

In German lexicography, there is a clear change in the evaluation of the Medea figure in the course of the eighteenth century (cf. Macintosh on France, this volume). The most important German encyclopaedia of the early eighteenth century was Johann Heinrich Zedler's *Grosses Vollständiges*

---

[1] See Herr (2000), 219–72; Winkler (2001); Glaser (2001); Luserke-Jaqui (2002); Schmierer (2005); Lü (2010); Cullhed (2017).
[2] See Schweitzer, this volume; Cullhed (2017), 89–90.

Universal-Lexicon Aller Wissenschaften und Künste, probably the most extensive encyclopaedic project in eighteenth-century Europe. It documents the state of knowledge of the late seventeenth and early eighteenth century in German-speaking countries. Volume 20 (published in 1739) contains a lengthy Medea article,[3] which is largely taken from the entry in Benjamin Hederich's *Gründliches Lexicon mythologicum* of 1724.[4] After presenting various ancient Medea myths, the encyclopaedia article concludes with a rationalist attempt at interpretation ('true history').[5] Many mythological elements are explained in accordance with an Enlightenment view: Medea's magical powers, for example, are explained by her knowledge of botany, the poison shirt is the result of naphtha, the dragons are really heraldic animals on Medea's ship, and so on.

In the final assessment of the figure, however, the author gets into difficulties. The evaluation itself is ambivalent: Medea appears on the one hand as a positive figure, who is able 'to help Jason in his plans, as well as to save him from the greatest danger; also to make people young again, who had become old in vice, that is, to bring them back to a good path'.[6] On the other hand, 'she is also an example of an indecent, misguided woman who, in order to satisfy her lust, left father, mother and fatherland and betrayed them; allured old fools to love, and made them, so to speak, young again, but who in the end plunged others and herself into extreme misery'.[7]

The lexicographer thus reveals fundamental difficulties in evaluating the figure. However, the infanticide is clearly negatively evaluated as a terrible atrocity by Medea, with which she 'surpassed even the most ferocious beasts in cruelty by laying her hands on her own flesh and blood'.[8] In 1770, however, a revised edition of the Hederich encyclopaedia was published by Johann Joachim Schwabe. There we find an addition, in which the child murder is

---

[3] Zedler (1739), vol. 20, cols. 61–71.

[4] Hederich (1724), cols. 1238–45; cf. Krämer (1998), vol. 1, 307.

[5] On similar attempts at rationalist interpretation in France, Spain, and Portugal (Bochart, 1651; Feijoo, 1742; Miravel y Casadevantes, 1753), see Lappin, this volume.

[6] '[...] so wohl einem, wie dem Jasoni, zu seinen Absichten verhelffen, als in der grösten Gefahr erhalten; allein auch Leute, die in Lastern alt geworden, wieder jung machen, das ist, wieder auf einen guten Weg bringen kan'. Zedler (1739), col. 70; cf. Hederich (1724), cols. 1244–5; Hederich (1741), cols. 1244–5.

[7] '[...] soll sie auch andern Theils ein Muster einer unzüchtigen ver=| laufenen Weibes=Person seyn, welche um ihrer Geilheit ein Gnügen zu thun, Vater, Mutter und Vaterland verlassen und verrathen, alte Gecken zu ihrer Liebe gereitzet, und gleichsam zu jungen Leuten gemacht, allein auch zuletzt andere und sich selbst in das äusserste Elend gestürtzet'. Zedler (1739), cols. 70–1; cf. Hederich (1724), col. 1245; Hederich (1741), col. 1245.

[8] '[...] daß sie auch die grimmigsten Bestien an Grausamkeit übertraf, indem sie die Hände an ihr eigen Fleisch und Blut legte [...]'. Zedler (1739), col. 68. Unlike all later dramatizations, this article mentions that the eldest son was able to save himself by escape.

now determined as slander by the Corinthians and thus has its provocative potential eliminated: 'Much has been added to their story, to make it the more miraculous, and to make the person the more hated.'[9] For in reality Medea had left the children 'in Corinth, where they were killed by the Corinthians themselves in the temple of the Akraian Juno'.[10] According to Schwabe's addition, Medea actually acted correctly and did not kill her children at all; her infanticide, on the other hand, appears to be propaganda concocted by Medea's victorious opponents who rewrote the story. Schwabe even suggests that Euripides received money for falsifying the myth. So around 1770, Medea is suddenly exonerated of one of the worst crimes traditionally attributed to her and is transformed from inhuman revenge monster to deceived woman, from an oversized figure of myth to a (at least partial) human woman. Similar changes in assessment can be found in the various representations of Medea in eighteenth-century German theatre.

German Musical Theatre around 1700: Bressand and Corneille

Musical theatre is a key mediator of mythological subjects in the German theatre around 1700. Although generally other mythological subjects were more popular,[11] Medea appears in an opera libretto by Friedrich Christian Bressand, the young 'Secret Chamber Writer' and de facto court poet at the court of Braunschweig-Wolfenbüttel. Bressand's 'Singe-Spiel' *Jason* premiered in Braunschweig in 1692 with (lost) music by Johann Sigismund Kusser;[12] libretto prints document performances until 1724.[13] Bressand cites his main sources in the 'Preliminary Report' [*Vorbericht*]: 'the magnificent Seneca and after him the inventive Corneille';[14] he also points out some changes in comparison to these two tragedies. Pierre Corneille's play remained his central model: in Bressand's recitative, the metre of the rhyming ('heroic') alexandrines of Corneille repeatedly shines through; and many

---

[9] 'Man hat vieles zu ihrer Geschichte hinzu gesetzet, solche nur desto wunderbarer, und die Person desto verhasster zu machen.' Hederich and Schwabe (1770), col. 1545.

[10] '[…] welche sie doch zu Korinth gelassen, wo sie von den Korinthern selbst in dem Tempel der akräischen Juno umgebracht worden.' Hederich and Schwabe (1770), col. 1545.

[11] Popular models from ancient myths in German musical theatre around and after 1700 were Ovid's *Metamorphoses* and the myths about the Trojan War as well as the figures of Hercules, Theseus, Odysseus/Telemachus, Aeneas, and Diana.

[12] Bressand (1692). A further *Medea* libretto by Postel (1695), staged in Hamburg, deals with a different part of the Medea myth; Postel's libretto goes back to Aurelio Aureli's *Medea in Atene*.

[13] Bressand (1695) (probably also played in 1697), (1715), (1724).

[14] 'der prächtige Seneca und nach ihm der wolausdenkende Corneille'. Bressand (1692), iii.

verses are almost literally translated from Corneille's *Médée* (1635). The integration of dances and choruses also points to the French *tragédie lyrique*. Almost contemporaneously with Bressand, Thomas Corneille wrote in Paris the libretto for Marc-Antoine Charpentier's *Médée* (premiered in 1693—see further Macintosh, this volume).[15] Although Bressand could not have known this *tragédie lyrique*, his German libretto nonetheless bears some structural parallels to it, especially in the characteristic love competition for Creusa between Jason and Ægeus.

Even though Bressand used Pierre Corneille's tragedy as basis, he was forced, for genre-specific reasons, to shorten the extensive text considerably for musical theatre. In addition, Bressand needed further space for the allegorical scenes which he added (the elevation of the ship *Argo* into the starry sky, including a genealogical interpretation of the House of Austria).[16] Therefore the characters tend to be flat and more unambiguous than in Corneille's spoken tragedy. Bressand's preface already conveys a clear perspective on Medea, who is described as 'the vicious and treacherous Medea', who 'evades punishment and revenge as she flees'.[17]

It is Jason's role that is significantly different from Corneille in Bressand's version. With Corneille, Jason blames his children after Créuse's death for handing over the poisoned gift from Medea; Jason also emphasizes that he himself wants to sacrifice his children (this was apparently first introduced into the history of the Medea plot by Corneille).[18] With Bressand, these negative shades of Jason's character disappear; Jason is consistently shown as loving father, while Medea is unscrupulously prepared not only to instrumentalize her children for revenge, but even to kill them. Both figures are thus reduced in their complexity. Medea's motherly love, present in Corneille, is completely omitted by Bressand, where she appears completely indifferent to her children and only uses them as a tool of revenge. Jason, on the other hand, shows nothing but fatherly love for his children. In a long dialogue with his confidant Idas, Jason also explains why he had courted Creusa: simply out of care for his children.

---

[15] See Leopold (1998), esp. 134–9.

[16] On comparable allegorical and political references of the Medea myth in Russia (for example to Catherine the Great), see Nikiforova, this volume.

[17] 'die lasterhaffte und treulose Medea', who 'der Straffe und Rache vermittelst ihrer Flucht entziehet'. Bressand (1692), f.iii–v.

[18] 'C'est vous, petits ingrats, que malgré la nature, / Il me faut immoler dessus leur sépulture' ['It is you, you ungrateful little ones, that despite nature I must sacrifice on their graves']. Corneille (1980), 591.

Ich hätte mich darzu auch nie erkühnet/
wenn das geschik/ mein allerhärtster Feind/
mich mit Gewalt darzu nicht zwänge.
[…]
weil ich Medeen doch nicht glüklich machen kann/
und keine sicherheit selbst neben ihr kann finden/
muß ich zum wenigsten mich unterwinden
was unsrer Kinder Heil und Wolfart gehet an.
[…]
weil ja Medea nicht der Straffe kann entfliehn/
muß ich die übrigen zu retten mich bemühn.[19]

[I never would have dared to do so, / if fate, my most hardened enemy, / didn't force me to do so. / […] because I can't make Medea happy after all, / and can't find any security next to her, / I have at least to seek / what's good for our children. / […] because Medea can't escape the punishment, / I must try to save the rest.]

There are no signs in the text that Jason's concern for his children was merely strategic and not meant seriously.

Similarly, in the sub-plot with Acastus, the son of the murdered King Pelias in Iolkos, all guilt is diverted away from Jason: 'because he didn't know about this murder / until the father's cold breast was already lifeless'.[20] It's all due to Medea's deception,[21] while Jason is exculpated. Creon sums up the position in the dialogue with Medea: 'Jason has no part in your vices'.[22] Bressand's Medea is a cold, calculating courtly figure who strategically plans her intrigues and carries them out by manipulating other people as well as by her magical powers. Moral concerns of any kind seem to be alien to the character. (Accordingly, Jason calls her 'O loath of nature / inhuman tiger!').[23] As another example, Medea immediately uses the opportunity to instrumentalize Acastus, who is in love with her, for her strategic purposes.

Jason is thus exculpated and significantly morally enhanced by Bressand in comparison to Corneille's version, while Medea becomes more culpable.[24]

---

[19] Bressand (1692), 24; see also Jason's requests for the protection of children at Creusa, 31–2.
[20] 'weil er nicht eh von diesem Mord gewust/ | als da schon leblos war des Vaters kalte Brust'. Bressand (1692), 4.
[21] 'der Medeen Trug'. Bressand (1692), 3.
[22] 'An deinen lastern hat der Jason keinen theil/'. Bressand (1692), 29.
[23] 'O abscheu der Natur / unmenschlichs Tygerthier!' Bressand (1692), 73.
[24] See Lü (2009), 21–39, esp. 37.

In the end, Bressand also cancels Jason's suicide introduced by Corneille. In this respect, it seems only logical that the title of the work has now shifted from Corneille's *Médée* to *Jason*. The reduction of the complexity of the figures compared to Corneille seems to be caused also by the different performance modes: for musical theatre around 1700, the plot was attractive not because of the potential for conflict between and within the characters, but because of its mythical material with the possibility of large visualizable effects, here in particular the magical powers of Medea (with the appearance of ghosts, and the use of flying machines, etc.). Bressand's libretto goes far beyond Corneille's tragedy in terms of spectacular effect because what matters in contemporary musical theatre is what can be visually represented.[25] Therefore, in the last act we find a large gypsy scene of a wedding 'Masquerade',[26] influenced by Italian *commedia dell'arte*. Here, a large dance scene is integrated into the *Medea* plot in a coherent way: during the wedding of Jason and Creusa, courtiers dance, 'partly dressed as gypsies and partly as Polichinelles and Harlequins'.[27] The 'gypsies' act as fortune-tellers for individual courtiers—a dramaturgically convincing, cheerful, and colourful scene, skilfully placed shortly before the terrible end of the play.

In a later version of the Bressand libretto, which was staged in Hamburg in 1695, a 'comic person' is additionally inserted (substituting the allegorical scene around the ship *Argo*). This also shows how strongly performance-related conventions—here from the reception of the Venetian opera in Hamburg—were taken into account. But despite the flexibility in musical theatre of the time, its basic generic traditions (its dramaturgy, unambiguous characterization of the figures, the significance of the visual) remained stable for a long time. Some sixty years later, in the libretto *Medea* by Johann Gottlieb Klest, printed in 1752,[28] there are similarly clear perspectives on the figures of Jason and Medea.[29] Musical theatre around and after 1700 favoured figures of low complexity; the complexity is found on other levels (e.g. in the combination of the various codes of music, language, scenery, and movement or in the combination of comic and serious figures and plots).

[25]   Gess et al. (2015).   [26]   Bressand (1692), 62–4.
[27]   'theils in Zigeuner und Zigeunerinnen/ theils in Polichinellen und Hartequins [*sic*] gestalt'. Bressand (1692), 62.
[28]   Klest (1752). The music was composed by Georg Gebel the Younger (1709–53).
[29]   See Lü (2009), 39–42.

Lessing's Marwood and Medea

From around 1750 onwards, theatre in the German-speaking world changed considerably. German-language musical theatre radically diminished in importance (and also in its institutional anchoring); the rise of the Italian *opera seria* at the courts led, among many other shifts, to a preference for historical material as models for libretti alongside traditional mythological subjects. In addition, musical theatre moved closer to neo-Aristotelian drama. There was a move away from the courtly musical theatre of the Bressandian type towards other genres in the German-speaking theatre: a newly conceived spoken drama with contemporary plots, later to comic *Singspiel* and to the new genre of melodrama. And in the field of ballet, the new model of *ballet d'action* developed as an independent form of theatre.

Despite all these changes, however, the interest in the figure of Medea remained. Gradually, there were changes in the representation of Medea, which entailed humanizing and psychologizing the figure, and increasing her complexity. And even though she remains predominantly a negative figure, evaluations of her character become increasingly difficult.

In Gotthold Ephraim Lessing's tragedy *Miß Sara Sampson* (premiered and published in 1755), the *Medea* plays of both Euripides and especially Seneca were central models.[30] The reference to the Medea myth is also made explicitly in the play itself when Marwood threatens her previous lover Mellefont to kill their daughter Arabella: 'Tremble for your Bella! Not her life shall bring to posterity the memory of my despised love; my cruelty shall perpetuate that memory. Look at me as a new Medea!'[31] Despite the modern setting, Lessing lets the figures of the ancient myth shine through here. This has occasionally led researchers to read the drama as an adaption of Medea in modern dress. Simonetta Sanna, for example, directly identifies Mellefont as Jason, Marwood as Medea, and Sara as Creusa;[32] Sara's father, Sir William Sampson, then becomes a modern, sensitive Kreon. Traces of more recent *Medea* adaptations can also be found in Lessing: and although he distinguished his work from Pierre Corneille's *Médée*,[33] with Mellefont's suicide he has clearly adopted the final motif of Jason's suicide from Corneille.

---

[30] See Barner (1973), 35–52; Woesler (1978); Levin (1979), 71–81; Ter-Nedden (1986); Sanna (1999), 19–50; Schmierer (2005), 94–111; Cullhed (2017).

[31] 'Zittre für deine Bella! Ihr Leben soll das Andenken meiner verachteten Liebe auf die Nachwelt nicht bringen; meine Grausamkeit soll dieses Andenken verewigen. Sieh in mir eine neue Medea!' Lessing (2003), 464.

[32] So explicitly in Sanna (1999), 19–20.

[33] Cf. Lessing's letter to Karl Wilhelm Ramler of 11 December 1755. Lessing (1987), 76–8, here 78.

However, these parallels do not work completely and they ignore, moreover, Lessing's numerous other intertexts. Further, they fail to grasp the central constellations of the play, such as the conflict between Sara and her father, or the internal conflicts in Sara herself. Lessing was certainly not interested in writing another Medea version in contemporary, bourgeois garb; his piece does, however, indirectly testify to the resonance of the Medea myth around 1750. For Lessing, the Medea myth seems to form a kind of framework that he used or transformed according to his own purposes. As Sanna points out, for example, at the beginning of the play Sara, too, is linked more to Medea than to the Creusa figure when she is to leave her homeland via the sea for a foreign culture:[34] 'So shall I leave my fatherland as a criminal? [...] In every wave that will strike our ship, death would rush against me; every wind would roar curses from my father's coasts after me [...].'[35] This imagined plight of the refugee aligns the figure of Sara not with Creusa, but with Medea.[36]

The actual new Medea figure, however, is the abandoned beloved of Mellefont, Marwood. She identifies herself as the 'new Medea' (see above), and when Mellefont calls her 'the greatest of the female monsters,'[37] he adopts the traditional evaluation of Medea (see above on Zedler) and thus confirms this identification. Marwood provides the tragic end of the piece, after a positive outcome seems to emerge from Act III onwards. Her murder of Sara by poison clearly ties in with the Medea myth (with the poisoned bridal gown), as does her triumphant escape across the sea at the end.

But the differences are just as obvious. Unlike Jason and Medea, Mellefont[38] and Marwood are not married, so Mellefont's move to Sara seems less serious than Jason's adultery. In the bourgeois value system around 1750, a married Mellefont would have been impossible: if Mellefont had already been married to Marwood, the whole play would no longer work; in the bourgeois system of the eighteenth century, intentional adultery would have meant an extreme, inexcusable violation of marriage as a central norm of the time. The transformation chosen by Lessing not only means a certain relief for Mellefont, but at the same time an indirect devaluation of Marwood (as mother of an

---

[34] Cf. Sanna (1999), 23–4.
[35] 'So soll ich mein Vaterland als eine Verbrecherin verlassen? [...] In jeder Welle, die an unser Schiff schlüge, würde mir der Tod entgegen rauschen; jeder Wind würde mir von den väterlichen Küsten Verwünschungen nachbrausen [...].' Lessing (2003), 445.
[36] Cf. Cullhed (2017), 90: 'In fact, Sara's as well as Marwood's traits contributed to shaping the new Medea.'
[37] 'der weiblichen Ungeheuer größtes'. Lessing (2003), 516.
[38] For Mellefont as a type of contemporary 'Libertin' see Sanna (1999), 24–5; Cullhed (2017), 93–6; differentiating critically Hillerkus (2017).

illegitimate child).[39] In Lessing's modern version, Marwood no longer possesses supernatural powers like Medea; the norms of the bourgeois theatre of the time seem to prohibit this as well. Finally, the infanticide is not carried out, but only articulated as a threat; in the end the child is even adopted by the old Sampson (which contradicts all variants of the ancient myth). However, despite all the negative qualities ascribed to Marwood in the play, Lessing also makes clear her dilemma. The demands she makes on Mellefont are not unjustified, and Mellefont also shows a certain sense of guilt towards her. Overall, Marwood is the most complex figure in the piece, a figure with an enormous capacity for strategic disguise and cold manipulation; but sometimes she also reveals very different traits. Compared to her, Sara appears as a relatively flat character, whose virtue at the end leads to a kind of sacralized exaltation ('already half an angel', 'saint');[40] as a figure, she clearly stems from Protestant *Empfindsamkeit*, not from pagan antiquity like the mythical Creusa.

Even though Marwood and Mellefont (both main characters without first names)[41] do not reach the complexity of the mythical figures of Medea and Jason, both are much more complex figures than the Medea/Jason figures of the opera libretti of Bressand or Klest. This seems, on the one hand, to be dictated by their performance modes: the dramaturgy of Lessing's spoken drama differs considerably from the dramaturgy of late baroque opera. On the other hand, changes in the systems of thought around the middle of the century are also reflected: Lessing now focuses on the nuclear family model of bourgeois *Empfindsamkeit* with its problems and limitations, which had not yet become relevant in Bressand's courtly context around 1700.

Medea and the Aesthetics of *Empfindsamkeit*: Lessing and Noverre

In his *Laokoon* of 1766, Lessing again deals casually with the myth of Medea, using the example of a painting by Timomachus, and again he emphasizes the complexity of the Medea figure. Lessing praises the painter for taking Medea 'not at the moment when she really murders her children, but a few moments before, when maternal love is still struggling with jealousy'.[42] Exactly this

---

[39] Cf. Woesler (1978), 80–1.   [40] Lessing (2003), 524–5.

[41] Lessing took the two surnames from works by William Congreve; see Lessing (2003), 1263.

[42] 'Die Medea hatte er nicht in dem Augenblicke genommen, in welchem sie ihre Kinder wirklich ermordet; sondern einige Augenblicke zuvor, da die mütterliche Liebe noch mit der Eifersucht kämpfet.' Lessing (1990), 33.

conflict was staged a few years earlier, in Jean-Georges Noverre's ballet *Médée et Jason*, first performed in Stuttgart in 1763.[43] The ballet was very successful and was shown in 1763, 1770, and 1771 in Paris, 1767 and 1776 in Vienna, 1771 in Venice, 1781 in London, and 1789 and 1791 in St Petersburg.[44]

This is the rare case of a tragic ballet with coherent action, still quite unusual around 1760. Even though Noverre basically follows Pierre Corneille's *Médée*, the ballet emphasizes the conflicts in the main characters. Here Medea is presented on stage in a dilemma, in the conflict of mother love and desire for revenge, which was neither the case with Bressand and Klest nor with Lessing. Jason too now appears as a split figure between his duty to Médée and his children, and his passion for Créuse. The tragedy is triggered by Créon, who fears Médée will have claims to his throne, and therefore wants to separate Jason from her and bind him to Créuse. He offers Jason Créuse's hand and the succession as king if he is willing to abandon Médée.

Médée is initially shown as a loving mother playing with her children. Her emotional appeal to Jason in the third scene, together with her children, first leads to Jason's stirring emotion, remorse, and the promise to return to her. But immediately in the next scene Jason changes his mind again and repudiates Médée. The piece now shows her inner conflict, especially in scene 6, for which the ballet programme states:

> Enyvrée de ses fureurs, elle appelle ses enfans, elle veut en faire ses premières victimes; mais son bras mal assuré refuse d'obéir, le fer échappe à sa main, & la nature semble lui reprocher l'atrocité d'un tel crime.[45]
>
> [Inebriated by her fury she calls her children, she wants to make them her first victims; but her insecure arm refuses to obey, the iron escapes from her hand & nature seems to reproach her for the atrocity of such a crime.]

She is therefore unable to murder her children and instead sends them to Créuse with the poisoned gifts. Only after Jason finally turns to Créuse and festively carries out the wedding does Médée turn into the avenger who, with the help of the allegorical furies of the underworld ('Jealousy, Hatred, & Vengeance [...] these three daughters of Hell are presenting her the Fire, Iron,

---

[43] The programme was printed in Noverre (1776). A modern reprint also in Abert (1913), xlv–xlvii.
[44] See Dahms (1991). See further, chapters by Macintosh, Dotlačilová, Nikiforova, and Hall, this volume.
[45] Noverre (1776), 9.

& Poison'),[46] carries out her revenge and kills the children, whereupon Jason kills himself.

Thus this ballet presents a process of development on stage, which finally leads from the contradictory feelings to a tragic decision. Despite the terrifying ending, this process is understandable for the audience and therefore convincing. The contemporary chronicler Joseph Uriot, from whom a description of the 1763 performance is preserved (Figure 7.1), emphasizes precisely this development as a special feature of the ballet: '[...] the scenes of the ballet are connected with such an art and power of estimation, and the interest in it rises step by step with such a strength that it deserves one of the most excellent places among the ballets [...]'.[47]

Through this process of development, Medea's behaviour and actions become fundamentally understandable despite the murder; the figure loses any barbaric and mythical distance. Medea has such severe internal conflict concerning the infanticide that she needs the help of external allegorical figures. It is precisely because of these problems that her horrible action is now comprehensible to the audience.[48]

This is central to the new mode of transmitting emotions on stage from *c.* 1750 onwards (and is also in evidence in Lessing's aesthetic of compassion). Now it becomes important for the audience to identify with the characters, and their inner conflicts must therefore be clearly presented on stage. This is a completely different concept from Bressand's. For this new concept, based on emotion, affect, and the emotional participation of the audience, Medea's children are now particularly important, and so the children in Noverre's ballet are given space on stage. The contemporary description of Uriot, for example, shows that this proved highly successful:

Zwey kleine Kinder der Medea, welche durch ihre Hofmeisterinn begleitet wurden, spielten ihre Rolen [*sic*] auf eine solche rührende Weise in den unterschiedenen Scenen wo sie zum Vorscheine kamen, daß sie den Zuschauern Thränen abloketen.[49]

---

[46] 'La Jalousie, la Haine, & la Vengeance [...] ces trois filles de l'Enfer lui présentent le Feu, le Fer, & le Poison'. Noverre (1776), 8.

[47] '[...] die Scenen desselben sind mit einer solchen Kunst und Beurtheilungskraft verbunden, und das Interessirende steigt stuffenweise darinn mit einer solchen Stärke, dass es eine der vorzüglichsten Stellen unter den Balletten verdienet [...]'. Uriot (1763a), 41–7, here 46–7; see also Dotlačilová, this volume.

[48] See Schweitzer, this volume.   [49] Uriot (1763a), 44.

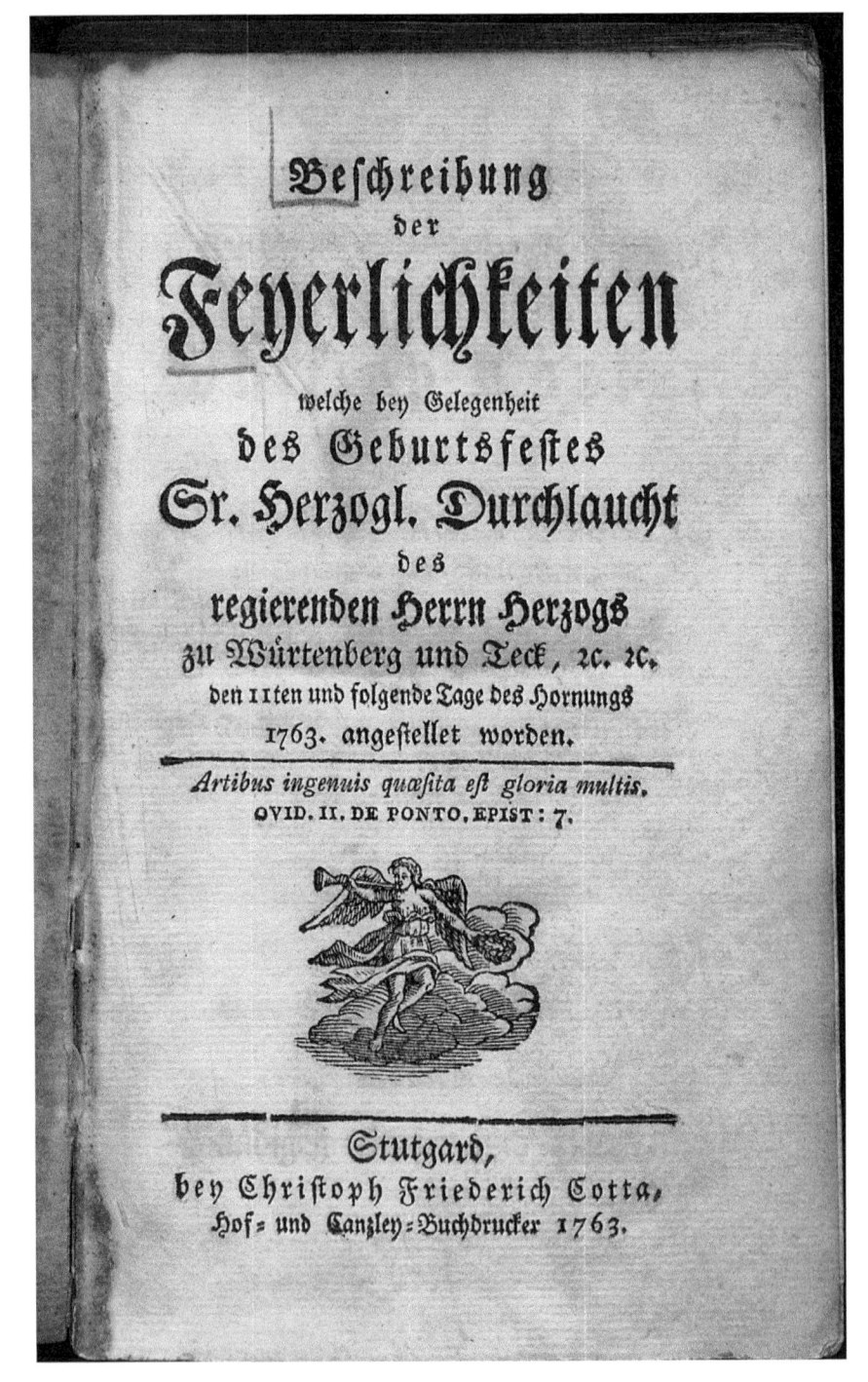

Figure 7.1 Frontispiece to Joseph Uriot, *Beschreibung der Feyerlichkeiten* (1763)

[Two little children of Medea, accompanied by their governess, played their roles in such a touching way in the different scenes where they appeared that the spectators broke out in tears.]

By showing Médée as a tender mother, giving ample space to Jason's injuries and her inner conflicts, the Medea figure is enhanced here. Noverre thus goes well beyond Lessing's procedure for creating the Marwood figure. Medea's complexity is increased in Noverre, and any assessment of her character is made more difficult for any audience by the numerous appeals to their pity. The contemporary chronicler Uriot uses the paradoxical concept of 'most terrifying beauties' and describes the fact that viewers sometimes had to turn away, their eyes full of tears.[50] The intended emotional participation of the audience seems to have worked in Stuttgart, to which the dramatically gripping music of Jean-Joseph Rodolphe supposedly also significantly contributed.[51]

The ballet was given in Stuttgart as an interlude to Niccolò Jommelli's opera *Didone abbandonata*, another female figure from ancient mythology in existential conflict. Médée abandoned by Jason is thus brought into parallel with Dido abandoned by Aeneas, in which Dido is clearly presented sympathetically. This might have brought the Medea figure even closer, in terms of affect, to the contemporary spectators.[52]

A New Genre: Medea Melodrama

The tendency towards the development of character in Lessing and Noverre is best illustrated by the most successful and characteristic piece of German theatre in the last part of the eighteenth century, the *Medea* melodrama by Friedrich Wilhelm Gotter and Georg Benda, premiered in Gotha in 1775.[53] *Medea* and its sister work *Ariadne auf Naxos* quickly spread throughout the German-speaking cultural area and stimulated a significant number of

---

[50] Uriot (1763a), 45: '[…] wo diese Prinzessinn, da sie gegen ihre Nebenbuhlerinn verlassen wird, aus einer gänzlichen Unmacht in die Wuth ausbricht, ist eine Vereinigung aller Arten der erschröklichsten Schönheiten: […]. Man zittert vor Schreck bey diesem Anblike. […] ein solches entsezliches Gemählde, das die Herzen zerfleischet und den Zuschauer nöthiget, die thränende [*sic*] Augen abzuwenden, aus Furcht, das Blut dieser Unschuldigen fließen zu sehen' ['when this princess, abandoned for her rival, breaks out of complete impotence into rage, this is a union of all kinds of the most terrifying beauties: […]. You tremble with terror at this sight. […] such a horrible painting that tears the heart to pieces and forces the spectator to avert the tearful eyes for fear of seeing the blood of these innocents flowing'].

[51] Score printed by Abert (1913), 243–98; unfortunately the exact assignment of the musical numbers to the scenes is not clearly recognizable. For the role of music in the *ballet d'action* see Nye (2011), esp. 185–207.

[52] Cf. Nye (2011).   [53] Gotter and Benda (2018).

similar melodramas.[54] In addition, they are the only works from the German-language musical theatre to garner success outside the German-speaking area and were translated into foreign languages.[55] For contemporaries, melodrama was regarded as a typically German form of musical theatre[56]—in spite of the genre's French origins.[57] For more than a decade after 1775, melodrama proved to be central to the discourse of German culture and led to a rethinking of the relationship between text, music, and the art of acting. In the wake of the new trends developed in *ballet d'action*,[58] melodrama went on to develop additional scenic innovations, not least in facial expressions, gestures, and costumes.[59] The discussions around melodrama sharpened the overall awareness of the different media in musical theatre. In Germany around 1780, melodrama formed an important and promising crystallization point for thinking about the connections between music, text, expression of 'feelings', and performative effects in musical theatre.[60]

In stage melodrama (as a monodrama) the events are reproduced completely from the perspective of one character, so the audience is automatically bound to the perspective of this (usually female) character. The new musico-literary medium of melodrama was gaining in popularity among contemporaries precisely because it offered in a new manner an internal perspective on a single, conflicted figure. In Gotter's case, this isn't Jason, but Medea. The play begins at a very late point of the myth, when Medea, already banished, secretly returns to Corinth.[61] There is hardly any external plot, nor are there any great arguments with other figures, but the piece, which lasts barely an hour, consists mainly of the depiction of Medea's internal conflict. She is torn between the desire for revenge, wistful resignation, and feelings of powerlessness and motherly love; and only through the wedding ceremony of Jason and Kreusa does she mutate

---

[54] Cf. Schimpf (1988), 219–23 and 263–7. On the classification of the two works as genre models in Germany see also Kühn (2001), esp. 123–40; Waeber (2005), 51–2, and Urchueguía (2015), 208; for the aesthetic-historical context see Lütteken (1998), 466–86. A list of performances until 1790 can be found in Urchueguía (2015), 206–7.

[55] Cf. Krämer (1998), vol. 1, 294–7; Schwarz-Danuser (1997), esp. col. 71; for Russia see Nikiforova, this volume.

[56] 'Germany's daughter, the melodrama'. *Über das Melodrama* in *Neue Bibliothek der schönen Wissenschaften und der freyen Künste* 37, vol. 2 (1789), [177]–197, here [177]–178. See also Krämer (1998), vol. 1, 293–353.

[57] Cf. Waeber (2005), 17–50; Hall, this volume. [58] Cf. Nye (2011).

[59] Benda's *Ariadne* is considered to be the first play in which historicizing (i.e. here: Greek-antique) costumes were used—a new interpretation of the past. Melodrama also played an important role in the development of facial expressions; cf. Engel (1785–6); von Goez (1783). For the development of the costume, see Dotlačilová, this volume.

[60] Last but not least, numerous contemporary parodies also confirm the enormous impact and popularity of melodramas. Schimpf (1988), 62–4; Krämer (1998), vol. 1, 347–9; Hall, this volume.

[61] For analysis see Krämer (1998), vol. 1, 293–353; Lü (2009), 46–57; Hall, this volume.

into a deadly Fury. Even contemporaries such as the playwright Heinrich Leopold Wagner emphasized the extraordinary diversity of the sometimes contradictory feelings as a special feature of the *Medea* melodrama: 'the eternal throng of love, hatred, and vindictiveness, the never-ending ebb and flow of so many completely opposite passions that toss Medea around [...]'.[62]

This variety of affect was intensified by the novel, intermedial interaction of music, gesture, and declamation. In the small-part interplay of spoken text and short musical interludes, the music follows the text and the dramatic course more closely than was usual in opera and *Singspiel* of the time, and the audience could not understand the piece with reference to traditional formal categories of opera.[63] Instead of traditional musical formal dispositions, Benda's melodrama music features many short interludes, often comprising only one to three bars, which musically capture the inner turns of the main character's mind. The music not only reproduces the character or change of affect, but can also prepare, guide, form, or subsequently intensify it. This can be seen everywhere in Benda's setting. The relationship between text and music in melodrama is as multi-layered as the relationship between music and gesture, facial expression and proxemics.[64]

Sometime around 1775, melodrama proved to be the ideal medium in the process of the development of a new conception of the art of acting. It became the virtuoso form for the greatest German actresses of the time. Theoretical writing on acting as well as theatre criticism[65] repeatedly called for a departure from the older, type-focused ('artificial') representation of affect towards a psychologizing ('natural') art of acting, an 'anatomy of the heart'.[66] For this reason, the *Medea* melodrama also receives due mention in Johann Jakob Engel's *Ideen zu einer Mimik* (1785–6) (Figure 7.2).[67]

In the libretto, Gotter looks more to Euripides than to the previously dominant Senecan tradition.[68] Medea is shown in Gotter's text as a deeply wounded woman, who was not only cast out of Corinth but also robbed of her children and who feels betrayed by Jason, to whom she had sacrificed everything. She enters the stage with a desire for revenge that immediately becomes insecure:

---

[62] 'das ewige Gedränge von Liebe, Haß und Rachgier, die nie stillstehende Ebbe und Fluth so vieler sich ganz entgegen gesetzter Leidenschaften, von welchen Medea herumgetrieben wird [...]'. Wagner (1777), 115.
[63] Glaser's assessment of the piece as a 'stirring piece', is completely inadequate; he even erroneously assumes that the text was sung in melodrama. Glaser (2001), 93–7.
[64] Betzwieser (2011).   [65] Heßelmann (2002), esp. 329–72.
[66] Curtius (1753), 394.   [67] Stephan (2006), 182–3.   [68] Lü (2009), 48–9, 53–5.

Figure 7.2 Engraving of Medea from Johann Jakob Engel, *Ideen zu einer Mimik* (1785)

Wo sind sie, die stolzen Entwürfe, mit denen du kamst? Wirft dieser Anblick sie schon zu Boden – o, was wird es seyn, wann du ihn selbst erblickst, den geliebten Verräther – [...] Stähle deine Brust, beleidigtes, verworfnes, ins Elend gebanntes Weib! – Mutter, ohne Kinder![69]

[Where are they, the proud concepts you came up with? If this sight already throws them to the ground – o, what will it be when you see him yourself, the beloved traitor – [...] Steel your breast, offended, discarded, miserable woman! – Mother, without children!]

[69] Gotter (1775), 5–6.

In the course of the play the psychological complexity of the character is fully on display: her decision to murder the children is made step by step against much internal resistance, which challenges and burdens her in the extreme. After the murder, which is not shown on stage but takes place behind the empty stage and conveyed only by music, Medea reappears on stage:

MEDEA. *(erscheint athemlos, betäubt, bleich und mit zerrissenem Haar am Eingang.)*

Es ist geschehen – geschehen – Schlummert sanft ihr Lieben! euch ist wohl – zerbrochen ist euer Kerker – Wer auch frey wäre, wie ihr! – *(sie will herunter und kann nicht)* Warum zittert mir jede Nerve, verläßt mich jede Kraft? –

(sinkt auf die Schwellen nieder.)

O du – wenn ich diese Hände voll Bluts noch gegen dich ausstrecken darf – erbarme dich der reinen schuldlosen Seelen, o, Juno! Ich war einen Augenblick lang ihre Mutter – sey du es nun ewig! –[70]

[MEDEA. *(appears breathless, numb, pale and with torn hair at the entrance.)*

It has happened – happened – slumber gently, dear ones! You are well – your dungeon is broken – Oh, to be as free as you are! – *(she tries in vain to get down)* Why does every nerve tremble, every power leave me? –

(sinks down onto the threshold.)

O you – if I may stretch out these hands full of blood against you – have mercy on the pure innocent souls, o Juno! I was their mother for a moment – be thou now forever! –]

Even though Medea finally mutates into barbaric revenge, *furia*[71]—Gotter once again borrows from Corneille Jason's suicide—any assessment of her ambivalent character here proves difficult. Yes, her murder of the children crosses a moral boundary and demands a negative evaluation of her character, but she was previously presented as a loving mother in an existential conflict that she is unable to resolve alone. This makes her appear credible and honest, and therefore acceptable to the contemporary audience. The tragic event was triggered solely by Jason's breach of faith; and unlike in many other Medea plays (such as Seneca, Corneille, and also Bressand), Jason is not exonerated for this. He violates the ideologically central value of marriage, which is defended by Medea (also in her invocations of Juno as guardian of marriage). Medea appears as an innocent victim of Jason:

---

[70] Gotter (1775), 19–20.   [71] See Albrektson, this volume.

Gotter eliminates the insidiousness of Medea in the tradition (such as her poisonous attack on Kreusa). Her revenge, even if it remains negative, is partly psychologized and thus made understandable. It is not the act of an inhuman, barbarian fury with magical powers, but the problematic act of desperation of a deeply wounded woman.

Johann Friedrich Schink emphasizes this precise point in his extensive review of the play in 1782. He argues that in contrast to the cold, inhuman (*menschlichkeitslosen*) greatness of traditional theatrical Medea characters, Gotter's Medea is

[...] ein armes, verlassenes, verspottetes, gedrüktes Weib. [...] Es ist die gepreste Leidenschaft, die überwältigte Menschheit, die sie zur blutigen Tat treibt. Nirgends ist sie ein kreischendes, sprudelndes Weib, immer nur die beleidigte, unglükliche, verstossene Medea; selbst noch in ihrer Raserei, selbst beim Mord ihrer Kinder unseres Mitleids, unseres Bedauerns wert.[72]

[[...] a poor, abandoned, mocked, depressed woman. [...] It is the pressed passion, the overwhelmed humanity that drives her to her bloody deed. Nowhere is she a screaming, bubbly woman, always just the offended, unhappy, outcast Medea; even in her frenzy, even in the murder of her children worthy of our compassion, worthy of our pity.]

In clear reference to Lessing's aesthetic of compassion, Schink formulates:

Darum, weil sie kein, unserer Gesellschaft fremdes Ungeheuer, sondern ein menschliches Weib ist, wirkt sie auf unser Herz und macht uns für sich empfinden, was wir sonst für keine Medea in der Welt empfinden würden.[73]

[Because she is not a monster alien to our society, but a human woman, she affects our heart and makes us feel for her what we would otherwise not feel for any Medea in the world.]

Medea's supernatural abilities from the mythological tradition are, by contrast, downgraded by Gotter. They are only a part of her inner conflict because she also feels torn between her roles as a demi-goddess and as a loving mother who can no longer reach Jason's heart:[74]

---

[72] Schink (1782), 662–3; Krämer (2019).
[73] Schink (1782), 665–6; Schweitzer, this volume.
[74] The passage alludes to Ovid's *Heroides*; Cullhed (2017), 98.

Unseelige Macht! – Die Elemente gehorchen meiner Stimme – und das Herz des Mannes, den ich liebe, verschließt sich ihr! Schatten bring' ich vom Orkus zurück – und ein Herz kann ich nicht erhalten. […] – Auch der elendeste der Menschen hat doch irgend eine gute Seele, die an seinem Schicksal Antheil nimmt – aber wen hab' ich? Für mich ist jede gesellige Freude vertilgt – ich bin allein in der Schöpfung![75]

[Unfortunate power! – The elements obey my voice – and the heart of the man I love closes itself to it! I bring back shadows from Orcus – and I cannot keep a heart. […] – Even the most miserable of human beings has some good soul, which commiserates his fate – but who do I have? For me every sociable joy is extinguished – I am alone in creation!]

Despite her magical powers, Medea cannot reach the heart of Jason. The modern autonomy of the subject can no longer be reversed by magic. According to this credo, love is the true crystallization point of human individuality and autonomy. Therefore love forced from outside by magic cannot be valid. With this painful insight, Medea again becomes an all too human, contemporary woman for the audience.

Benda's music enhances the intensity of the piece. It clarifies the dilemma of Medea non-verbally on an additional, highly emotional level and affectively deepens it. Furthermore, Gotter, like Noverre, also dramaturgically uses the sentimental effect of the innocent children's appearance on stage. Here the children (as with Euripides) even receive speaking roles, which certainly increased their impact on the spectators. The scene with Medea and her children visually and performatively demonstrates the high values of motherhood[76] and family (see Figure 7.3).

However, the significant increase in the inner complexity of the figure Medea is offset by a certain overall loss of complexity. Medea's supernatural powers are considerably reduced and the figure thus loses her mythological greatness as she is reduced to the role of a human, abandoned wife and a loving mother.[77] In particular, all external conflicts are no longer included in the play—the large conflict scenes between Medea and Jason, Medea and Kreon, or between Medea and Kreusa (which also shine through in Lessing's large dialogue scenes between Mellefont and Marwood or Marwood and Sara), the hallmarks of the older Medea dramas, are completely absent. Jason now becomes a flat character, who can neither be compared to Lessing's Mellefont

---

[75] Gotter (1775), 7.
[76] For Medea's motherhood, see Cullhed (2017), 96–8.   [77] Cullhed (2017).

Figure 7.3 Engraving by Daniel Nikolaus Chodowiecki from Gotter's *Gedichte* (1788)

nor to Noverre's Jason, and who oscillates between duty and passion. The gain in complexity afforded by the interior view is achieved in the melodrama at the expense of a loss of complexity in the dramatic whole—this fundamental problem of the genre may later have contributed to its decline in importance and relatively rapid disappearance after 1790.

However, the great popularity of Gotter and Benda's *Medea* is reflected in many contemporary reactions. One of the most interesting is an untitled dramatic sketch by Ludwig Tieck, written around 1790 in Berlin.[78] As Albert Browning Halley has already pointed out, the sketch is clearly influenced by Gotter's text; it almost seems, in places, like a copy.[79] The still very young Tieck (only 17 years old) had obviously watched a performance of Benda's melodrama in Berlin, where it had been performed repeatedly since 1777, and in 1789 it was performed (at the very least) on 8 May and 1 August.[80]

However, it is unclear whether Tieck's manuscript was actually intended as a real melodrama, as Browning Halley insinuates. This is contradicted by the large space occupied by dialogue scenes: four of the eleven scenes of his piece are dialogues, occupying more than two thirds of the text. This is Tieck's response to the problem of the missing dialogue scenes in Gotter described above—but it violates some of the constitutive rules of the genre. While in Tieck's short monologue scenes one can certainly imagine the melodramatic interruption by the music, this is difficult to imagine in the dramatic dialogue scenes with their often high tempo one-line exchanges. Here the constant interruption by music would disturb more than it would support the effect.[81]

Tieck presents the figure of Medea from the beginning as a furious revenger, as a 'raging woman' ('*rasendes Weib*').[82] The complexity of Gotter's figure is again narrowed and significantly reduced. Tieck touches upon Medea's inner dilemma (so broadly unfolded by Gotter between motherly love and the desire for revenge) only in a single half-sentence, immediately before the infanticide:

[...] nur Rache sei mein Gefühl, Rache mein Gedanke! [...] Ihn soll mein Stahl nicht treffen [...] aber er hat Kinder – Kinder; fort aus meiner Seele ihr

---

[78] Manuscript in the Staatsbibliothek Preußischer Kulturbesitz Berlin; first published under the title 'Medea' in Browning Halley (1959), vol. 2, 1–11; this transcription of the manuscript contains some misreadings in detail. A new print can be found under the title 'Jason und Medea' in Luserke-Jaqui (2002), 315–20.

[79] Browning Halley (1959), vol. 1, 37–81.   [80] See Urchueguía (2015), 207.

[81] Moreover, Tieck does not, as is often the case in melodrama libretti, mark possible uses of music (e.g. by asterisks, dashes, or the like). The dashes in Tieck's manuscript have mainly a function of structuring the content. On this problem, see Krämer (2022).

[82] Scene 6. Luserke-Jaqui (2002), 318.

weichen Muttergefühle, peitscht sie fort ihr grinsenden Eumeniden! – Auf Rache, beflügle mich, leite mich! *(sie geht in den Pallast)*[83]

[revenge alone be my feeling, revenge be my thought! [...] My steel shall not strike him [...] but he has children – children; vanish from my soul, you soft motherly feelings, whip them away you grinning Eumenides! – Come, Revenge, inspire me, guide me! *(she enters the palace)*]

In addition, Tieck consistently erases all the few remnants of Medea's supernatural traits present in Gotter. The dragon-drawn machine in Gotter's text, in which Medea appears and disappears like a baroque goddess,[84] is no longer present in Tieck's work. Tieck also avoids any reference to Medea's superhuman abilities; only the invocation of the Eumenides brings something of the mythological potential into the sketch. In contrast to Gotter, however, Jason is now given more space, trapped between two women. Jason is involved in three of the four dialogue scenes and also receives three of the seven monologues. Tieck's version thus distances itself from the constitutive principle of melodrama as monodrama. The introspection into the inner life of one single figure gives way here to a more traditional dramatic conflict. Tieck thus indirectly confirms what is unique and novel in Gotter's text as he tries to integrate the radically monodramatic inner view of Gotter with more traditional dramatic techniques, thus creating a kind of combination of melodrama and the traditional one-act play. For the depiction of Medea, this means that the richly developed complexity in Gotter is reduced and Medea is returned once more to traditional negative assessment.

Klinger's Figure of Power

In 1787 Friedrich Maximilian Klinger presented a kind of counter-model to Gotter and Benda's monodrama with his own dramatic version, *Medea in Korinth*.[85] Klinger, as a theatre poet (1776–8) of Abel Seyler's *Schauspielergesellschaft*, was certainly familiar with Gotter's play, which was performed extensively in German-speaking countries during these years (also in Seyler's repertoire from 1777 onwards). Individual formulations and also some details (such as the invocation of Hecate) in Klinger's play clearly refer

---

[83] Scene 7. Luserke-Jaqui (2002), 319.
[84] For Medea's dragon chariot see Cullhed (2017), 90–3.
[85] Klinger (2012), vii–xxiii, xxxi–xxxix, 1–96.

to the text of Gotter. All in all, however, Klinger is aiming for a completely different dramatic model. He prefixes the first edition of 1787 with the remark: 'I did not use the Greek, nor the Latin, nor the French Medea. This one, and how she is, is my work.'[86] Despite this claim of originality so typical of the 'genius period', Klinger's play resides firmly in the world of the rhetorically influenced, 'high' spoken drama of neo-classical provenance. He develops the events in five acts through long dialogues (Medea and the children, Medea and Kreon, Medea and Kreusa, Medea and Jason, Medea and Hecate, etc.). They are contrasted by only two monologues from the main character (a short one at the beginning of Act II; a longer one delivered over the sleeping children in Act IV).

Instead of Gotter's radical isolation of Medea and focus on her inner perspective, Klinger unfolds a variegated panorama that also presents supernatural figures such as the allegory of fate or the Eumenides on stage. The goddess Hecate is only represented as a voice, which reinforces her uncanny greatness. In the first act Medea is characterized externally, from the point of view of others, as a cold, terrible and inhuman figure, as an evil sorceress. Medea's banishment is ordered by Kreon already at the beginning of the piece (scene I, 2); Jason's relationship to Kreusa doesn't play any role here yet. It is only in Act II that Medea herself enters the stage, accompanied by her children. Her appearance immediately contradicts her previously established character and she now appears completely different. Even though the accent in Klinger's character is generally more on a female 'power figure', his Medea is also complex and full of inner conflicts. In her, the consciousness of superhuman power (as granddaughter of the sun and daughter of the goddess Hecate) struggles with anxiety and with the desire to integrate herself into human society as an equal by renouncing this power.[87] Klinger completely reconceives her inner dilemma here—in the conflict between the superhuman and human parts of her still unsettled identity.

In addition, Klinger shows the problem of an apparently failed cultural transfer: Medea is not accepted by the Greeks and, conversely, cannot integrate herself into their culture. This is further complicated by the fact that her superhuman side is also split, which is indicated by the contrast between her misanthropic mother Hecate and her grandfather Hylios (in the version of 1815: Helios), who is more friendly to humans. These conflicts are not

---

[86] 'Ich benuzte weder die griechische, noch die lateinische, noch die französische Medea. Diese hier, und wie sie sey ist mein Werk.' Klinger (2012), [5].
[87] Lysell, this volume; Albrektson, this volume.

resolved in the play itself; only the subsequent second Medea drama of 1791 (*Medea auf dem Kaukasos*)[88] traces a purification process that marks Medea's conversion to humanity. The first Medea drama, however, is open-ended: Medea announces that she will retreat to the Caucasus and think about herself[89] (which the second drama will show). In an unusual dramaturgical arrangement, the actual climax, the infanticide, takes place here in the fourth act, while the fifth act brings mainly the tribunal of the Eumenides over Jason, Kreon, and Kreusa. At the very end, Medea appears—as with Gotter—'on her dragon carriage,'[90] mocking Jason with ironic questioning. Jason does not commit suicide, but together with Kreon and Kreusa he is grasped by the Eumenides. Despite several revisions, especially of the final act (1791, 1794, 1815), Klinger's drama made little impact.[91]

In many ways Klinger's Medea behaves differently from the earlier versions—due to the very different approach of the play. Medea doesn't use her children to bring Kreusa poisoned gifts. She also does not kill the children on her own initiative, but only carries out an order from her divine mother Hecate. Medea's own desire for revenge was initially not directed at the children, but only at Jason, Kreusa, and Kreon.[92] However, Hecate then demands of her the murder of the two children as atonement for the fratricide that Medea committed during her escape from Colchis with Jason (Klinger, in an extension of the myth, even mentions two brothers, Absyrthos and a 'suckling babe', who were killed by Medea).[93]

Despite all the emphasis on the 'terrible greatness' (*'fürchterlichen Größe'*)[94] of the Medea figure so typical of the time, Klinger also presents a conflicted figure who cannot solve her inner turmoil on her own.[95] The murder of the children only becomes possible after Medea, under pressure from Hecate, has

[88] Klinger (2012), 97–166.

[89] Klinger (2012), 88: 'Dann flieh' ich von meinem Drachen gezogen in die Felsen-Höhlen des Caucasos, starre hin in meiner schrecklichen Größe, betrachte mich in meinem schrekbaren Selbst!' ['Then I flee, pulled by my dragon, into the rock caves of Caucasus, staring into my terrible immensity, contemplating my dreadful self!']

[90] Klinger (2012), 86.

[91] On Klinger, see Lü (2009), 57–85; Glaser (2001), 99–110; Luserke-Jaqui (2002), 125–9; see also chapters by Hall, Lysell, and Albrektson, this volume.

[92] Klinger (2012), 60: 'Wohin schleudre ich die Blitze meiner Rache? – Nach ihm! Nach ihr! Und alle drey!' ['Where do I hurl the lightning bolts of my revenge?—After him! After her! And all three!']

[93] Klinger (2012), 61–2. The infant is indirectly murdered through neglect. Presumably the reason for this extension can be seen in a certain wish for 'poetic justice': the two children of Medea as atonement for the two children of Hecate.

[94] Klinger (2012), 86.

[95] Glaser fails to recognize this when he stylizes Klinger's Medea as 'Titanin des Sturm und Drang' ['Titan of Storm and Stress']. Glaser (2001), 99. He tries to classify the figure as 'eines der wenigen weiblichen Kraftgenies' ['one of the few female power geniuses']. Glaser (2001), 100.

explicitly denounced her maternal role in Act IV (which she had emphatically confirmed in Act II):

> FERETOS. Hilf uns, Mutter! [...]
> MEDEA. Ich bin Medea, bin nicht eure Mutter.[96]
> [FERETOS. Help us, Mother! [...]
> MEDEA. I'm Medea, I'm not your mother.]

The murder of the children is not primarily aimed at revenge on Jason, but at the solution to the problem of Medea's residence in human Greek culture and her reintegration into barbaric pre-history.[97] Lü concludes: 'Less Medea's revenge than her inner conflicts have become the main theme of the play'.[98] Here, again in contrast to tradition, the murder of the children marks only a temporary end, which does not resolve the actual conflicts within the protagonist. This happens only at the end of the second drama (*Medea auf dem Kaukasos*),[99] when Medea ends in an almost euphoric suicide.

Some elements of Klinger's piece can be related to later seventeenth-century traditions.[100] However, the recourse to allegorical figures, furies, and magical powers has a clear function in regaining the mythological 'greatness' of the figure. In this way, the play sets new accents in the reception history of the Medea myth. More strongly than in Gotter, Noverre, or even Lessing, the complexity of Medea as a conflicted mixture of the demonic and the human is delineated— and is used here to address the strangeness of the extraordinary in culture.

Conclusion

The Medea plays in the German-speaking theatre between 1692 and 1791 show very different ways of dealing with the complexity of the mythological Medea. On the one hand, she becomes increasingly humanized and psychologized, and her inner dilemma becomes the focus of attention. Gotter's highly successful monodrama of 1775 marks a high point in this process. This increasing focus on the character's inner problems makes their actions

---

[96] Klinger (2012), 64–5.   [97] See Glaser (2001), 104–6; Albrektson, this volume.
[98] 'Weniger die Rache Medeas als ihre inneren Konflikte sind zum Hauptthema des Stücks geworden'. Lü (2009), 68.
[99] On political aspects of *Medea auf dem Kaukasos* (1791) in the context of the Russian annexation of Georgia see Hall, this volume.
[100] Cf. Lysell, this volume. He sees in Klinger's text 'affinities with baroque German drama rather than with the theatre of Lessing and Schiller'.

partially understandable and thus any evaluation more and more difficult: the evil, barbaric monster of Bressand's libretto 1692 is now a human woman and mother whose irresolvable inner conflicts make her deed, to a certain extent, an understandable consequence of her injuries. Even in the modifications of lexicography during the course of the century, a similar process of a partial apology of the figure is indicated. At the very end of the century, Klinger then shifts Medea's inner conflict and reshapes her as a complex figure in the direction of an ingenious female figure of power, who must remain alien in the shallow everyday human society.

During the century, the focus shifts from the terrible act of infanticide itself to its aetiology and background. The scandal of the murder of children is thereby attenuated by different strategies: it is made plausible as an act of affection in the face of insoluble inner conflicts (Noverre, Gotter), or it appears as an externally arranged atonement against which the conflicted and divided Medea cannot defend herself (Klinger), or it is completely avoided, reduced to mere threat and replaced by an enlightened final solution (as in Lessing).

We need to ask whether these modifications are also related to formal shifts dictated by genres. While the operatic model around 1700 seems to be strongly determined by categories such as the clear evaluation of unambiguous characters, dramatic contrast, and the alternation of clearly fixed affects, the new *ballet d'action* of the Noverre-type requires a closer connection and higher continuity of the non-verbally presented plot. Now developments and consistent deviations become more important than contrasts or sub-plots full of affects. Finally, in melodrama, the radical focus on a single figure in the dilemma allows for an intensive view into the interior that makes even the scandalous act understandable to the audience and arouses their pity. The monodramatic melodrama thus corresponds also to the *Erfahrungsseelenkunde* (experiential psychology) formed by Karl Philipp Moritz during this period. But equally in spoken theatre the conflict-laden complexity of Medea's character becomes important. From Lessing to Klinger, this complexity appears to have been further increased and provided with additional functions. And the murder of children remains an important theme in contemporary drama even beyond reference to the Medea myth. As a glance at Johann Wolfgang von Goethe's *Faust* or Heinrich Leopold Wagner's *Die Kindermörderinn* demonstrates,[101] it now becomes part of a current socio-critical diagnosis.

---

[101] See Luserke-Jaqui (2002).

8

Visual Narrative

The Role of Costumes in Noverre's *ballet d'action*, *Médée et Jason*

Petra Dotlačilová

Theatrical costume is an active element in the performance, which communicates with the audience, together with actors' words, movements, sets, lights, and music. While in each period, costumes are influenced by current trends in fashion, aesthetics, by particular customs and morals, at the same time they acquire another role. Theatrical costume transforms the body of an actor into that of the character; it defines the character on stage (in terms of status, personality, age, or even nationality), more or less accurately—according to the aesthetics of the period. In the past, theatrical costume also reflected the status of the patron who sponsored the performance, the status of the dramatic genre and not least that of the actor, that is if they owned their costumes. At the same time, the costume had to reflect—literally—the light, which was of importance especially when the stage was lit by the flickering light of candles.

In French opera and ballet of the eighteenth century, costumes were strictly designed by an artist—the designer. Costuming strategies and the visual symbolism go back to the first performances of *ballet de cour* and even earlier to the Italian spectacles.[1] Since most designers were artists, it is not surprising that they used conventions from the fine arts, albeit now in their costume drawings. So, despite the costume being related to current fashion, in one way or another, it is always a particular type of dress, with specific features and materialities, and thus not the same as any dress worn off stage.

In this chapter, I focus on the costuming strategies used by designer Louis-René Boquet for Jean-Georges Noverre's ballet *Médée et Jason* (1763). This famous work, considered one of the first works of the innovative

---

[1] See Dotlačilová (2020), (2021).

Petra Dotlačilová, *Visual Narrative: The Role of Costumes in Noverre's* ballet d'action, Médée et Jason In: *Mapping Medea: Revolutions and Transfers 1750–1800*. Edited by: Anna Albrektson and Fiona Macintosh, Oxford University Press.

eighteenth-century genre of *ballet d'action*,[2] or 'danced drama',[3] has been investigated by several researchers from various perspectives.[4] Furthermore, Edward Nye, together with Fanny Thépot and Ruth D. Eldredge, have investigated in detail the relationship between dance, gesture, and music in this ballet, arguing that music assumed a specific and strategic role in the intelligibility of danced drama.[5] This chapter develops Nye's hypothesis around *ballet d'action*'s dramaturgical tools, namely the role of the visual element. I argue that the costumes and other visual effects are as important as music in the staging of mime, and they both contributed greatly to the development and success of this new genre.

The ballet *Médée et Jason* was immediately successful and was performed many times between 1763 and 1804 in several cities—Stuttgart, Paris, Vienna, Venice, Milan, London, St Petersburg—staged either by Noverre or by his disciples.[6] However, the costumes were not always designed by Boquet, and the various stagings are by no means documented equally. Therefore, this chapter only employs sources where the connection to the original creative team (Noverre and Boquet) can be established, in order to trace their development of dramaturgically effective and physically practical costumes for this particular danced drama. These sources are both visual and textual (costume lists, inventories, drawings, programmes, reviews), and they record the costumes' materiality, visuality, and the intended or actual effect that these garments ought to have on the spectators. In particular, I examine sources relating to the first performances of *Médée et Jason* in Stuttgart and Paris in 1763 (which already differ one from another), and to Boquet's later drawings, present in the so-called 'Stockholm manuscript', compiled by Noverre in 1791. I investigate how these ballet costumes relate to the well-established codes from both

---

[2] While the term *ballet d'action* is commonly used in contemporary historiographical discourse, it should be mentioned that Noverre himself never used this expression, on the contrary he consistently writes *ballet en action* in all his texts. Michael Burden and Jennifer Thorp state that the term *ballet d'action* was probably used for the first time by the translator of Noverre's *Letters* into English, J. P. MacMahon in 1782–3. Burden and Thorp (2014), xiii–xiv.

[3] This modern—but very fitting—term is used by Edward Nye. See Nye (2008).

[4] In this volume alone, the ballet is discussed in other chapters, notably in Macintosh (in relation to tragedy), Krämer (in the German-speaking theatre), and Nikiforova (in theatre in Russia).

[5] Nye and Thépot (2007); Nye (2011), 194–207.

[6] While Noverre later stated that the premiere of *Médée et Jason* took place at the Württemberg court in 1762, no other evidence supports this. However, the 1763 Stuttgart production is well documented. The ballet was then performed at the French court (at Choisy) in June 1763, at Académie Royale de Musique in Paris in December 1770, in February 1771, and from 1776 it was also presented independently of the opera several times until 1804. The ballet was also performed in Vienna in 1767 and later in 1776, in Venice 1771, in Milan 1772 and 1773, in London 1781, and in St Petersburg in 1787 (cf. Nikiforova, this volume). Most of these productions were mounted either by Gaëtan Vestris or by Noverre's pupil, Charles Le Picq. Cf. Piot (2014), 41–4; Dahms (2010), 407.

musical theatre and the fine arts, how they relate to previous costume practices, to current fashions, to ballet's physical techniques, and, most importantly, to the dramaturgy of the piece. What does the visual depiction tell us about the characters? How do the costumes reflect the dramatic development of the ballet, and how do they emotionally affect the spectators? In order to place Boquet's costumes in context, I start this enquiry with an account of the principles of costume design for musical theatre earlier in the century before analysing the new ideas about costume that challenged established practice starting from around the 1750s.

While theatrical costume generally, and that of *ballet d'action* in particular, have received surprisingly scant attention, the costumes for *Médée et Jason* have in fact been investigated by French art historian Albane Piot in her MA thesis at École du Louvre.[7] Piot has assembled various sources from several European archives and provided a very helpful overview. My chapter extends her visual and material analysis of these collected sources in order to relate it to the broader historical context of theatrical costume, and asks how the specific material and visual agency within Noverre's danced drama contributes to new understandings of Medea in the late eighteenth century.

Drama without Words

The development of the genre called variously *ballet d'action/ballet en action/ ballet-pantomime/ballo pantomimo* in various European countries has been thoroughly researched by scholars in the last few decades.[8] Currently it is agreed that while Jean-Georges Noverre is still considered as one of the first choreographers of tragic ballets, the tradition of dramatic dance, or danced drama, has its roots considerably earlier. Dance historian and musicologist Rebecca Harris-Warrick detected dramatic dance in Lully's operas in Paris,[9] while the efforts of John Weaver in London at the very beginning of the eighteenth century are sometimes considered 'the first modern ballet'.[10] The lively activity in the area of pantomimic dance in the Parisian fairground theatres during the first half of eighteenth century has been explored by Marian Hannah Winter. Dancers and choreographers such as Jean-Baptiste De Hesse or Franz Anton Hilverding, albeit working with mainly lighter comic themes, also

---

[7] Piot (2014).
[8] Winter (1974); Guest (1996); Nye (2011); Sasportes (2011); Fabbricatore (2017).
[9] Harris-Warrick (2016).   [10] Ralph (1985).

developed the dramatic potential of dance (through acting, gesture, and dramaturgy) and trained a generation of skilled dancers/actors.[11] Marie Sallé was another of the pioneers in dramatic dance, as both performer and choreographer, who even introduced rather progressive stage costume.[12]

The theoretical grounds of *ballet en action* had also been laid before Noverre, notably by Louis de Cahusac (1706–59), the author of *La danse ancienne et moderne* (1754),[13] and by the many articles on the topic of dance and music in the *Encyclopédie*. While focusing mainly on the history of dance, without much analysis of present developments, Cahusac coined the term *ballet en action*, considering it the most ideal dance form for the future. Such an art form would combine dancing, gesture, and facial expression in order to depict emotions and dramatic situations. In accordance with other authors of dance history before him (such as Claude-François Ménestrier or Jacques Bonnet), Cahusac hailed ancient Roman pantomime as the highest form of art and the ideal for modern dramatic dance to follow.

Noverre assumed and developed these ideas, including the term *ballet en action*, both in his writing (*Lettres sur la danse*),[14] and in his practice. In a campaign to proclaim dance as an independent art form on the same level with the others, perfectly capable of conveying all the emotions, he emphasized the role of gesture and expressions, which could have more power than words. This statement echoes ideas of Charles Batteux and Denis Diderot, who also acknowledged in their writings the power of gesture as a prolongation of words.[15] However, Noverre also considered danced drama as a fusion of dramatic art with the fine arts, as silent drama and painting set in motion:

> [a] ballet is a painting, the stage is the canvas, the mechanical movements of the dancers are the colours, their physiognomy is, I dare say, the brush, the composition and liveliness of the scenes, the choice of the music, scenery and costumes is its palette; in short, the Composer is the Painter.[16]

Noverre seems to refer here to the important distinction between line/drawing and colour in eighteenth-century art theory, which became the topic

---

[11] Winter (1974), 83–99.   [12] McCleave (2007); Chazin-Bennahum (2005).

[13] Cahusac (2004).   [14] First edition 1760, last edition 1807.

[15] Cf. Batteux (1746), 210–23; Diderot (1875–7), vol. 7, 378.

[16] 'Un ballet est un tableau, la Scène est la toile, les mouvements méchaniques des figurants sont les couleurs, leur phisionomie est, si j'ose m'exprimer ainsi, le pinceau, l'ensemble et la vivacité des Scènes, le choix de la Musique, la décoration et le costume en font le coloris; enfin, le Compositeur est le Peintre.' Noverre (1760), 1–2. Translation mine, in consultation with Mickaël Bouffard. The 'mechanical movements' refer in Noverre's terminology to the dance technique.

of disputes among artists and theoreticians.[17] The scene of ballet—the canvas—is outlined with lines drawn by the dancer's movements and expressions, and coloured with the music, set design, costume, and distribution of people on stage. Together, this drawing and colouring make up the whole of the ballet. But the comparison to painting was not just a metaphor: Noverre mentions the importance of studying the paintings themselves (together with other subjects). The great variety of depicted expressions, gestures, and positions can serve the dancer as inspiration for his acting. Furthermore, the paintings should also offer inspiration to the costume and set designer when drawing historical and/or exotic settings.

In practice, Noverre often used well-known mythological and historical stories as subjects for his ballet, which facilitated the understanding of the action. The emerging genre of danced drama emphasized the dramaturgical development of the plot, where dance was only one element. The 'dialogues' were executed in mime, alternating with other stage action such as solo and group dance and movement (including for instance marching and fighting), in a way similar to the alternation of *recitative* and *aria* in opera.[18] Nye proposes that the programmes may have assumed the 'choreographic' function in *ballet d'action*, in the sense of 'notation'; while admittedly 'not designed to give a complete account of stage design, but [they] were nevertheless a blueprint for interpretation by an "intelligent dancer".[19] Such a dancer should apply his own imaginative faculties to a dramatic situation and perform the role according to his stage experience. So, Nye concludes, 'programmes do not tell us much about the dance steps, but they do tell us about something which arguably is much more important, the dramaturgical construction'.[20] In this new construction, the music, costumes, props, and scenography play a crucial role—the choreographer (in today's meaning of the word) controls all of the aspects of the performance, and coordinates the theatrical or narrative expression of the music together with the material and visual effects and the movement of performers. The choreographer in this eighteenth-century danced drama 'often uses visual techniques to express the sense of the drama'.[21] It is these visual techniques that will be thoroughly examined in *Médée et Jason*.

---

[17] See Lichtenstein (1993), 138–68.   [18] Nye (2008), 53.

[19] Nye (2008), 55. The 'intelligent dancer' is a reference to Diderot's 'intelligent actor' in his *De la poésie dramatique*, where he describes the ideal performance of his kinetic drama, how the action in his text should be mimed without the use of words.

[20] Nye (2008), 56.   [21] Nye (2008), 56.

Between Convention and Reform

Early forms of musical theatre in Italy had already incorporated costume and decor as important parts of the whole spectacle. However, the principal characteristic of opera in the seventeenth and early eighteenth century was the '*meraviglioso*'—'*le merveilleux*'—'the marvellous' or 'the spectacular'.[22] This term refers to epic tales that include interventions of Graeco-Roman gods and allegorical characters, whose appearance and actions—being out of the ordinary—amaze the mind. The supernatural appearances were enhanced through illusion-building scenery, the grand effects of scene changes, big crowds, fireworks, and of course rich costumes. At the same time, as with all artistic creations, opera was expected to address the dictates of verisimilitude in an aesthetic balancing act. According to Giovanni Battista Doni's *Trattato della musica scenica* (1640),[23] verisimilitude was in the case of musical theatre subordinate to the *meraviglioso*, a point he illustrates with reference to the costumes of the characters:

> Verisimilitude in the imitation and expression of those matters that are represented on stage should be a concern; but in the right way and in that manner that inspires the '*meraviglioso*' and the beautiful. Otherwise, when introducing shepherds one should dress them with nothing else but a few simple pieces of leather, or a similar rustic attire, and not the golden trimmed cloths, as it is commonly done; and the same is true for servants and other humble people; who despite the fact that they commonly wear nothing but primitive and poor clothes, because they appear on stage, wear rich garments, or at least so they appear, and beautiful to look at, so as to balance on one hand the delight and admiration of the audience, and on the other the verisimilitude of the imitation; this is done so that the action does not lose completely its verisimilitude, nor become too simple or ordinary.[24]

---

[22] See Lappin, this volume.

[23] Doni (1763 [first ed. 1640]). Cited in the De Lucca (2013), (2019).

[24] '[...] si ha da procurare bene la verisimilitudine nell'imitazione, ed espressione delle cose, che si rappresentano in Scena; ma con debito modo, e in quella forma, che ha più del meraviglioso, e del vago. E altrimenti quando s'introducono Pastori, non si dovrebbono vestire se non con qualche semplice pelle, o simile addobbamento rustico, e non di tele d'oro, come si fa; e così i servi, e altre persone vili; che sebbene non usano se non panni rozzi, e plebei; tuttavia perchè compariscano, si vestono in Scena di guernimenti ricchi almeno in apparenza, e alla vista vaghi, bilanciandosi da una parte il diletto, e l'ammirazione delli spettatori e dall'altra la verisimiglianza dell'imitazione; in modo, che l'Azione non divenga del tutto inverisimile, nè troppo semplice, e ordinaria.' Doni (1763 [first ed. 1640]), ii, 29. The original has been translated by Valeria De Lucca.

Therefore, the beautiful and spectacular dimension of the genre exceeds, in this early period, all clothing that is visible in real life.[25]

Another Italian treatise, *Il corago* (*c.* 1630),[26] mentions that models for the costumes of different characters should be sought in various sources. Paintings, travel books with illustrations, coins, medals, descriptions of garments in antique and modern poetry are deemed the most usual sources for the designer. However, again here we hear of the necessity to change or adorn the original in order to tailor it to the local stage and expectations of the audiences. The treatise also suggests that different types of clothing and shoes need to be used according to different types of movement. For example, dancers should have their legs free, not covered with buskins, and only wear stockings and shoes, and their waist should not be restricted.[27] In the case of battle scenes (*abbattimento*), the performer must be dressed in a heavier garment that covers most of the body, even if not exactly in armour in the ancient style. Furthermore, they should wear shoes with no heel so that they do not slip during the battle.[28] This might be one of the first mentions of special shoes for dancing and proves that already in the seventeenth century garments are adjusted to the demands of the performance. Indeed, *Il corago* explicitly states that 'dressing for the scene is different from dressing every day for the city.'[29]

A similar approach to costume making could be observed in French genres of *ballet de cour* and *tragédie en musique* that emerged in the sixteenth and seventeenth centuries. If we compare the drawings by Stefano della Bella,[30] created for the Florentine entertainments in 1661, and those by Ludovico Ottavio Burancini,[31] who was active in Vienna in the same period, with those by Henry Gissey and Jean I Berain the Elder for the French court,[32] very similar approaches to the characterization via costume emerge.

---

[25] De Lucca (2013), 462, 469.

[26] *Il corago, o vero Alcune osservazioni per metter bene in scena le composizioni drammatiche* (1983); De Lucca (2013).

[27] 'Quelli che devono ballare si deve avvertire di vestirli di maniera che la vita non resti impedita e la gamba rimanga scoperta e libera, e perciò non dovranno adornarsi le gambe con i borzacchini, ma con semplice calzette e scarpe.' *Il corago* (1983), 114.

[28] 'Quelli che dovranno barreggiare o fare altro combattimento non si potranno armare con corazze all'antica, ma dovrannosi coprire con l'arme proprie da barriera, cioè con petto, schiena, bracciali, manopole e buffa; il restante de l'abito sarà calza intera alla spagnola ricoperta da un girello o faldiglie riccamente adornate che pendino intorno dall'armadura, la gamba con semplice calzetta e scarpa bianca fatta col suolo arrovescio e senza calcagnino acciò non possa sdrucciolare.' *Il corago* (1983), 114.

[29] '[…] differentemente è il vestire in scena et il vestire ordinariamente per una città…'. *Il corago* (1983), 11.

[30] De Lucca (2013), 464–5; Massar (1970).   [31] Ferrero (2002), 53–4.

[32] Selection of designs and their description, divided into categories or typologies can be found in Christout (1987); La Gorce (1997), (2011).

Jean-Baptiste Dubos dedicated part of his treatise to costume and especially interesting is his distinction between garments used in the tragic and comic plays, in relation to the effect and *bienséance* of each genre. The rules of propriety, known from real life, and their application to clothing, are here transferred to the theatre and require a specific type of dress for each 'rank' of theatrical representation and character. Tragedy, placed highest in the hierarchy, required an image of dignity and elevation, while comedy aimed to approach the conditions of real life more closely.

The costume designs preserved from the end of the seventeenth and beginning of the eighteenth century confirm this practice. The costumes for tragedy, representing characters from ancient Greece and Rome as well as from ancient myth, adapt some features of Roman uniform, which was considered the most noble attire. Such costume contains structured bodice and skirt (*tonnelet*) imitating the *lambrequins* for men, and are richly decorated with embroidery or painted ornaments (Figures 8.1–8.2).

However, female costumes, though also rather sumptuous, were more like the court dresses of the period.[33] But certain sartorial elements, such as the so-called *petit jupon*, seem to have been reserved exclusively for the stage (Figures 8.3–8.4). Art historian Mickaël Bouffard developed a theory that

Figures 8.1 and 8.2 Jean Berain, costume design for a warrior from *Amadis* (premiere 1684) and for Thésée (1677–8)

---

[33] Christout (1987); La Gorce (1997), (2011).

Figures 8.3 and 8.4 Jean Berain and workshop, designs for Minerva's high priestess and Hunter in the suite of Diana

these shorter overskirts could be said to imitate the folding of Greek dress as depicted on ancient vases and medals.[34]

Such theatre costume conventions and the particular relation between the *merveilleux* and verisimilitude still prevailed on the operatic stage in the mid-eighteenth century. In 1751–2 Louis-René Boquet entered the services of Les Menus Plaisirs du roi—the department of the French court organizing concerts, performances, and other entertainments—and started work under the designers Jean-Baptiste Martin and François Boucher. These artists continued to depict characters according to tradition, as a comparison of their drawings with those of Henry de Gissey and Jean Berain reveals.[35]

However, by the middle of the eighteenth century, new ideas relating to theatre costume began to emerge. The requirements of verisimilitude now appear to prevail over the need for *le merveilleux*. Instead of depicting the characters in spectacular ways, more emphasis began to be put on the verisimilar representation of ancient Greek and Roman dress and of those from other periods and places. Pierre Frantz has connected this trend to the new concept of theatre as *tableau*, which put emphasis on the visual side of theatre

[34] Personal conversation with Mickaël Bouffard.
[35] Bouffard (2019).

(gesture, distribution and acting of characters on stage, set and costume design) as opposed to its rhetorical aspects that prevailed in the French classical theatre.[36] This could be also a reaction against the particular development of fashion during the first half of the eighteenth century, which brought on stage large and impractical *paniers* (hoops) for women and the male *tonnelets* that also grew sideways in order to match them in size. Regarding theatrical clothing as such, this new approach to costume, emerging in the mid-eighteenth century, can be described as an aesthetic of truthfulness, replacing an aesthetic of propriety that had governed theatrical costume in the previous centuries.[37]

Among the first to put these ideas into practice had been the French dancer Marie Sallé, in her performance of *Pygmalion* in London (1734). According to the editor of *Mercure de France*, Philippe Bridard de La Garde, the costumes for Lully's *Alceste* at Fontainebleau in 1754 were similarly dictated by a desire for verisimilitude.[38] In the genre of spoken theatre, it was the actress Claire Josèphe Hippolyte Leris, *dite* Clairon, supported by Voltaire and other playwrights in the course of the 1750s, who started to change her wardrobe in order to dress her characters in a more appropriate way in relation to their age, origin, and dramaturgical situation, as did her colleague Henri-Louis Lekain.[39]

These new ideas and critiques of conventional costume practices resonated with Jean-Georges Noverre, who summarized them in his *Lettres sur la danse*. He demanded costume get rid of extravagant decoration and tinsel, abolish heavy hoops and *tonnelets* to allow the performer to move freely, and remove the mask so the dancer could act with the face. He also demanded that the costumes be inspired more by historical painting, which would inform both dress and gesture. However, he was aware of the limits of authentic representation in costume. He acknowledged that the clothing on stage required decency and grace, but considered certain items unnecessary:

Decency, you will say, is requisite on the stage. – This I readily acknowledge:
But must not also nature and verisimilitude govern the action? Does not the picture, to be good, require a proper energy, vigour, and a certain pleasing disorder wherever it is needful? – I would leave off those stiff

---

[36] Frantz (1998).

[37] See Dotlačilová (2020), 53–168.

[38] La Garde wrote 'programmes of costumes' where he described what they should look like—based on these programmes, Boquet designed the actual costumes. See Dotlačilová (2019), 102–3.

[39] Chardonnet-Darmaillacq (2014); Terrier (2015). I treat the development and arguments of the reform in chapter 2 of my thesis, Dotlačilová (2020), 108–64.

hoops or *tonnelets*, which, when the body is in a peculiar position, raise the hip nearly upon a line with the shoulders, and thus disfigure their natural conformation. – I would expunge all that affected symmetry in their dresses, which only serves to denote an artist without taste, and betray a want of gracefulness.[40]

When the ballet master describes how theatre costume should look, he takes into consideration the ideal of imitation and the specific nature of theatre:

> Every art has its laws and rules of convenience; the theatre has its own. They are based on pleasure [*agrément*], taste and decency, which is sufficient reason to ban all the types of costumes that would offend against one of these and to add elements to the clothing that do not degrade its character, but make it less hard and more theatrically picturesque. We conceive that these augmentations or reductions are a question of taste and they have to be made with great caution to maintain the principal traits and distinct character of each nation.[41]

Furthermore, Noverre emphasizes that theatre has its own manner and its own particular 'magic', independent of the visual arts: costume should be inspired by art, but still separate from it. For this reason, he does not approve of a total imitation of ancient dress because such slavish imitation would, in his view, create an unpleasant and shocking effect on stage.

Noverre's concept of theatre costume, thus, embraced the propriety of dress and the verisimilitude of imitation (which required some adaptation of the natural model for the sake of each art form)—both of which demonstrate a rather cautious approach to the imitation of historical costume, which was emerging as a new ideal in theatre. Yet the way in which he sought verisimilitude was different from previous theatrical conventions. The ballet master liked for the most part to adopt drapery, according to nationality, age, and the type of character that the actors had to represent. He preferred simplicity to pompous decoration, asymmetry as opposed to symmetrical arrangements,

---

[40] Burden and Thorp (2014), 310–11.
[41] 'Chaque Art à ses Loix, et ses Régles de convenance; le Théâtre à les siennes; elles sont fondé sur l'agrément, sur le Goût et sur la décence; raison suffisante pour en bannir tous les genres de costumes qui blesseroient l'un ou l'autre & pour ajoûter à tous ces vêtemens des choses qui n'en dégradent point le caractére, mais qui les rendent moins durs, et d'un Pittoresque plus théâtral. On conçoit aisément que ces augmentations ou ces diminutions sont l'ouvrage du goût; qu'on doit les faire avec beaucoup de ménagement à fin de conserver les Principaux traits et le caractére frapant et distinctif de chaque nation.' *Théorie et pratique de la danse simple et composé* (1766), Gabinet Rycin, Biblioteka Uniwersytecka w Warsawe, Inw.zb.d. 20818, 238. Translation mine.

lightness of fabric and folds as opposed to the stiff hoops and *tonnelets*. The loose drapery also enhanced the movement of the performer, which is of course especially important for the dancers.[42] He also emphasized the import-ance of a varied cut for the garments, which were to be different for all the characters—able to distinguish nations, allegories, gods and passions, and so on, as opposed to the unified cuts and forms used on stage in the period when he was writing. On the other hand, he did not oppose rich or heavy garments when they were appropriate for particular characters, for instance a princess on the day of her wedding (for the decorated garment) or an old king (for the heavier and rich garments). For dance costumes specifically, Noverre insisted that they should always be adapted for dancers—with a volume that affords freedom of movement to the legs as well as the waist. And most importantly, he insisted on adaptation of the costume to the dramatic situation of the character. Throughout his descriptions of ideal stage costume in general, and dance costume in particular, Noverre constantly names Louis-René Boquet as the person with the right knowledge and taste to design it. He criticized Boquet's predecessors, Charles-Louis Perronnet and Jean-Baptiste Martin, who made all the above mistakes, stating that they had 'neither taste nor knowledge of this genre'.[43]

Collaborating on *Médée et Jason*

Noverre and Boquet collaborated from 1754 onwards, when Boquet created costumes for Noverre's divertissement *Les fêtes chinoises*, presented at the Opéra-Comique. Their collaboration continued over the next few decades, despite the two Frenchmen rarely residing in the same place. While Boquet lived and worked in Paris for most of his long life, having a permanent

---

[42] 'I should certainly prefer a simple and light drapery of opposite colours, and so laid on as to shew the shape of the materials: Foldings properly managed, and a pleasing ensemble is all I require. – The extremities of those draperies being loose, and floating in various forms, in proportion as the action grows more animated, would give ease and life to the whole.' *Théorie et pratique de la danse simple et composé* (1766), 311.

[43] 'J'ai conservé soigneusement les dessins des Srs Péronet et Martin, et en les confrontant avec ceux de M. Boquet, il est aisé de voir qu'il y avoit ni goût, ni intelligence dans ce genre, que l'on ne présentoit que la charge grossière des différents peuples; que les divinités et les passions personnifiés annonçoient l'ignorance la plus crasse, et que tous les habits caractéristiques auroient eû besoin d'un écriteau pour indiquer ce qu'ils devoient représenter.' *Théorie et pratique de la danse simple et composé* (1766), 243.

position at the Paris Opera and at court,[44] Noverre travelled all over Europe to earn his living as a ballet master.[45]

An especially productive period for Noverre, and for his collaboration with Boquet, was offered by his engagement at Stuttgart. Between 1760 and 1766, Noverre was employed at the court of the Duke of Württemberg in Ludwigsburg and Stuttgart, where he encountered unusually generous conditions for creating his *ballets en action*, while also choreographing dances for operas. He could even afford to invite Boquet as an external collaborator for the costumes; and this was the case for *Médée et Jason*, premiered in Stuttgart on 11 February 1763, during the celebrations for the Duke's birthday. This ballet entered into dance history as one of the first ballets with a tragic ending, together with Gasparo Angiolini's *Don Juan*, presented in Vienna in 1761. *Médée et Jason* was certainly one of Noverre's most famous ballets, although not the first to be inspired by a Greek tragedy. Before that he had created *Alceste* (*ballet tragique*), based on Euripides' pro-satyric tragedy and loosely inspired by Lully's and Quinault's famous opera.[46] However, unlike *Médée*, *Alceste* had a happy ending followed by a celebratory apotheosis, so it was generally less controversial.

According to Noverre, the use of well-known plots as subjects for dramatic ballets was an important factor in overcoming the limited communicative/narrative capacity of dance and pantomime. The story of Medea was very much present in the European repertoire of both theatre and opera: after the presentation of Corneille's tragedy in 1635, it featured in Quinault's and Lully's *tragédie en musique Thésée* (1675)—which had been revived many times during the following century.[47] Before 1700, Medea featured in two more operatic versions: *Médée* by Thomas Corneille and Marc-Antoine Charpentier in 1693; and *Jason ou la Toison d'or*, with text by Jean-Baptiste Rousseau and music by Pascal Collasse in 1696.[48] Furthermore, Longepierre's *Médée, tragédie* was published in 1694; and at the beginning of the eighteenth century, François Joseph Salomon composed the music for the libretto of Simon-Joseph Pellegrin's *Médée et Jason, tragédie lyrique* (1713).[49]

---

[44] For more details about Boquet's career, see Tessier (1926); Fischer (1931); Kerhoas (2007); Piot (2014); and Dotlačilová (2020).

[45] For more recent publications about Noverre, see Dahms (2010); Mourey and Quentin (2011); Burden and Thorp (2014).

[46] For analysis of the ballet *Alceste* and its costumes, see Dotlačilová (2019), 136–42.

[47] For one eighteenth-century revival, see frontispiece to this volume.

[48] See Macintosh, this volume, for the Corneille/Charpentier opera.

[49] Russo and Smart (1994); Hall et al. (2000); Wygant (2007).

The premiere of Noverre's *Médée et Jason* was recorded by librarian Joseph Uriot in his *Descriptions des fêtes données pendant les quatorze jours à l'occasion de jour de naissance de S.A.S. Monseigneur le Duc* (1763).[50] Uriot also confirms the regular employment of Boquet as designer for these festivities (the last being perhaps in the winter of 1764):[51]

> The costumes of the actors, the dancers and the great quantity of people employed in this grand spectacle are invented by Mr. Boquet [...]. The richness, elegance, variety and perfection of costume in the clothing of so many characters that represent such different nations and conditions, have been pushed so far by this clever designer, that we can assure that he never gave better proofs of his skill in his art and of the extent of his knowledge.[52]

A collection of costume drawings for the ballet of *Médée*, together with the score written by Jean-Joseph Rodolphe and Noverre's programme, have been preserved in the so-called Warsaw Manuscript.[53] This collection contains fourteen designs for the characters drawn by Boquet, most likely the ones originally designed for the Stuttgart premiere.[54] And since soon after the first performance, in June 1763, the ballet was presented twice at the royal residence of Choisy in front of Louis XV, the costumes have been recorded also in written form in the *Programme* of Menus-Plaisirs.[55] The

---

[50] On Uriot, see Krämer, this volume.

[51] According to several letters discovered by Albane Piot in the Stuttgart archives, Boquet was not able to participate at the festivities in February 1765 due to an 'accident', and in 1766 his contract was cancelled at the last minute—probably due to the bad financial situation of the Duke at the time. Piot (2014), 37–9.

[52] 'Les habits des Acteurs, des Danseurs, & de la prodigieuse quantité de Personnes employées dans ce grand Spectacle sont de l'invention du Sieur Boquet [...]. La richesse, l'élégance, la variété, & la perfection du Costume dans l'habillement de tant des Personnages qui représentoient des Nations & des Conditions si différentes, ont été poussées si loin par ce sçavant Dessinateur, qu'on peut assurer que jamais il n'a donné des preuves si éclatantes de son habilité dans son Art, & de l'étendue de ses connoissances.' Uriot (1763b), 37–8.

[53] A series of eleven volumes, which assemble Noverre's theoretical writings about dance, programmes and music for twelve of his tragic and heroic ballets, together with 445 watercolour costume designs by Boquet. Noverre addressed his manuscript to the Polish King Stanislas August Poniatowski with the hope of getting employment at his court in 1766. Despite the application not being successful, this precious source has been held in the Warsaw archive ever since for posterity. For more about the Warsaw Manuscript see Mourey (2011); Dotlačilová (2014).

[54] *Médée et Jason*: Médée, Jason, Créuse, Créon, Corinthien/Corintienne, les 2 enfants de Médée, Gouvernante, La Haine, La Jalousie, La Vengeance, Le Poison, Le Feu, Le Fer. *Habits de Costume pour l'Exécution des Ballets de Mr Noverre dessigné par M. Boquet, dessinateur des Menus plaisirs du Roi de France.* Vol. VII. Gabinet Rycin, Biblioteka Uniwersytecka w Warsawe, Inw.zb.d. 20824/7-37. While these drawings are presented by Noverre as Boquet's work, a comparative analysis with his other drawings shows that they are copies drawn by another hand. This fact is not very surprising, since Boquet is known to have had several assistants in his workshop. Therefore, I still consider them the products of Boquet's imagination.

[55] *Programme des opéras représentées avant leur Majestés*, année 1763, Archives Nationales, O/1/3266.

visual sources can be thus compared to the written descriptions, complementing each other, but also uncovering alterations that apparently took place from one staging to another. In my analysis I work primarily with the drawings preserved in the Warsaw Manuscript, although some of the drawings from the productions in Choisy and Paris between 1763 and 1770 have been preserved in the Bibliothèque nationale de France. This collection, however, is not as complete as the set of drawings preserved in Warsaw, and I have not found any considerable differences between those that are in both collections.[56]

Noverre's ballet concentrates on the episode covered by Euripides in his tragedy. Composed of nine scenes, the ballet is indeed packed with action, changing emotions and passions. As Krämer explains in this volume, although Noverre's version of the story basically follows Pierre Corneille's *Médée*, it is original in its emphasis on the conflicts felt by the main characters. In order to communicate these inner conflicts, the ballet required a cast of skilful dancers-actors—the annotations of the libretto and score emphasize the precise mime and expressions, which were complemented with an eloquent, almost 'cinematic' music composed by Jean-Joseph Rodolphe.[57] Médée was performed by Nancy Levier (or Nancy Levrier, married to Trancard), Jason by the famous *premier danseur* from Paris, Gaëtan Vestris, Créuse by Mlle Toscani, and Creon by Angelo Vestris. The cast was completed with Médée's confidante and governess of her children (Mme Noverre), the two children (sons of dancer Delaître) and numerous extras representing princes, princesses and people of Corinth, as well as the important roles of Furies and allegories.[58] The latter become instrumental in visual representations of Médée's rage and revenge, combining conventional operatic practice with modern tools.

The programme suggestively recounts the ballet's action in great detail, including even the dialogues. Alongside Uriot's accounts of the performance, it offers interesting insights into its execution and use of various communicative tools, mostly visual, from mime to stage design. It recounts how the king of Corinth wishes to build an alliance with Jason, and tries to separate him

---

[56] For more about the drawings preserved in Paris see Piot (2014), 78–89. One set of drawings can be found in the Department of Manuscripts, in the volume *Dessins et croquis de costumes pour les opéras représentés à Paris et à Versailles de 1729 à 1767*, accession number Rothschild 1462; another set of costumes is in the collection of Bibliothèque-Musée de l'Opéra, in the volume *Menus-Plaisirs du Roi-Ballets—Costumes—1765–1789*, accession number D 216 O-7 (2) to D 216 O-7 (15); and in another volume, accession number D216 VIII-18 to D216 VIII-24, and D216 VIII-55. These drawings are also consultable online on gallica.fr.

[57] Nye and Thépot (2007); Nye (2011), 194–207.

[58] For the cast list, see the original libretto: *La Didone abbandonata Dramma per musica da rappresentarsi nel teatro ducale di Stuttgart/Festeggiandosi Il felicissimo Giorno Natalizion di Sua Altezza Serenissima Carlo Duca regnante di Wirtemberg E Teck* (1763), 75.

from Médée: he organizes a feast at the court, during which he encourages his daughter Créuse to approach Jason. It does not take long before Jason is charmed by her beauty, which is observed by jealous Médée. Jason hesitates at the offer of Créusa's hand, while Médée appears with their children and tries to convince him to stay with her. Uriot writes that this was a very moving scene, during which Nancy Levier fell on her knees and together with the two children embraced the legs of Gaëtan Vestris. However, the arrival of Créuse spoils this last attempt and Jason decides to abandon Médée. After Jason's rejection, the programme says that Médée remains motionless for a moment, eyes fixed on the floor, while all the disgrace sinks in and the anger accumulates.

Such action—and/or non-action—packed with inner tension, required a highly skilled actress, which Nancy Levier reportedly was. In the next moment, she sends away her children and with a single wave of her magic wand changes the scene from the peristyle hall to a horrible cavern and evokes the demons from the underworld. The demons are led by the allegories of Jealousy, Hatred, and Vengeance. During this scene, Médée orders the allegorical figures to create deadly gifts for Créuse, Créon, and Jason. This allows the dancers to be paired up, well indicated by the costumes: Jealousy and Poison make a poisoned bouquet for Créuse, Vengeance and Fire put deadly smoke in a box for Créon, and Hatred with Iron bring the dagger that will in the end kill the children and will be thrown to Jason to finish his own life. The allegories were of course representing Médée's inner feelings, and at the same time created a horrific spectacle with their appearance, surrounded by snakes and fire, wearing frightening masks, which seems to be necessary even in Noverre's ballet in order to achieve the 'right' terrifying effect.

The costumes of the main characters clearly characterize them using the sartorial codes of opera. For instance, Créon would be recognized by the eighteenth-century audience as a Greek king: he wore *habit à la grecque*—a sort of tunic wrapped around his body, in gold and red, with a royal mantle of ermine, crown, and high feather panache (Figure 8.5). Similar drawings by Boquet for other ballets and operas, as well as material descriptions, show that the combination of gold/yellow and red was frequently used for kings (such as Égée in *Thésée* (Figure 8.6)), and also for Jupiter, the 'king of Gods'.[59] The asymmetrical costume *à la grecque* seems to be new invention by Boquet, as it does not appear on designs by his predecessors, who would dress all the Greek characters *à la romaine*, following Berain's example. This innovation, together with the simpler drapery, can be seen as a moderately reformed way

---

[59] Dotlačilová (2020), 251.

Figure 8.5 and 8.6 Boquet and workshop, design for Créon from *Médée et Jason* (1766) and Boquet, design for Egée from *Thésée* (1765)

of fulfilling the new aesthetic requirements. Furthermore, compared with the operatic costumes for the singers, we can see how the costume for similar characters was adjusted for the sake of dance: the mantle is obviously a necessity because it marks the status of the character, but it needs to be shortened to enable more animated movement.

Jason (Figure 8.7), on the other hand, was dressed in the heroic *habit à la romaine*—inspired by Roman uniform with an armour-like structured bodice (*cuirasse de moire acier*, embroidered with golden thread)—which was a standard garment for a hero on stage. Again, we can find many similarities with Boquet's operatic costume for *Thésée* from Paris, in a lighter, 'danceable' version.[60] It is noteworthy that despite this rather traditional garment, the size and form of his skirt are diminished and loose, which suggest the absence of the stiff *tonnelet*. In the programme of the costumes from Menus-Plaisirs, we can read that the costume was composed of rather light materials such as gauze and satin, especially the sleeves and cape, and the dancer wore a *rotonde* (a round skirt) instead of the *tonnelet*. Yet Jason still wore a helmet richly equipped with feathers and a 'diamond necklace'.

---

[60] Thésée en Géliot, F-Po D216, f. 24, probably 1754. See Dotlačilová (2020), 105.

Pas-seul – Jason – M. Vestris

Costume: Cuirasse made of 'steel' moire embroidered in gold, golden gauze drapery and fringes, 'rotonde' of silver glacé decorated with blue satin and golden net, upper sleeves in golden gauze, amadis sleeves in silver glacé, cape of golden gauze lined with blue taffeta.

Accessories: white feathers on a helmet with black egret, helmet of golden 'steel' moire, diamond necklace. Hair and allongé wig decorated with seven blue and golden rosettes. White gloves and stockings, black shoes.[61]

Figure 8.7 Boquet and workshop, 'Jason' from *Médée et Jason* (1766)

Comparing the costumes of Médée and Créuse, we can see that they communicate the opposites that these two women represent. Médée (Figure 8.8), despite the fact that her human and motherly sentiments are emphasized in the ballet, is still dressed in a 'uniform' of a sorceress/magician. The design shows that the costume was made in a wild combination of red, green, and yellow, with prevailing sharp edges, embroidered bats, and magical symbols (astronomical signs). And of course, she holds the necessary prop of this *rôle à la baguette*—the magic wand.[62] All of these elements are the clear iconological *topoi* for wicked and infernal characters, which can be observed throughout the history of design over the previous hundred years, at least.[63] Such a depiction of Médée, on the one hand, is purely conventional with her attributes signifying her magical, rather than her human side; on the other hand, it tries to limit unnecessary decorative elements, such as the extensive

---

[61] 'Habit: Cuirasse de moire acier brodée en or, draperie de gaze d'or et franges, rotonde de glacé d'argent ornée de satin bleu et reseau d'or haut de manches de gaze d'or amadis de glacé d'argent; mante de gaze d'or doublée de Taffetas bleu/ Ajoustement: Plumes en casque blanches avec une aigrette noire; casque de moire acieret or; Colier de diamants. Ses cheveux et allonges sept rosettes bleues et or. Gants, Bas blancs, Souliers noirs.' *Programme des Opéras representée devant leur majestés*, 1763, F-Pan O-1-3266. Translation mine.

[62] See Dratwicki (2019).   [63] See Dotlačilová (2017).

³ Pas-seul – Médée – Mlle Lyonnois

Costume: The base dress in red satin with borders embroidered with golden sequins, green amadis, upper sleeves and skirt, 'roll up' of golden gauze, small golden gauze cape lined with florence yellow taffeta.

Accessories: chain and clip of diamonds for attaching the cape, bouquet of red and black feathers, black wig, magic wand, pearls for the hairdo, white shoes and stockings, pearl and diamond necklace.[64]

Figure 8.8 Boquet and workshop, design for Médée from *Médée et Jason* (1766)

decorative embroidery, which can be seen for instance on Martin's opera costume design for Médée (Figure 8.9).

So, by resorting to a more stylized depiction, Boquet seems to distance the costume from fashionable dress. However, the programme from Menus-Plaisirs does mention a chain of diamonds for fastening Médée's cape and a pearl and diamond necklace. Even if probably not real jewels, the accessories might have been necessary in a court representation, or in order to emphasize the noble status of her character and reflect the status of the spectators and patrons of the performance. Furthermore, the description of the costume for the Choisy production refers to luxurious materials such as satin, taffeta, and golden gauze, as well as a slightly different distribution of colours in contrast to the design (predominantly green on sleeves and skirt); however, the colour scheme—red, green, and yellow—remains the same.

---

[64] 'Habit fond de satin ponceau avec armures brodées en paillette d'or, amadis, haut de manches et Juppe verte, retroussée en gaze d'or: petite mante de gaze d'or doublée de taffetas de florence jaune. Ajoustement: Barrière, agraffe et chaine de diamants qui porte la mante. Bouquet de plumes noires et ponceau; Coeffes en cheveux noirs; une baguette de magicienne; boucles et filles de perles pour coeffure. Bas et Souliers Blancs. Colier de perle et de Diamants.' *Programme des Opéras representée devant leur majestés*, 1763 F-Pan O-1-13266, translation mine.

Figure 8.9 Jean-Baptiste Martin, 'Médée' (designed between 1748 and 1761)

Pas-seul – Creuze – Mlle Vestris

Costume: The base dress in white taffeta buffered with gauze, white taffeta drapery covered with silver gauze, silver glacé bodice, white taffeta sleeves and amadis, bracelets and 'court sleeves' in silver net.

Accessories: bouquet of white feathers, gauze veil, three white rosettes, silver chenillée, bracelets, chain of diamonds, white gloves, stockings and shoes.[65]

Figure 8.10 Boquet and workshop, 'Créuse' from *Médée et Jason* (1766)

By contrast, Créuse's costume is typical for a young princess, with soft colours of white and pink (or just white in the Choisy production), with the undulating cuts to the draperies, decorated with flowers, ribbons, pearls, and veils. Such a costume symbolizes beauty, youth, noble origin, but also a certain coquetry to which such excessive decoration has been connected. The seductive character of Créuse was apparently emphasized in later versions of the ballet, particularly when the role was performed by Marie Guimard. For this famous dancer, coquetry and seduction were, according to contemporary sources, 'her true genre',[66] and colours such as white and silver were her favourites.[67]

Two drawings of the costumes of the chorus of Corinthians feature a similar colour scheme to Créuse's dress, predominantly pink, but with a simpler decoration than that used for the princess' costume (Figure 8.10). Both of these

---

[65] 'Habit fond de Taffetas blanc Tamponné de gaze, draperie de Taffetas blanc couverte de gaze d'argent, Corps de glacé d'argent, manches en amadis de Taffetas blanc, brasselets et manches de Cour de reseau argent / Ajoustement: Bouquet de plumes blanches un Voile de gaze nouée. Trois rosette blanches Chenillée argent; brasselets, Barriere et chaine de diamants. Gands, bas et Souliers blancs.' *Programme des Opéras representée devant leur majestés*, 1763, F-Pan O-1-13266, translation mine.

[66] Bachaumont et al. (1781), 43.   [67] Goncourt (1893), 147–8.

Figures 8.11–8.12 Boquet and workshop, designs for 'Corinthien' and 'Corinthiene' from *Médée et Jason* (1766)

costumes are *à la grecque* style with the asymmetrical wrap-tunic, showing how this garment looked in its female version. At the same time, they represent the most formal type of costume—with its contained shape and high plumes—signalling that the dancers performed in the so-called *genre sérieux*, which was considered to be the highest in the hierarchy of genres and characters. The female costumes in Boquet's designs are all adjusted for dance with the skirts shortened so that the feet can be seen, and they lack a long train. Their operatic colleagues would still wear longer skirts and trains in this period (Figures 8.11–8.12).

It is, however, the contrast between the shapes visible on the costumes of the two female characters which carries particular significance: Créuse's costume is full of soft curves, while Médée's features straight lines and sharp edges. According to William Hogarth's theories from *The Analysis of Beauty*, the former costume would invoke the wavy and serpentine lines that are the embodiments of grace and beauty.[68] In fact, undulating lines prevail in all the costumes for the human characters, in accordance with the contemporary rules of taste. Médée's design is in striking contrast to these qualities, visually distinguishing the character from the other humans and disturbing the

[68] Hogarth (1753), 37–9.

normative standard of beauty. Furthermore, the shapes on her costume link Médée directly to the underworld, whose representatives display similar linearity and colour scheme.

These underworldly and allegorical characters are invoked by Médée in scene five: Vengeance, Hatred, and Jealousy who resemble the Furies in their appearance, especially with the omnipresent snakes, draperies with sharp edges, and *mascarons* (masks of grimaces) drawn on the fabric (Figures 8.13–8.18). Furthermore, Jealousy is blindfolded, and on its chest appears an interesting detail of a heart being bitten by several snakes, which expressively portray the blind fury and all-consuming passion represented by the allegory. The roles of Fire, Iron, and Poison are even more eloquent, especially due to their accessories in the form of flames, daggers, and herbs attached to their costumes. On the drawings, we can see clearly the difference between costumes for men and women (which is here only that of Hatred)—men wear draperies above the knee, while women have longer skirts underneath; there is no sign of a *tonnelet*.

Although Boquet's use of symbolism was quite traditional, his designs break with the formal shape of the dance costume developed during the first half of the eighteenth century. Designs by his predecessor Martin, for example, show a Demon in a *tonnelet* and with high feathers, and a Fury in wide hoops (Figures 8.19–8.20). These costumes, embroidered or painted with snakes and grimaced masks, feature sharp edges, but also other ornaments that are almost elegant. Boquet removed the *tonnelets* and hoops from the costumes of these characters, and instead used loose draperies with irregular arrangements and angularity. His drawings suggest naked arms and partially naked torsos. However, it should be mentioned that the drawings represent the costume as it should appear, rather than showing accurately the various components of the garment. As the descriptions in the *Programme* reveal, all of them wore shoes, stockings, breeches, bodices with long sleeves and gloves, often in plain fabrics without embroidery in order to create the effect of naked bodies. Appearing on stage without such covering would have still been considered indecent—and it would perhaps, in turn, ruin the illusion of the supernatural creatures.

The programme, which recorded the costumes for the Choisy performances in 1763, shows an interesting alteration in the number of performers in this scene: the allegorical figures were played by only two women and one man, and they combined the emotions and the objects within the costume. Vengeance had a costume covered with poisoned herbs, Jealousy was in red and orange like Fire, and Desperation (instead of Hatred) was covered with

Figures 8.13–8.18 Boquet and workshop, designs for 'La Vengeance', 'Le Feu', 'La Haine', 'Le Fer', 'La Jalousie', 'Le Poison' from *Médée et Jason* (1766)

daggers.[69] This alteration might have happened owing to the shortening of the ballet on this occasion.[70] Finally, all of these characters were also decorated with numerous serpents—a 'mémoire' recorded that seven dozen snake heads were made of coloured and gilded papier-mâché.[71] These details uncovering the materiality of costume design also show an original move by Boquet in contrast to his predecessors. By making the traditional attributes three-dimensional, and more realistic as they completely enveloped the body of the dancer, they certainly contributed to the terrifying effect of these costumes. The elimination of unnecessary decorative elements and the emphasis on the parts evoking disgust and fear reveal Boquet's striving for emotional truthfulness in the costuming of his allegorical figures.

Finally, the Stockholm Manuscript, composed by Noverre in 1791 using copies of Boquet's designs from the previous decade, shows how the portrayal of Médée's character developed over time in convergence with the new ideas on costume (Figure 8.21). Here, the infernal and/or magical attributes are reduced to symbols painted on the edge of her skirt, while the colour scheme transformed from red, green, and yellow to blue and yellow. Instead of bats her dress is adorned with flowers and ribbons. The whole ensemble creates a somewhat softer and calmer effect than the previous one, which emphasized Médée's relation to the underworld. While she still holds the magic wand, the costume now seems to emphasize more her role of princess, woman, and mother. This indeed corresponds to the eighteenth-century reinterpretations of her character and with the tendency of costume reformers not only to portray the type, but also to reflect the psychological features of the characters.

Conclusion

When creating the revolutionary tragic ballet, Noverre and his designer Boquet combined conventional visual symbols together with the new ideas about choreography and costume. The emphasis on the visual is evident in the ballet programme and in the review of the performance, which recounts stark moments of mime and tableaux—notably, Médée and children embracing

---

[69] For further analysis of the garments of these characters, see Dotlačilová (2017), 63–5.

[70] In Choisy, the ballet was directly incorporated into the *tragédie lyrique Ismène et Isménias ou la fête de Jupiter* by Jean-Benjamin Laborde as a part of the second act, and therefore it needed to be considerably shortened. See Nye (2011), 194–207.

[71] *Mémoire de Peintures*, Archives Nationales, O1 3008, pièce 66. Cited in Piot (2014), 58–9.

Figures 8.19–8.20 Jean-Baptiste Martin, designs for 'Démon' and 'Furie' (between 1748 and 1761)

Jason's legs, her moment of stillness at the point of desperation, and finally the embodiment of her rage through the change of setting and the arrival of infernal characters. Regarding the costumes, each of the characters was visually differentiated, and the traditional operatic costume was updated for dance: with shorter skirts and capes, less fabric and more varied drapery, it was easier to dance and move on stage. Boquet reduced the sizes of women's hoops and of men's *tonnelets*, which for certain characters disappeared completely, depending on their role and the technical requirements of their dance. But, despite the growing demand for simplicity, the costumes designed by Boquet, and especially those described in the French programme, still contain some pearl and 'diamond' decoration, sequins etc., to keep some of the splendour for its royal spectators.

Skilful blending of the familiar with the new facilitated the understanding of the plot of the danced drama through visual appearance. For instance, with the imitation of a naked torso through plain coloured garments, green or red, for the allegorical characters, the designer created an otherworldly appearance. Furthermore, the terrifying effect of these characters was emphasized by three-dimensional items on their bodies, and by the removal of unnecessary (from a dramaturgical point of view) decorative elements. The decorations didn't entirely disappear from Boquet's costumes, but were only used when appropriate for the character. The designs also clearly distinguished the roles

Figure 8.21 Boquet and workshop, design for *Médée* (1791)

and their characters, which is perhaps most recognizable in the costumes of Médée and Créuse. And in the case of Médée, there are two different approaches to her representation: as witch or as 'human'. Unfortunately, Créuse's later costume has not been preserved, therefore we cannot be sure what changes (if any) were made.

These subtle changes in design are a typical feature of the first wave of costume reform that took place during the eighteenth century, and of which both Noverre and Boquet were proponents. They did not aim for radical change in relation to previous traditions, but pushed the boundaries in order to put on stage dramaturgically effective costume which supported the eloquence of the danced drama. This strategy entailed clearly distinguished characters, adjustment of their clothing to the situation, as well as effective use of material in order to create extraordinary effects: in other words, it was the right degree of verisimilitude with a touch of the *merveilleux* that made Noverre's ballets and Boquet's costumes so celebrated and alluring.

9

Medea as Infanticidal Mother in the Late Eighteenth-Century Theatre

Zoé Schweitzer

Creating a *Medea* play was a perilous enterprise in eighteenth-century England, France, or Italy, since its scandalous plot pushes the boundaries of representing extreme violence on stage. Indeed, in this historical context, a regicide and a maternal infanticide, which both remain unpunished, could hardly be viewed as tropes appropriate for tragedy. However, this subject enjoyed enormous success in this period, and it is this paradox that this chapter seeks to understand. It is the infanticide that provides the focus, both in its ancient and modern representations.

There were serious ethical and practical problems relating to the infanticide from antiquity onwards. As Horace argued in his *Ars Poetica*,[1] a mother who is both a ferocious woman and the murderer of her children raises issues of verisimilitude. Moreover, according to Horace, the tragedy is unbearable because the criminal remains unpunished; and such an immoral ending makes the plot faulty. The association of morality and plot is problematic: Medea is described as a '*ferox*' infanticidal mother; but Horace recommends that theatrical poets follow tradition when they represent an illustrious character.[2] Thus, Medea, who kills her own children,[3] must be '*ferox invictaque*' ('fierce and unvanquished').[4]

However, this Horatian definition of verisimilitude in relation to Medea gave rise to two difficulties for eighteenth-century playwrights.[5] The first was that such a female character was at odds with the prevalent view, shared across

---

[1] Horace (1929), l. 123, l. 185.   [2] Horace (1929), l. 119.   [3] Horace (1929), l. 185.
[4] Horace (1929), l. 123. Whereas lines 185–8 are ambiguous, this is not the case for line 123 if we compare the different translations proposed between the sixteenth and nineteenth centuries.
[5] The two contradictions appear when reading poetics from the seventeenth and eighteenth centuries focusing on Medea and translations and commentaries of Horace's *Ars Poetica*; to follow the evolution of these references during the two centuries and for analysis of the various positions adopted by theoreticians and translators, see Schweitzer (2016).

Zoé Schweitzer, *Medea as Infanticidal Mother in the Late Eighteenth-Century Theatre* In: *Mapping Medea: Revolutions and Transfers 1750–1800*. Edited by: Anna Albrektson and Fiona Macintosh, Oxford University Press.

Europe, that women were primarily mothers.[6] Thus, there was a conflict between eighteenth-century *decorum* on the one hand, and the theoreticians' demand for continuity with antiquity on the other.[7] This conflict resulted in a lack of verisimilitude in the Colchian infanticidal mother's character, either from an ideological viewpoint, because she broke the rules of eighteenth-century propriety, or from a mythological standpoint, since the character differed from the original myth. The second contradiction stems from the first: in the age of triumphant motherhood, the infanticide could only be committed by a mother led astray by passion; Medea could not be a ferocious woman. Character and plot, in this sense, seemed incompatible. Indeed, leaving out the infanticide, mentioned by both Aristotle and Horace, was a delicate matter since it had contributed to making the Corinthian story a stand-alone episode of the Argonautica and was key to the appeal of the plot.[8] Turning the barbarian enchantress into a 'very submissive' woman—in the words of Corneille[9]—was an equally complicated strategy. The Corinthian story thus posed a serious problem of verisimilitude (Figure 9.1).

However, the plot and its *dénouement* are equally problematic: Medea is an unpunished murderess. Since the mid-seventeenth century, most theoreticians had been recommending that a tragedy should end with the culprits being punished. Yet, following Horace's precept, Medea is to remain 'unvanquished',[10] but such a dénouement was no longer appropriate in the eighteenth century,

---

[6] This idea appears during the first part of the century and reaches a larger audience during the course of the century. See, for example, Hill (1989); Hoffer and Hull (1981); Jones (1990).

[7] See, for example, Marmontel (2005b), art. 'vraisemblance', 1170–1: 'Horace nous donne le choix ou de suivre la renommée ou d'observer les convenances. Mais ce choix est-il libre ? Non; et si les caractères et les faits sont connus, l'altération n'en est permise qu'autant qu'elle n'est pas sensible. On peut bien ajouter aux vertus et aux vices quelques coups de pinceau plus hardis et plus forts; on peut bien adoucir, déguiser, effacer quelques traits qui dégraderaient ou qui noirciraient le tableau, mais on ne peut pas insulter en face à la vérité, en changeant les événements et en dénaturant les hommes […]' ['Horace gives us the choice either to follow tradition or to observe *decorum*. But is this choice free? No; and in the case where characters and facts are well known, their alteration is possible only as far as it remains imperceptible. We can add to vices and virtue a few brushstrokes more daring or stronger; we can soften, disguise, or erase a few features which would degrade or blacken the picture, but we cannot offend grossly against truth in changing events or misrepresenting men […]' (my translation).

[8] This situation is described precisely by Pigna (1554), 22: '& falsa è tutta la Medea d'Euripide; & di coloro che seguito l'hanno: & pure è stata permessa. & la vera Medea di Carcinos no non è stata accettata. Tal chez una bugia d'un buon poeta ogni verità sepellisce. […] Ma pure Euripide una falsità prese per oggetto: & biasimato non fu. […] Ma se bene in sul vero non saremo fondati, in sul verisimile almeno staremo talmente, che egli mai trapposto non sarà' ['Euripides' *Medea* and other *Medeas* from authors inspired by him are the result of an invention, but they had success, whereas Carcinos' *Medea* got none, which proves that a good poet's lye is superior to truth. […] Euripides has also presented invented events and was not misjudged for this reason […] But if a fiction is not founded on truth, it must at least always respect verisimilitude'] (my translation).

[9] Corneille (1987), 132.

[10] Dryden (1912 [1671]), 83: 'Medea is the only example I remember at present who escapes from punishment after murder.' According to this point of view, Medea is for Dryden the exact opposite of Oedipus because he was punished for a crime committed unknowingly.

Figure 9.1 Final scene of Pierre Corneille's *Médée* by François Chauveau

whether in treatises or in *Medea* plays. This might be one of the reasons why Glover's *Medea* met with great success in England.[11] Medea in this version is now a devoted mother, who kills her beloved sons by accident. By means of an apparent paradox, the nature and number of the differences with the original plot made it possible for the audience to overlook the mythological

---

[11] Richard Glover's tragedy, printed in 1761, then played from 1767 and reprinted in 1777 and in 1792; it was translated into French by Jean-Florimond Boudon Saint-Amans in 1784 and used as a reference by Jean-Baptiste Gabriel Marie de Milcent for his opera, *Médée et Jason* (1813). See Hall (2000).

tradition, and turned an outstanding woman, an exemplary mother, into a plausible Medea.

Thus, in order to guarantee the verisimilitude of the infanticide on the tragic stage, it was necessary to alter Medea's character considerably according to the changing ideological contexts: in the Renaissance, she was cruel; at the beginning of the seventeenth century, she was a proud princess who was the victim of an iniquitous husband; and by the end of the century, she had become passionate and jealous. In the second part of the eighteenth century, Medea had eventually been turned into a loving mother, whose crime the audience was able to bear and believe in, solely and precisely because she herself could not bear it.[12]

In order to please the audience, playwrights and translators resorted to censorship and rewriting, the impacts of which were sometimes difficult to foresee. This chapter seeks to analyse some surprising configurations, which illustrate both the inventiveness of eighteenth-century playwrights and the plasticity of the plot of the original myth. My analysis will fall into two parts. First, I will present three original solutions found by playwrights to make Medea and her crime bearable. Secondly, the focus will be on two plays from the end of the eighteenth century, which bring out a renewed form of violence under the guise of sensibility. The first is a French translation of Seneca's *Medea* (1795) by Jean-Marie-Louis Coupé; the second is Glover's version, which is remarkable because it is the very radically modified plot and the very suppression of violence under the guise of sensibility that results paradoxically in both the heightened presence and impact of the violence.

The Playwrights' Inventiveness

However implausible to us nowadays, some solutions did lend verisimilitude to the plays back in the eighteenth century. Yet, such verisimilitude had to be found outside of the theatrical or even mythological fields, notably in treatises on women and in medical books, two areas in which writers had been trying to solve the mystery of Medea since antiquity. Thinking about women's identities or defining passions and pathologies, the writers encounter this terrifying and original mythological figure and many treatises quote the infanticidal mother. Authors try to analyse her actions, to understand her mind and motives;

---

[12] See Schweitzer (2015), focusing on Shaftesbury's moral conception linked to Medea's crime and its influence on theatrical rewritings from this period.

and their interpretations provide material to playwrights, keen to grant verisimilitude to their theatrical characters.

Given that they associate a pedestrian plot line (a husband's infidelity) with extreme violence (a deserted wife's infanticide), Jason and Medea's adventures in Corinth provide those who study gender relations—and usually focus on their conflictual dimension—with a *locus classicus*. The more womanhood, and then motherhood, became valued,[13] the stronger the justification for the maternal infanticide had to become. Thus, whilst in the seventeenth century, as we have heard, the explanation is to be found in the husband's cruelty and his wife's passion, in the eighteenth century, it lies in the torments undergone by a woman's sensitive soul.

Those who made passion, sensibility, or maternal love women's defining qualities dug the grave of Medea as a cruel female character, which was precisely what makes her unique. On the other hand, they provided playwrights with theatrically efficient solutions to make the infanticide acceptable, as evidenced by the success of *Medea* plays in the eighteenth century. The argument of the weight of passions finds new momentum in the eighteenth century. Indeed, the intensity of the passions became one of the principal female character traits, either in a positive or in a 'baneful' way when it takes the form of jealousy, which 'is generally accompanied with anger, mischievousness, & a desire for revenge'.[14] Thus, Medea ceases to be an unnatural mother murdering her children. Rather, she is a woman so deeply in love that she cannot resist the excess of her passion—in other words, she is a victim of her own nature. In this way, maternal love is not called into question and neither is the verisimilitude of Medea's crime, since the mother perpetrates the infanticide in a moment of extreme passion, when she has lost control over herself, and will immediately regret her crime. Such a configuration is specific to the eighteenth century.[15]

Charles Johnson, who asserted that a tragedy must have a moral ending, published *The Tragedy of Medea* in 1731 without the infanticide.[16] Not only the characters but the plot too is profoundly changed: Creusa dies because of Medea's jealousy but her father, speaking as a Christian, recognizes his own

---

[13] See, for example, treatises written by Philippe-Florent de Puisieux, published anonymously (1750), or by John Andrews (1783).

[14] Steele (1719), 85.

[15] It is recommended, for example, by Baculard d'Arnaud or Marmontel (1763), 183; this text was reused for the entry on 'Mœurs' in Marmontel [2005a], 731.

[16] Johnson (1731). For morality, see the introduction, 8: 'With a Preface containing Some Reflections on the new Way of Criticism': '[...] Morals recommended in this Tragedy [...] Justice, *and not to do Evil that Good may come of it.*'

culpability and commits suicide. Moreover, the play does not end with the traditional infanticide, but with a double suicide, Jason's and then Medea's, because the wife is incapable of surviving the loss of her husband.[17] The cruel magician has become a new Hermione, slave of her love. Such a singular ending appears to be less surprising in the light of contemporary treatises on women, according to which an infanticidal mother would be an insuperable contradiction. For instance, there is a treatise about how even an offended wife is not permitted to make an attempt on the life of her children.[18] The verisimilitude of this Medea's suicide is also supported by the notion that women's submission to their husbands is their own greatest manifestation of virtue.

In Clément's tragedy,[19] infanticide is caused by temporary madness. Within the framework of Clément's poetics, which does not permit marvellous elements and emphasizes *decorum* and strict morality, the use of hallucination as a plot device is a relevant strategy. In his 1779 version of *Medea*, the bereaved mother surfaces within moments after Medea, the jealous wife has murdered her children in a fit of rage—Medea has hallucinations through which she relives her atrocious crime and such an overwhelming memory leads her to her suicide. Nevertheless, the playwright cannot be blamed for failing to abide by Horace's precept. In fact, he boasts about following it:

> Mais si l'on se contente de représenter Médée, comme l'a peinte Horace, fière & intraitable, d'un caractère ardent & impétueux, incapable de fléchir, sinon pour se venger: [...] au lieu d'en faire une dégoûtante Canidie [...].[20]

What is at stake here, however, is the very understanding of Horace's lines:[21] choosing the ethical term '*intraitable*' ('uncompromising') for '*invicta*', Clément implies Medea's nobility. The other Latin adjective is not even translated:

---

[17] On the importance of virtue in this version of *Medea* and its ending for the two young women, 'innocent victims of circumstance', see Hall and Macintosh (2005), 86–8. The play 'was still an outstanding failure', not so much because of its morality as for its 'fidelity to the original, resulting in a sombre tone and lack of love scenes'. Hall and Macintosh (2005), 93.

[18] See the anonymous (female?) author of *Triomphe du beau sexe sur les hommes* (1719), who recognizes that cruel women exist ('Jesabel, Dallila, Herodias', 63), but, like Renaissance authors, thinks that they were driven to violence by men and that their number is largely inferior to male criminals. The treatise takes as its model the case of a woman who, legitimately offended by her husband, asks God for help. Nonetheless, concludes the author, it would not be believed that such an offended woman, even convinced by her husband's treason, killed her children (47).

[19] See further Albrektson, this volume.

[20] Clément (1779), 'Préface', [iii]: 'But if one is content with representing Medea, as Horace did, as a proud & inflexible woman, with a fiery & impetuous character, incapable of giving in, except to take revenge: [...] instead of turning her into a foul Canidie.'

[21] Clément, who criticizes plays from his time, names some possible opponents. Clément (1779), iv, xi.

'*ferox*' is no longer 'fierce' but rendered with the positive, evaluative adjective, '*fière*' ('proud'). Clément thus significantly bridges the gap between his own *Medea* and that of the theoretician without deviating significantly from other contemporary translations of Horace. By doing this, it seems the playwright is not betraying Horace on purpose, and this reading is not an isolated one: other translations of these lines from the same period are broadly similar.[22]

The sight of the evidence of her crime (the dagger in hand,[23] the steaming blood) triggers a hallucinatory process in the course of which Medea believes she is hearing an infernal voice calling for the punishment of the Furies to fall on her. With all her senses alert, she believes she has begun her descent into the underworld where the ghost of the late Absyrtus denies her much wished-for relief from punishment. Thus, Clément completely reinvents and distorts the role of the hallucination in the plot, since the aim is no longer to exhort Medea to commit a crime, as in Seneca's version. Rather, and to the contrary, it aims to increase her pain by forcing her to relive her actions.[24] Medea progressively comes to guess the identity of those lying under the 'bloody veil'. Through the references it conveys, the phrase compensates for the absence of the sight of the crime on stage, since it refers both to Timanthes' veil[25] and to the piece of cloth that covers up Clytemnestra's murdered body.[26] Thus, Medea is made to relive her crime, to play it over again, in a sense, and the audience too is gradually able to picture it as it witnesses its effect on her. Therefore, the solution imagined by Clément is an efficient and original use of Horace's interdict. Representing the crime through the lens of Medea's hallucinating gaze succeeds in renewing the pathetic of the infanticide—the terror caused to the mind of the criminal on account of the scandalous crime makes even her more pitiful.

---

[22] Some French translators in the second part of the eighteenth century understand this line similarly; for example, Le Bel (1769), 75, who translates 'que rien ne puisse abattre le cœur barbare de Médée' ('nothing can tear Medea's barbarous heart'), and the abbé Batteux (1750), 373, whose translation is similar to Clément's: 'Médée sera fiere, inébranlable' ('Medea will be fierce and unwavering'). This is why Clément doesn't deliberately dilute the two adjectives but, on the contrary, through this reading reflects contemporary sensibility.

[23] The stage direction which opens the scene is very clear: 'Médée *seule, un poignard à la main*' ('Medea, *alone, a dagger in her hand*'). Clément (1779), 45.

[24] Clément reconnects with the Latin invention, which used the slow pace as an increasing factor for pain, but Medea is taken for Jason here because she is the one suffering.

[25] Painting the moment when Iphigenia is led to sacrifice, a pitiful scene painted by the Greek painter Timanthes from the fourth century BCE, who chose not to show the face of Agamemnon: the father has covered his face and his body is turned in the opposite direction. Thus Agamemnon's emotions remain invisible and the spectators can only imagine his pain. This solution has led to many commentaries. See for example Perdichizzi (2008).

[26] In *Electra* from Euripides, Clytemnestra's corpse is stretched out under a shroud at the back of the scene so that Aegisthus can only guess there is a body but not its identity.

Nevertheless, such a rewriting of the plot poses problems with the dramatic genre itself, as if the choice of including the episode has been to the detriment of the structure of the tragedy. Indeed, Clément's *Medea* seems to hover between a myth-based tragedy and a domestic drama. In this respect, the play reveals a lot about the evolution of French theatre at the end of the eighteenth century. The infanticide in Clément is the desperate gesture of a mother who wishes to spare her children the torments of exile and servitude. This motive, first hinted at in Euripides' *Medea* and then given more prominence in Longepierre's version of 1694,[27] was fully developed in the eighteenth century, in Gasparo Gozzi's *Medea*,[28] when the motive is dependent upon the glorification of maternal love. In Gozzi's tragedy, Medea is no more a cruel spouse eager to take revenge, but a mother motivated by the love of her children whom she wants to protect from a future necessarily pathetic and dire because of the cruelty of their father, the sadness of the exile and the wrath of the Corinthians.[29] Her suicide after she reveals her crime to Jason appears as an ultimate proof of her motherly nature and the virtuous motive of her crime. Committed by a forlorn mother who wants to protect her children from an even more sinister fate, the infanticide becomes a motherly crime.

In the second half of the eighteenth century, then, Medea's infanticide became tolerable inasmuch as it was unbearable to its perpetrator—she was thus represented as a good mother whose only way of overcoming the horror of her crime was either suicide, as in Clément's play, or exile, as in Glover's. Therefore, a sea change can be observed as far as the representation of the infanticide is concerned, which led to a revolution regarding the character of the criminal—while, in the Renaissance and early seventeenth-century works, the infanticide was an unacceptable act, the violence of which was insurmountable and beyond compare, and could only be committed by a singular heroine who was the most inflexible figure of otherness; in eighteenth-century tragedies, the children's murder stems from an excess of passion, and Medea is but a woman who is the victim of her own nature. However, laying emphasis on sensibility and virtue is not without its own ambiguities—it may well

---

[27] Longepierre's Medea thinks that death is preferable to enslavement which is threatening her children (Act IV, scene IV, l. 986–8; scene VII, l. 1056–70; scene VIII, l. 1122–6).

[28] Gozzi (1758). We can also observe that Potter (1781) and Prevost (1782) give a translation from Euripides' *Medea* in which the main character appears very pathetic at the moment where she decides, after long hesitation, to commit infanticide, of which she is partly exonerated.

[29] Gozzi (1758), Act V, scene V, p. 172.

turn out to foster the expression of a disturbing form of latent violence, as a counterpoint to a discourse that seemingly aims to adhere to the predominant moral ideology at the end of the century.

Violence that Eludes Censorship

There are two peculiar *Medea* tragedies that show how violence in fact eludes censorship by revealing itself despite the playwright's intent. The first example, a translation from the Latin of Seneca in 1795, involves a deliberate choice on the part of the translator, Coupé, who plays a double game in his translation.[30] The translator censored the Latin text by leaving out sexual allusions, which are nevertheless discreetly revealed in the accompanying footnotes. For instance, Coupé translated the problematic lines 990–1: 'Voluptas magna me inuitam subit, / et ecce crescit'[31] as 'Malgré moi une grande volupté entre dans mon âme: je sens cette volupté s'étendre.'[32] Though he has censored the sexual overtones in the body of the text, they are restored in the footnote: 'Voilà une terrible Métaphore, tirée des plaisirs les plus secrets de l'amour, et appliquée à la jouissance abominable de la vengeance.'[33] Though the translator dulls Medea's words above the line, he oddly sheds light on their true meaning in the footnote, which is of course equally available to all readers.

A similar semantic shift occurs at line 1016: 'perfruere lento scelere, ne propera, dolor',[34] which is translated as 'Ô mon ressentiment, jouis à longs traits de ton bonheur, et ne précipite pas une volupté si douce.'[35] The slowing down of the pace does not concern the revenge itself here—as is the case in the Latin text. Rather, it has to do with the feeling of triumph upon taking revenge,[36] which is more common and less disturbing. Nevertheless,

---

[30] Coupé (1795).

[31] The Loeb edition (2018) gives this translation: 'A great sense of pleasure steals over me unbidden, and it is still growing.' Seneca (2018), 401. About these lines from Seneca and their various translations, see Lecercle (2000), (2001).

[32] Coupé (1795), 85, 'A great voluptuousness is entering my soul despite my will— / I feel that this voluptuousness is spreading' (my translation).

[33] Coupé (1795), note I, 85. 'Here is a horrendous metaphor, drawing upon love's most secret pleasures, and applied to the vile enjoyment of revenge.'

[34] The Loeb edition from 2018 translates: 'Relish your crime in leisure, my pain, do not hurry.' Seneca (2018), 403.

[35] Coupé (1795), 87. 'O my resentment, relish in your happiness, and do not hasten such (a) sweet voluptuousness' (my translation). The translator doesn't give up the vocabulary of pleasure but the words concern Medea's resentment after her crimes were accomplished.

[36] When such a displacement is not possible, for example lines 1012–13, in which Medea thinks about scouring her womb, the note is openly critical making it clear that this is the only way to distance itself from the violence that the translation cannot reduce: 'Il est impossible de pousser plus loin

the amplification of the lexicon of pleasure in comparison to the original suggests that the crime has been enjoyable and seems to echo the Latin words 'ne propera' ('hasten not'). In his translation, Coupé plays on two different levels of interpretation, according to which neither sensibility nor condemnation of the crimes appears to prevent a far more provocative, possibly Sade-inspired combination of pain and sexual pleasure rising to the surface. Such a hypothesis seems all the more convincing given that Sade's *Philosophy in the Bedroom*—one of his best, completed works from a philosophical point of view—was published in the same year as Coupé's translation. A similar conception of nature emerges in both the translation and in the philosophical works against the revolutionary backdrop, which is alluded to by Coupé when he evokes the 'blood shed by Robespierre'[37] in his 'Historical, literary and critical notes on *Medea*'.

My second example comes from Glover's *Medea*. Given that the infanticide is committed offstage by a Medea who is beside herself,[38] who is unaware of what she has done, the murders need to be brought to the criminal's knowledge, as well as to that of the other characters, and the audience itself. Still, the unfolding of the crime itself is never described and the audience waits for it to be relayed in vain—not only does the crime remain unseen, it also remains unheard. Such an excessive take on Horace's interdict leads Glover to a radical restaging of the infanticide—the scandalous crime may only be represented through the account of its consequences. Therefore, the spectacle of the aftermath of the crime becomes a muted, metonymical substitute for its representation (see Figure 6.3).

The three scenes dedicated to uncovering the crime and commenting upon it resort to three different types of dramatic configurations. In the first scene, secondary characters learn from the priestess, a moral authority, about what has happened. She does not recount the infanticide, since she did not witness it, and only gives details about the discovery of the crime, merely saying that the murder weapon was a sacrificial knife and that madness has overcome Medea.[39] Such an announcement causes terror, distress, and compassion among the other characters, who are but internal doubles of the audience. The latter are thus invited to feel terror and pity: 'Behold, where, dropping with

l'esprit et la profondeur de la haine, de la vengeance, de l'inhumanité.' Coupé (1795), note I, 87. 'It is impossible to go further in the spirit and depth of hatred, revenge and inhumanity' (my translation).

[37] Coupé (1795), 96: 'blood shed by Robespierre' (my translation).

[38] About madness as motive of the infanticide, Hall and Macintosh (2005), 93–4, write that this circumstance would have probably led a tribunal to acquit Medea in the eighteenth century.

[39] Richard Glover (1761), *Medea*, Act V, scene I, 83: 'A knife of sacrifice she seiz'd, / And in their tender bosoms plung'd its point!'

her children's blood, / The lost Medea comes!'[40] In the following scene, everyone, except Medea herself, knows that she has killed her children. Medea calls for her beloved children to be brought to her before eventually finding out about her crime through the Colchians' strange silence and the blood on her hands.[41] In the third, and final scene, the poor Jason learns what has happened from Medea herself. The playwright makes full use of a protracted, but occluded, infanticide based on the fragmentation of information and on the disparity in knowledge among the characters.

Representing Medea as a terrifying, terrified, and pitiable mother lends verisimilitude to the fact that she is a child-killer. Glover experiments with the devices of a poetics of frustration, which leaves out storytelling to the benefit of the expression of the passions, and turns the spectacle of their effects into the very substance of tragic efficacy. Without ever risking to disrupt the *mimesis* or to flout the *decorum*, the playwright renews the very source of the effect of violence (*pathos*) in a way that arouses terror and pity without resort to storytelling or staging (*opsis*) devices.

However, subversion lurks under the moral tone of the play, as violence breaks through the mask of *decorum* and sensibility. Glover's *Medea* can be interpreted as a strange combination of late eighteenth-century sensibility[42] with Senecan poetics,[43] and illustrates the paradox of a moralizing interpretation of the Corinthian story.

The text is ambiguous from the start, as if there were two separate levels of interpretation. Though the playwright's moral purpose is asserted in the prologue, in which he explains his wish to show the misfortunes that befall the powerful and 'Teach private life to prize its tranquil state', he lays greater emphasis on the description of passions and their effects, inspired by Seneca. Indeed, 'love and fury, grief and madness join'd', overcome Medea's 'Pow'r,

---

[40] Glover (1761), Act V, scene II, 84.
[41] Glover (1761), Act V, scene III, 87–8: '[...] Sure, my faithful friends, / From my sad heart no evils can erase / Maternal gladness as my childrens' [*sic*] sight. / Go, lead them from the temple – They will smile, / And lift my thoughts to momentary joy. / Not gone my virgins? wherefore this delay? / Why all aghast? why tremble thus your limbs? / Ha! whence this blood? My hands are deep in slaughter. / Speak, ye dumb oracles of terror, speak? [rising] / Where are my children? My distracted brain / A *thousand dreadful images* recalls / Imperfectly remember'd – Speak, I charge you; / Where are my children? – Silent still and pale' (my italics).
[42] *Medea*'s 'Prologue' is concluding by these words: 'The characters and passions hence exprest / Are all submitted to the feeling breast; / Let ancient story justify the rest.'
[43] The editor in 1792, J. Bell, underlines the parenthood between Glover' *Medea* and Seneca's: 'This is the last produced of four plays by different authors upon the same subject. For those previous to the present, it is enough to stile them bad translations of a bad original—they are all from SENECA. Mr. Glover however has taken a scope less servile and better suited to his powers; for though he has kept Seneca constantly in his eye, yet his poem bears very frequent marks of originality and skill.' Glover (1792), [iii].

wisdom, science, and her birth divine', and her pain is so great that 'In vain to shield her from distress combine: / Nor wisdom, pow'r, nor science yield relief'.[44] Although Glover's tragedy aims at being the epitome of a moral and sensitive kind of theatre, the ambiguity perceived in the prologue is never resolved, as if an abundance of fine feelings, far from putting the audience at ease prompts curiosity and suspicion instead.

Beside the many changes that tone down the violence, other changes, which are less easy to perceive, actually seem to increase it. The expected moment of the infanticide epitomizes how such changes result in paradoxical effects, as they contribute to enhance the violence of the episode under the pretext of moralizing it. While it is no longer either the resolution of the sentimental drama or a crime committed knowingly, the infanticide is foregrounded and its scandalous nature emphasized. The two elements play a key role in this context: first, allusions to the murder which can only be understood by the audience and the readers—mostly through the use of tragic irony—and, secondly, paradoxical though it may seem, through Medea's new character. The first technique appears patently in Hecate's speech, when she foretells, sibyl-like, the children's death:

> What thou dost love shall perish by thy rage,
> Nor thou be conscious when the stroke is given; [...].[45]

The prophecy throws Medea into despair, and she decides to change her attitude towards Jason since she does not understand that Hecate is alluding to her children. Medea is no longer a revenge-seeking wife, nor is she a mother thinking about killing her sons. As a result, the crime appears all the more terrifying to the audience, who is aware of Medea's error and can therefore sense her forthcoming pain and devastation. Glover uses maternal love and Medea's state of oblivion as she commits her crime to devise a remarkably pathetic scene. Alone, in not knowing about the crime, Medea speaks of her love for her children and her desire to see them:

> I will at least possess the short relief
> To see my infants. Sure my faithful friends,
> From my sad heart no evils can erase
> Maternal gladness as my children's sight.[46]

---

[44] Glover (1761), 'Prologue'.   [45] Glover (1761), Act III, scene VII, 53.
[46] Glover (1761), Act V, scene II, 87.

The recognition scene is both slow and built upon sensibility,[47] which makes it possible to reconcile *decorum*, the audience's taste for tears, and the tragic efficacy of the crime, without dampening in any way the scandal of the murder of two sons at their own mother's hands.

Under the guise of informing the other characters, the infanticide is evoked in a number of scenes. As a result, the violence of the crime keeps on being reiterated without ever losing its intensity. The first time, as we have heard, Theano shares the news with the Colchians, Aeson, and the audience while Medea is absent from the stage. At first, she evokes the deed without naming the criminal or the victims. She then goes into detail about how the event unfolded. The audience first feels surprise then terror, a terror which is increased both by reference to the sacrificial knife and by the personification of the passions—'Revenge' and 'Madness'—which presided over the impious sacrifice.[48] Furthermore, in order to lay stress on the pathos of the event, Theano describes the crime in concrete terms: 'her savage hand / Unclos'd the jaws of slaughter on her children', 'in their tender bosoms plung'd its point!' and the mother now stands beside 'their welt'rings limbs'.[49] Thus, the language paints a singular picture in which the children's martyred bodies are described with an accuracy well in excess of what is needed, as if the aim were not to highlight the horror of the crime and its unfortunate victims, rather to elicit a form of tragic pleasure based on the enjoyment of suffering under the guise of *pathos*.

Furthermore, the resurfacing of a Senecan intertext is at odds with the apparent moral of the *dénouement*, in which Medea is prevented from killing herself by Juno. However, according to the desperate woman, such an intervention to prevent her suicide is by no means a benevolent gesture. Rather, Medea insists, it proceeds from the goddess' sadistic wish to prolong her 'pain' as a mother:

> Malignant goddess, to prolong my pain,
> Dost thou unbrace the firmness of my arm![50]

---

[47] Medea wishes someone is searching for her children, but, confronted by the stillness of the other protagonists, she asks twice anxiously 'where are [her] children' before discovering the truth (Act V, scene II, 87–8): 'Go, lead them [my children] from the temple – They will smile, / […] / Not gone my virgins? wherefore this delay ? / […] / Where are my children? My distracted brain / A thousand dreadful images recalls / […] / Where are my children? – Silent still and pale.'

[48] Glover (1761), Act V, scene I, 83: 'A knife of sacrifice she seiz'd, / And in their tender bosoms plung'd its point! / We found her planted near their welt'rings limbs; / Her fiery eye-balls on their wounds were fix'd; / A ghastly triumph swell'd her wild revenge, / And madness mingled smiles with horror!'

[49] Glover (1761), 83.   [50] Glover (1761), Act V, scene III, [93].

The use of an almost slow-motion process in order to increase the suffering is precisely reminiscent of the Latin delineating Medea's desire (line 1016), discussed above, which was so scandalous to philologists and translators.

The changes, then, that are clearly designed to tone down the violence serve instead to highlight it and thereby allow for the emergence of a kind of a pre-Sadean logic, which inverts normal moral codes and asserts in their place the primacy of pleasure. Hence scandal lurks behind the *decorum*, and the excess of sensibility leads to the emergence of a form of violence, which is even more ambiguous than the explicit violence of the original plot. This kind of theatrical poetics relies on a double level of interpretation—on the one hand, an explicit discourse spoken by the characters, which conforms to contemporary ideology, and, on the other, theatrical representation that denounces its very artificiality.

Conclusion

As a deliberate infanticidal mother, in both the Euripidean and Senecan versions, Medea was not acceptable on the late eighteenth-century stage. Medea could only be staged with considerable changes that privileged ideological conformity over aesthetic continuity. These moral constraints applied to all European playwrights but they didn't necessarily lead to absolute conformity or uniformity. Fine sensibility, as we have seen, did not preclude enjoyment of a theatre of violence representing disturbing situations. In this sense, some of these late eighteenth-century Medeas show unequivocally that theatre could both conform to ideological norms and yet still appeal to and even reveal audiences' darkest fantasies.

AFTERTHOUGHTS

10

Medea—Sorceress or Woman? *c.* 1750 and Beyond

Roland Lysell

In an essay entitled 'Divine and Human in Euripides' *Medea*', Edith Hall emphasizes that the chief strategy since the early twentieth century has been to make the religious aspects of the play comprehensible to modern audiences through allegory; and the play has consequently been read in the light of feminist or ethnic and racial questions.[1] It is, indeed, essential to consider the religious and metaphysical aspect of the ancient Greek tragedies in order to make the actions of the protagonists as logical and explicable as they are in the myths. Euripides' Medea acts in a fit of despair, madness, or hysteria, if we look upon her as a human being. As Hall explains, Medea 'has rather offbeat divine associations in Hecate and Helios', meaning she is 'not exactly a goddess, but neither is she susceptible to most of the constraints of mortality'; and her transactions with Hecate and Helios remain murky. There is, as Hall reminds us, no Greek or Roman tradition according to which Medea in fact dies.[2]

This chapter builds on Hall's insights by reflecting upon Medea's degree of agency as a descendant of the gods Helios (the Sun) and Hecate. I am inspired by Roland Barthes' discussions in *Sur Racine* concerning Phaedra's similar descent: Phaedra's maternal grandfather is the Sun, her father is Minos, one of the judges in the underworld. This means that her sinful actions are observed by the Sun and that she can expect severe punishment in the realm of the Dead. She has nowhere to turn: to live on in the daylight is to live on in the cruel light of her father and to commit suicide means to enter the realm of the dead and be the victim of his severe punishment. Just as Barthes makes Phaedra's actions understandable to an audience who had read Sartre,[3] Medea's actions can be seen as rational and consequential, and not monstrous, in a Greek metaphysical context. With these afterthoughts, I proceed in two

---

[1] Hall (2014), 148.   [2] Hall (2014), 145.   [3] Barthes (1963), *passim.*

Roland Lysell, *Medea—Sorceress or Woman? c.1750 and Beyond* In: *Mapping Medea: Revolutions and Transfers 1750–1800.* Edited by: Anna Albrektson and Fiona Macintosh, Oxford University Press. © Anna Albrektson and Fiona Macintosh 2023. DOI: 10.1093/oso/9780192884190.003.0010

directions: on the one hand, I briefly return to excavate the divine in Medea in antiquity and the pre-eighteenth-century context, and on the other, I consider a demonic exception to the rational eighteenth-century rule before tracking her demonic legacy into the nineteenth century. Both moves are intended to frame the fifty-year period that is the dominant focus of this volume, and to reflect further, with the help of modern performance, on its importance in relation to Medea's divine identity.[4]

Euripides' Demi-Goddess *Medea*

The famous *Schaubühne am Lehniner Platz* production of *Medea* in Berlin in 1996, when Edith Clever directed and also appeared as the protagonist (Figures 10.1 and 10.2), was of particular note.

Clever emphasized honour and revenge in her interpretation, which was highly convincing in its presentation of Medea as a descendant of the gods, with a sense of honour and a strong belief in the necessity of revenge. The combination of a Stanislavskian detailed study of character and post-Brechtian distance between character and performer was striking. However, some critics, notably Urs Jenny in *Der Spiegel*, blamed Clever for her too brilliant, too sublime, and too stainless performance.[5]

Jenny may well be correct in his observation that Clever's Medea missed out on the vulgarity of the Aegeus scene. But he certainly missed the point that the semi-divine appearance of Clever made Medea's infanticide, other-wise grotesque and hard to understand, evident, logical, and even possible to defend. The literary scholar Inge Stephan is clearly aware of the metaphysical aspect in her study, *Multimediale Karriere einer mythologischen Figur*,[6] but she does not seem to appreciate the full consequences of this. Euripides' Medea's paternal grandfather is explicitly the Sun; her mother, though not explicitly in Euripides' play, is Hecate, who in Euripides, at least, is a close ally ('By the goddess I worship most of all, my chosen helper Hecate, who dwells in the inner chamber of my house' (l. 397)). This monologue, as Clever high-lighted in her performance, is key, during which Medea tries to make herself strong enough for her revenge plan: 'You must not suffer mockery from this

---

[4] For Euripides and Seneca, line references follow the Loeb editions (Euripides, 2001; Seneca, 2018), and for Corneille (1980), the Pléiade edition. For Klinger and Grillparzer, page numbers are from the De Gruyter (2012) and Hofenberg (2015) editions respectively.
[5] Jenny (1996).   [6] Stephan (2006), 29.

Figure 10.1 Edith Clever as Euripides' Medea (1996), Schaubühne am Lehniner Platz, Berlin

Sisyphean marriage of Jason, you who are sprung from a noble father and have Helios for your grandsire. You understand how to proceed' (l. 404 f.). Already from the Nurse's prologue onwards, it is made clear that Medea is dishonoured and cannot bear the sight of her children. If we consider Medea a demi-goddess (and her position as a human woman a disguise caused by her love for Jason), her disappearance in the winged chariot at the end of the play is completely logical.

Jason's hubris lies in his blindness not only to the justice of Zeus but to the supernatural power of his wife as well. But he finally realizes that she is more

Figure 10.2 Edith Clever as Euripides' Medea (1996), Schaubühne am Lehniner Platz, Berlin

sorceress than woman. Medea is injured in love and, just like Dionysos in *Bacchae*, her revenge is cruel—you could even speak of an excess.[7] The sons are not so much hers as Jason's—as a person of divine descent (who is probably not bound to die), she is not dependent on children in the same way.

One could argue that Medea, being a sorceress, through her love for Jason has taken the shape of a human woman for a while, giving birth to two sons;

[7] This is not always the interpretation of the final scene, which sometimes (e.g. Zé Celso's *Os Bacantes* at the Teatro Oficina) is euphoric. But Ingmar Bergman kept this dimension in his productions at Kungliga Dramatiska Teatern, Stockholm, 1996, and Kungliga Operan, Stockholm, 1991. The concept of 'excess' is central to contemporary tragedy theory, cf. Lehmann (2013).

and through her fatal love for Jason, she realizes in turn that 'Of all creatures that have breath and sensation, we women are the most unfortunate' (l. 230).[8] Love between gods and human beings is always dangerous according to the ancient Greeks. For a while Medea also considers herself an exile: 'Where am I now to turn? Kolchis? Iolcos? To my own kin I have become an enemy' (l. 502 f.). At the end of the play, however, Medea is not a human woman anymore, leaving Jason alone in his despair—just as the triumphant Dionysos leaves the people of Thebes in their misery.

From the Demonic to the Aristocratic *Medea*

Seneca's Medea is more violent and demonic than Euripides' Medea and her first aim is to kill Creon and his daughter. She is so cruel and strong that she does not need to deceive Creon and Jason as Euripides' Medea does. She searches for strength by appealing to Hecate and her paternal grandfather Helios (the Sun), just as she does in the Greek play. There is no Aegeus, however, and Medea leaves Jason in a chariot supported by snakes. Seneca's Medea wants Jason, who is an affectionate loving father, to wander in want for the rest of his life.

When Medea disappears at the end of Seneca's play, Jason is left alone with their dead sons and asks his disappearing wife to 'bear witness where you ride that there are no gods' (l. 1027). Maybe Seneca's final message is that of an atheist concerning the good forces in life. However, his Medea appeals to the evil forces which dominate the action. Thus, Seneca's play might rather be described as demonic and similarly demonic traits are found in eighteenth-century Medeas. As Stoic philosophy does not accept the ancient Greek belief in the revenge of Zeus for law-breaking, notably the laws of marriage, Medea's revenge takes a personal character and Seneca turns out to be, if not an atheist, at least a defender of religious scepticism. His gods are more aesthetic devices than metaphysical forces.

In the baroque world of Corneille, royalty seems to be more important than divinity. In Corneille's world there are no impeccable heroes: Créuse is killed by the gown she wanted; Créon stabs himself when he sees his daughter dying; the children, being criminal in the eyes of Médée having Jason as their father, are killed behind the stage; and Jason commits suicide. Even if the gods are mentioned, the actions of the play appear—apart from the winged

---

[8] Melchinger (1980) describes the situation of women in Euripides' Athens (38–9).

chariot—as purely human. Corneille's *Médée* is a seventeenth-century aristocratic psychological play in disguise.

Friedrich Maximilan Klinger's *Medea in Korinth*

Klinger wrote two Medea plays late in his career, the five-act drama *Medea in Korinth* (1787), the focus of the discussion here, where he remains loyal to Euripides' plot, and *Medea auf dem Kaukasus* (1791), which treats Medea's fate beyond the Euripidean tragedy, when she is in exile.[9] None of Klinger's Medea dramas was performed, in marked contrast to Gotter/Benda's *Medea* (1775), but they remain important in the reception of Medea in this period.[10] Since the metaphysical and divine aspect is more important in Klinger's versions, the question that needs to be asked is: does Klinger treat problems that are otherwise neglected in the eighteenth century?

In many aspects Klinger's *Medea in Korinth* seems less modern than Pierre Corneille's *Médée* from 1635; and he claims that he was indebted neither to Greek, Roman, nor his French predecessors. Klinger starts his version with an allegory: *Das Schiksal* [sic] (Fate) speaks.[11] The scenography is well described: we are in the grove of Artemis and to the right of the stage there is a passage with pillars leading to the royal palace; to the left is the temple of Aphrodite. This allegorical technique seems much closer to German baroque plays, notably the tragedies of Lohenstein, than contemporary plays by Lessing and Schiller, and it is also very far from the style of Corneille. My focus here is on the character *Schiksal* [sic]/Fate and the elements of the action that are important to the divine/human question.

The steps of Fate are silent. She calls the mortals from their sleep. *They* give her the name Fate, she says. She is far from them, although she sways above them. We do not realize her importance, however, until the last act. Everything is still calm. In the exposition *Schiksal* [sic]/Fate explains the situation (7–9). The Sun will bring pain and distress to the kingdom: his granddaughter Medea is protected there and the king, Kreon, is tortured by bad dreams sent from

---

[9] A detailed discussion of the Medea plays is to be found in the 'Einleitung' to Klinger (2012), pp. vi–lv.

[10] Cf. Krämer, this volume, who discusses the contrast between Gotter's more psychological play and Klinger's 'rhetorically influenced, "high" spoken drama of neo-classical provenance' in five acts. He also discusses the panorama of divine powers.

[11] In William Shakespeate's *The Winter's Tale* Time appears on stage in the beginning of Act IV, scene I, lines 1–32 (Shakespeare, 1963). For a detailed discussion of Klinger's version, see Karl-Heinz Hartmann et al.'s edition of the play (Klinger, 2012).

Zeus. Kreon is worried about the future of his citizens. Then Fate turns to mythology: Aphrodite is said to have shot one of her arrows into Medea's heart, who is said to be suffering, not realizing the force of her magical powers anymore; another arrow was shot into Jason's heart. Both these arrows represent Aphrodite's vengeance on the descendants of the Sun, because the Sun a long time ago revealed her relationship with Ares. Metaphorically Kreusa, Jason's new love, is tied to the wheel of Clotho, one of the three *moirai*, and the Eumenides, the goddesses of revenge, are rising from Tartaros, the realm of death. Fate here is obviously a metaphysical power, but totally separated from the world of the actors. On one level the powers are more evident than in the ancient plays, but their completely external character, which transforms them into allegory, turns the religious or existential problem into pure fiction.

In Seneca's *Medea*, it is Creon who fears Medea, who is said to be plotting against him. In Klinger's play, Kreon declares that Medea must leave the city because people are scared of her. The gods will no longer accept the sacrifices as long as she is there. As the king and father of the people, Kreon can no longer protect Medea; and Jason praises Kreon's restraint. Though the gods exist in this world, Kreon is made into a more 'modern' king who is less concerned about his own safety than about the opinion of his citizens (Act I, 7–18).

Medea tries to be a human being, although her relationship to her two sons is problematic. When she enters the shrine to sacrifice the flowers to Aphrodite, she discovers Kreusa's sacrifice and becomes furious. She asks the children to run away from her because of her demonic powers. It is a surprise to Medea that Jason and the children are allowed to stay whilst she is not (as Kreon thinks of the well-being of his people). Medea is thrown back on herself and her demonic powers. She fears the '*Nichts*'—the emptiness. In Act III it is explicit that Medea has tried to be a human being but Jason fears the flames of her eyes—in other words, he feels her mythical power (19–28).

The demonic/human contrast is skilfully presented in a dialogue between Medea and Kreusa. Medea tells Kreusa how she helped Jason to obtain the Golden Fleece, how she fell in love and how she became the victim of the Love Goddess. Kreusa declares that she has only followed the voice of her heart. Kreusa suggests that Medea limit her vengeance by killing her alone, not her father or anyone else—an evidently sentimental *Sturm und Drang* change. It is rather surprising that Medea mentions her *human* problem: Jason makes her leave Korinth but she has nowhere to go—she will be a refugee. Is this Medea's strategy to reach her goal, or Klinger's, to show a Medea who tries to be human? (Act III, 29–50).

How does Medea the wife and mother become Medea the sorceress? Act IV opens in the cypress bower near the fountain of the nymphs, with an idyllic scene with Medea and the boys. The scene turns very emotional, the boys want to stay with their mother. In a long passage Medea concentrates on her demonic character and appeals to the dark powers—now she finally becomes the Senecan Medea; and Hecate, now her mother, appears and we hear her voice. Murder of the sleeping boys would be Medea's atonement in her relationship to Hecate for having killed her brothers. Medea wants to break her bonds with humanity and accede to the dark powers, to Erebos. Medea calls the Eumenides and at last she herself joins her mother and becomes one of the dark powers. The killing of the children dominates the act and is a long, drawn-out process. Klinger thus explains his Medea: reminded of her background, she eventually acts on the commands of her divine mother. One could even say that she *becomes* Medea once she is exiled on Kreon's command (51–67).

There are two extant versions of Act V, and I comment here on the longer one. Now Medea is the sorceress and this final act is dominated by theatrical devices such as the three Erinyes, or the Furies, servants of Fate who are not present in earlier versions of the play: Klinger calls them by their euphemistic title, the Eumenides. Medea enters in her dragon-drawn chariot: she wants her revenge on Jason and takes the bodies of the sons and tells him that she will bury them in Pallas' temple, and having done so will flee to Caucasus (68–89). To a certain extent, as with Noverre's *ballet d'action*, the Furies serve to enhance the spectacle of horror on stage. Each Fury takes her victim: Jason, Kreon, Kreusa. However, it is important to recall that Klinger (just like Corneille) is a Christian author who does not believe in Greek gods; therefore, he can regale his reader/spectator with a spectacular 'divine' panorama.

Klinger's drama, as we have heard, is very different from Corneille's tragedy. Corneille's characters are all more or less evil and act according to their egoistic interests—his Jason is a cynical seducer of princesses and his Créuse covets Médée's gown. In Klinger's drama, by contrast, innocence dominates the human characters. His Jason simply wants to be human and liberated from Medea, the sorceress, and Kreon has explicit ethical motives for his action: his way of making Medea leave Korinth so that his people are safe. Kreusa is like the *ingénue* of his later plays and this ushers in the *Sturm und Drang* aspect of the play. But the allegorical personification of Fate, corresponding to the overlong vengeance scene of the Furies in Act V and possibly also Act IV, has embarrassing affinities with baroque German drama rather than with the theatre of Lessing and Schiller.

Hecate and the demonic powers still exist in Klinger's *Medea in Korinth* and are to be respected. When a possible sorceress is provoked, they can be invoked. More than most eighteenth-century writers, Klinger is aware of the distance between men and gods. Transition to and contamination from them are neither possible nor desirable. And something else has happened in the rendering of the human/divine problem here: whereas in Euripides' tragedies, the vengeance of the gods is devastating, in Klinger's tragedy, the gods are reduced to horrific forces of terror. Whereas Euripides' Jason thought he could use the arts of a sorceress, marry her and then reject her, Klinger's Jason just wants to be a human being and distance himself from the deeds of his demonic wife. Klinger's *Medea in Korinth* is definitely not an Aristotelian tragedy: there is no *catharsis, anagnorisis*, or *peripeteia* in evidence. It is closer to Hans-Thies Lehmann's concept of *excess* in *Tragödie und dramatisches Theater* (2013): Medea is a character with only a few limited, but very extreme, traits.

The Human Medea of the New Century

The distance between human beings and gods, seldom reflected upon in Enlightenment literature, is acutely present in the German idealistic literature after Herder. In Friedrich Hölderlin's *Hyperion's Schicksalslied*, the gods, high above, 'walk up there in the light / on soft ground'; 'But it is our fate / to have no rest anywhere. / [. . .] suffering human beings'.[12]

This does not mean, of course, that the early Romantic poets believed in heathen gods as the ancient Greeks did, but they reflected upon religious contrasts between Greeks and Christians and the development of religion. Gods might be cultural entities or abstract positions, but they are nevertheless relevant in ways that they were not to eighteenth-century Enlightenment poets.

The Austrian author Franz Grillparzer (1791–1872), though beyond the timescale of this volume, is nonetheless central to the understanding of Medea from 1750 to 1800. Grillparzer's trilogy emanates from an era later than early Romanticism and the brothers Schlegel: the Biedermeier period. His five-act

---

[12] Friedrich Hölderlin (1796–8), https://www.textlog.de/17824.html. English translation by John Glenn Paton: https://www.lieder.net/lieder/get_text.html?TextId=22407 [last accessed 2 July 2023].

tragedy *Medea*, the third part of the trilogy *Das goldene Vlies* [*sic*] (*The Golden Fleece*), performed in March 1821 and at least twice at the Burgtheater in Vienna during the last thirty years, wrestles with similar problems to those of Hölderlin, which had been repressed by late eighteenth-century dramatists such as Klinger.

Grillparzer's Medea hides any signs of her supernatural descent: in the first scene of Act I, Medea appears, with a large black and golden chest containing her magical belongings, in front of a tent talking to a slave. The slave is digging a hole in the ground to hide her chest. She tells Gora, her old nurse, what she hides: her veil, the goddess's staff, and her banner with the Golden Fleece. In future she will only rely on her husband Jason. In Corneille's and Klinger's plays, Jason wanted to escape from the demonic deed; here Medea too wants to hide her past (123–5).

In Grillparzer's tragedy Jason is in exile, falsely accused of the murder of his uncle in Iolcos because the old king was in fact killed by his sons (134, 136–8). Born a prince, Jason must nonetheless sail around Greece begging for protection: once he triumphed, now he is despised (Act II). Grillparzer's Jason only wants to be a normal human being, just like Klinger's Jason; and Jason and Medea need to be accepted by King Kreon in Korinth. Jason asks Medea not to talk to the moon or continue with her witchcraft, but instead to wear the garments of her new country. 'Be a Greek among the Greeks!' (132), he asks and Medea takes off her red veil and gives it to Gora. Jason is also aware of Medea's love for him (134), which is stronger than in the versions discussed above. Medea is accused of not taking part in the sacrifice to Poseidon (signalling her status as a religious foreigner). Jason asks Kreon to accept Medea (148) but the king hesitates through fear of Medea.

In Act II, Kreusa tries to teach Medea how to play the lyre but without success (149, 162). Medea admiringly recalls the appearance of Jason in Kolchis, but she also reveals that Jason seduced and cheated his victims; Jason is an egocentric. Medea tries to sing but cannot; she weeps and finally breaks the lyre. Now regarding both musical skill and friendship, as previously with religion, Medea reveals herself to be an outsider.

In Grillparzer's play, Medea has nowhere to go, the Greeks hate her and she cannot go back to Kolchis (174). The Korinthians' critical attitude towards Medea means that Kreon cannot allow Medea to stay, but promises Jason that he might free himself if he still has the fleece and gives it to the king. Jason does not have the fleece (which is important in Kreon's strategy because of its magical power)—it is still in Medea's possession—but Kreon is duped into accepting Jason as his future son-in-law. Kreon declares that Medea must leave today, because she has threatened his daughter. He also declares that the children will stay.

In Act IV Medea expresses the idea of killing her sons because they are the children of Jason and look like him (198). Medea seems to want total destruction and now she even hates her own past. She hates her children explicitly. This Medea is a deeply reflective Medea, like most of Grillparzer's protagonists, but once she opens the chest, she returns to her former dark personality. She asks Gora to take Kreusa the ointment and the gown. The sons are extremely afraid of their mother and do not want to leave Korinth; first Medea thinks only of her crime, but finally she embraces the sons (213). At the end of Act IV the palace is in flames and Kreusa's death is reported. Medea escapes with the sons for a while and suddenly reappears with a dagger (215). Chaos ensures: everybody blames everybody. In the short final act, Kreon accuses Gora of having brought the fatal gift to his daughter. Gora reports that the sons are murdered but Kreon seems only to think of Kreusa. Jason asks for the sons but Gora tells him that they are dead (218). Instead of Klinger's Furies, in this human-centred world everybody blames everybody else. Gora blames both Kreon and Jason and Kreon blames Jason.

In a final dialogue Medea tells Jason that death is not the worst. Medea laments not the death of the boys, but that she and Jason had ever met and that the children had ever been born. She will bring the fleece back to Delphi and accept her punishment. What is earthly fame and happiness? A shadow and a dream. Now the dream is over, but not the dark night (222–4).

Grillparzer's tragedy makes Klinger's *Medea*, only a little more than three decades earlier, seems very dated in its flamboyant style. In Grillparzer's tragedy religion is reduced: Hekate is only mentioned once (202); and is only glancingly present through the burial and the digging up of a chest. The possession of the fleece appears in the play as if it were a prop in a bourgeois comedy. What matters here is the fact that Medea is an outsider, a woman in exile who cannot adapt herself to Greek customs. She wants to be accepted, but the Greeks provoke her to return to her original identity as a sorceress. But still atonement is necessary: Medea brings the Golden Fleece to Delphi. In Biedermeier literature, with its ideal of harmony, there is no obvious place for metaphysical forces.

A 1994 Burgtheater production, directed by Hans Neuenfels (1941–2022)— who has several Medea versions to his name—with Elisabeth Trissenaar in the leading role, emphasized both the feminist aspect and the immigrant dimension, which signalled the tragedy's modernity. The elegant and beautiful Trissenaar, who was then about 50 years old, appeared in a simple and dirty dress, her hair dishevelled and her movements clumsy. Neuenfels and Trissenaar, who are committed to interventionist performances, emphasized that this was a play about exile: Medea is a foreigner. Medea, the sorceress, was neglected entirely in this production.

Grillparzer's version is the first in which Jason and Medea appear as exiles begging for protection. Both end up wandering in a spiritual darkness since after Kreusa's death, Jason cannot remain in Corinth. This early nineteenth-century version is more existential than earlier versions, including especially Euripides' play, of course. There is usually a split between thought and action in Grillparzer's works and Medea here reflects on her actions and regrets them, but unfortunately is totally lacking in the skills of diplomacy. Love seems to be a curse, especially for the innocent Kreusa who loves and dies.

In Klinger's play, Jason is the victim but Medea looks upon herself as a victim of love. She confesses her sins, but maintains that they were inspired by her love for, and the demands of, Jason. In Grillparzer's trilogy the sons are sentimentalized and, even more than in Klinger's play, they fear their mother. She cannot let the children accompany her, simply because they do not want to do so. Grillparzer's Medea uses magic, but only reluctantly when nothing else works. *She* has not exhumed the chests; others have. Like Jason she wants to leave behind mythology and create a new human identity; but the tragedy is that they both fail. We are very far from both Euripides' demi-goddess and Klinger's demonic figure of myth. But we are also lightyears away from the eighteenth-century sentimentalized Medeas because with Grillparzer we enter the realm of the Medeas of the twentieth century.

Grillparzer's *Medea* is not explicitly ironic, of course. But its consequences are. The protagonists do what they can to escape from the magical force of the ancient demonic forces, but the effect is the opposite. The neglected divine background confirms its existence and the human beings are left in despair. Like Euripides' Jason, not realizing how serious metaphysical forces are, has serious consequences.

Epilogue

In twentieth-century literature many authors try to defend Medea, notably Christa Wolf in her prose text *Medea. Stimmen*, where Medea does not even murder her own sons.[13] There are two main twentieth-century traditions:

---

[13] Stephan (2006), 11.

one looking upon Medea as a foreigner—in Hans Henny Jahnn's play *Medea* (1924), where the protagonist is African; and the other looking at Medea from a feminist perspective.[14] Rolf Liebermann's opera *Freispruch für Medea* (1989) based on a novel by Ursula Haas is an exception, however: Medea is a member of a matriarchal community, destroyed by young men, and Jason here is young and macho. One way of understanding Medea in this opera is to see her affected by sudden madness, as in many late eighteenth-century versions; another is to emphasize her mental struggle between revenge and love for the children.

The twentieth-century versions do not simply find eighteenth-century solutions to their versions. Sometimes, they too modify the Euripidean Medea's divine origins and not always to good effect. On other occasions, they too find ways of tapping into divine Medea that don't preclude her humanity, in ways that the eighteenth century only managed to achieve in *ballet d'action*. The twentieth-century's most celebrated Medea, Maria Callas (1923–77), who was an impressive Medea both in Luigi Cherubini's opera (1797/1953) and in Pier Paolo Pasolini's film *Medea* (1970), was one of the few able to bring the human and the divine convincingly together in her performances. Her biographer David Bret writes:

> Maria told *The Observer*'s Kenneth Harris, in 1970, 'She kills her children because she feels she has no other choice, and because, being a goddess, she can remove them from this bitter and bloody world and enable her to join them in everlasting life. She kills so they may live in peace and dignity. She knows there will be no hope for that in this world, so she commits them to the next.'[15]

---

[14] Stephan (2006), 12. For further performances se Hall (2014), 150–4.
[15] Bret (1997), 78; concerning Cherubini's *Medea*, see Stephan (2006), 187.

Bibliography

Anon. (1719), *Triomphe du beau sexe sur les hommes*. Hamburg.

Anon. (1722), *Ovidievy figury v 226 izobrazheniayh* [*Ovid's Metamorphoses in 226 images*]. St Petersburg.

Anon. (1744), *Theatro comico portuguez, ou collecção das operas portuguesas, que se representarão na Casa do Theatro Público deo Bairro Alto de Lisboa. Offerecidas á muito nobre Senhora Pecúnia Argentina, por* [...]. Lisbon.

Anon. (1746), *Theatro cómico portuguez*. Lisbon.

Anon. (1777), 'Ueber Inkle und Yariko', in *Berlinisches Litterarisches Wochenblatt* 37 (13 September). Berlin, 578–89.

Anon. (1780), *Volshebnaya shkola: V prolog na otkrytiye novopostroyennogo Petrovskogo teatra; I pri nyom volshebnaya shkola; balet pantomimicheskiy* [*The Magic School. In prologue at the opening of the newly–built Petrovsky Theatre; and a Magic school at it; a Pantomime ballet*]. Moscow.

Anon. (1787), *Theatro cómico portuguez*. Lisbon.

Anon. (1789), *Programme du ballet de Médée et Jason*. St Petersburg.

Anon. (1789), *Über das Melodrama*, in *Neue Bibliothek der schönen Wissenschaften und der freyen Künste* 37, vol. 2. Leipzig, 177–97.

Anon. (1810), 'Moskovskie zapiski' ['Moscow Notes'], *Vestnik Evropy* [*Herald of Europe*] 24: 309–14.

Anon. (1874), *Fabula de Jazaõ e Medea*. Rio de Janeiro.

Anon. (1983), *Il corago, o vero Alcune osservazioni per metter bene in scena le composizioni drammatiche*, ed. P. Fabbri and A. Pompilio. Florence.

Abert, H. (ed.) (1913), *Ausgewählte Ballette Stuttgarter Meister aus der zweiten Hälfte des 18. Jahrhunderts*. Denkmäler deutscher Tonkunst, 1st series, vol. 43/44. Leipzig.

Adelung, J. C. (1793–1801), *Grammatisch-kritisches Wörterbuch der Hochdeutschen Mundart mit beständiger Vergleichung der übrigen Mundarten, besonders aber der oberdeutschen. Zweyte, vermehrte und verbesserte Ausgabe*. Leipzig.

Aeschylus, Sophocles, and Euripides (1567), *Tragoediae selectae Aeschuli, Sophoclis, Euripidis. Cum duplici interpretation Latina, una ad verbum, altera carmine*. Geneva.

Aguilar Piñal, F. (ed.) (1972), *Manuel Lanz de Casafonda: Diálogos de Chindulza (sobre el estado de la cultura española en el reinado de Fernando VI)*. Oviedo.

Aguirre, J. (dir.) (2006), *Medea 2*. Spain: Actual Films.

Agulló, M. (1972), 'Documentos sobre las fiestas del Corpus en Madrid y sus pueblos', *Segismundo* 8: 51–65.

Algarotti, F. (1767), *An Essay on the Opera written in Italian*. London.

Almeida, F. A. de (1733), *La pazienza di Socrate: dramma comico da contarsi nel carnevale di quest'anno nel Real Palazzo di Lisbona*. Lisbon.

Amosov, A. (1998), *Licevoj letopisnyj svod Ivana Groznogo. Kompleksnoe kodikologicheskoe issledovanie* [*The Illustrated Chronicles of Ivan the Terrible. Comprehensive Codicological Research*]. Moscow.

Andioc, R. (1976), Teatro y sociedad en el Madrid del siglo XVIII. Madrid.

Andreozzi, G. (1793a), *Giasone e Medea. Dramma per musica. Da rapprasentarsi nel Real Teatro di S. Carlo nel dì 4 di Novembre 1793. Per festegiarsi il glorioso nome di sua maestà la regina. Dedicato alla real maestà di Ferdinando IV. Nostro amabilissimo sovrano*. Naples.

Andrews, J. (1783), *Remarks on the French and English Ladies in a Series of Letters; Interspersed with Various Anecdotes and Additional Matter Arising from the Subject*. London.

Andújar, R. and K. P. Nikoloutsos (eds.) (2020), *Greeks and Romans on the Latin American stage*. London.

Angiolini, G. (1770), *Noviye argonavty: Balet pantomimno–allegoricheskiy, predstavlenniy na Imperatorskom teatre 24 dnya 1770 goda, po sluchayu preslavnoy pobedy, oderzhannoy nad flotom ottomanskim pri ostrove Hio* [New Argonauts: Pantomime–allegorical ballet put in the Imperial Theatre on September 24, 1770, to commemorate the glorious victory over the Ottoman fleet at Chios Island]. St Petersburg.

Anguio Egea, M. (2006), *Luciano Francisco Comella (1751–1812): otra cara del teatro de la ilustración*. Alicante.

Angulo Díaz, R. (ed.) (2020), *Cayetano Brunetti: Obertura de la zarzuela Jasón o el vellocino de oro (1768)*. Santo Domingo de la Calzada.

Apollodorus (1787), *Apolodora Afineiskogo Basnosloviye, ili Bibliot'eka o bogah* [Apollodorus of Athens's Library], vol. 1–2, trans. V. S. Podshivalov. Moscow.

Arellano, I. and A. L. Cilveti (eds.) (1992), *Calderón de la Barca: El divino Jasón*. Pamplona.

d'Arnaud, F. T. M. de Baculard (1782), *Oeuvres dramatiques*, vol. 1. Amsterdam.

Azara, J. N. de (1846), *Cartas de Don Manuel de Roda*, 2 vols. Madrid.

[Bachaumont, L. Petit de, M.-F. Pidansat de Mairobert, and B.-F. Moufle d'Angerville] (1781), *Mémoires secrets pour servir à l'histoire de la République des lettres en France depuis 1762 jusqu'à nos jours*, vol. 15. London.

Bachmann-Medick, D. (ed.) (2016), *The Trans/National Study of Culture: A Translational Perspective*. Berlin and Boston.

Balsamo, O. (1798), *La vendetta di Medea, dramma serio per música da rappresentarsi nel Real Teatro di S. Carlo nella giornata de' 13 agosto 1798 in cui si festeggia il fausto nascimento di S. M. Maria Carolina d'Austria, Regina di Napoli, nostra signora, dedicato alla real maestà di Fernando 4. Borbone nostro amabilissimo sovrano*. Naples.

Barner, W. (1973), *Produktive Rezeption. Lessing und die Tragödien Senecas*. Munich.

Bartel, H. and A. Simon (eds.) (2010), *Unbinding Medea: Interdisciplinary Approaches to a Classical Myth from Antiquity to the 21st Century*. Abingdon.

Barthes, R. (1963), *Sur Racine*. Paris.

Bastide, J. F. de (1773), *Dictionnaire des mœurs*. Paris. https://www.google.co.uk/books/edition/_/-kdaAAAAcAAJ?gbpv=1.

Bate, J. (1997), *The Genius of Shakespeare*. Basingstoke.

Batteux, C. (1746), *Les Beaux Arts réduit à un même principle*. Paris.

Batteux, C. (1750), 'Art poétique d'Horace', in *Les Poësies d'Horace, traduites en François*, vol. 2. Paris, 358–407.

Bauer, W. A., O. E. Deutsch, and J. H. Eibl (eds.) (1962–75), *Mozart: Briefe und Aufzeichnungen*, vol. 2. Kassel.

Bauman, T. (1985), *North German Opera in the Age of Goethe*. Cambridge.

Beales, D. (1990), 'Social Forces and Enlightened Policies', in H. M. Scott (ed.), *Enlightened Absolutism: Reform and Reformers in Later Eighteenth-Century Europe*. Ann Arbor, 37–54.

Bergamín, J. (1954), *Medea la encantadora*. Montevideo.

Berkov, P. (1973), 'Ovidij v russkoj literature 17–18 vekov' ['Ovid in Russian Literature of the 17th and 18th Centuries'], *Vestnik Leningradskogo universiteta* [*Bulletin of the Leningrad University*] 14: 88–92.

Betzwieser, T. (2011), 'Text, Bild, Musik: die multimediale Überlieferung des Melodrams *Lenardo und Blandine* (1779): Eine Herausforderung für die Editionspraxis', *Editio* 25: 74–100.

Betzwieser, T. (2018), 'Compositional Gestures: Music and Movement in *Lenardo und Blandine* (1779)', in K. Hambridge and J. Hicks (eds.), *The Melodramatic Moment: Music and Theatrical Culture, 1790–1820*. Chicago and London, 95–115.

Bianconi, L. and G. Pestelli (eds.) (2002), *Opera on Stage*. Chicago.

Bibileishvili, I. (1997), 'The Tragedy of the Kolchian Maiden', *People Newspaper*, 7–13.

Blüher, K. A. (1983), *Séneca en España: investigaciones sobre la recepción de Séneca en España desde el siglo XIII hasta el siglo XVI*. Madrid.

Bluteau, R. (1721), *Vocabulario portuguez & latino*. Lisbon.

Bluteau, R. (1736), 'Prosa enigmática, interpretativa', in *Prosas portuguesas, recitadas em diferentes congressos académicos*. Lisbon, 365–90.

Bocage, M. M. de B. du (1802), *Rimas*, vol. 2. Lisbon.

Bochart, S. (1651), *Geographiae sacrae pars prior: Phaleg seu de dispersione Gentium et terrarum divisione facta in aedificatione turris Babel*. Caen.

Boggio, G. (1791), *La conquista del vello d'oro, dramma per música da rappresentarsi nel Regio Teatro di Torino nel Carnovale del 1791*. Turin.

Boileau Despréaux, N. (1674), *Le traité du sublime ou du merveilleux dans le discours, traduit du grec de Longin*. Paris.

Boletsi, M. (2013), *Barbarism and its Discontents*. Stanford.

Bolotov, A. (1873), *Zhizn' i priklyucheniya Andreya Bolotova, opisanniye samim im dlya svoikh potomkov* [*Andrey Bolotov's Life and Adventures, Described by Himself for his Descendants*], vol. 4 (1735–95). St Petersburg.

Bonecchi, G. (1753), *Eudossa incoronata o sia Téodosio II: Dramma per musica da rappresentarsi all'Imperial Corte di Russia: Il di 25. aprile 1751: Per festeggiare l'annua solennità dell'incoronazione di Sua Maestà Imperiale Elisabetta Prima [...] La poesia é del signor dottor G. Bonechj Fiorentino, poeta di Sua Maestà Imperiale etc.; La musica è del signor Francesco Araya Napolitano, maestro di cappella di Sua Maestà Imperiale etc.; I balletti sono d'invenzione e composizione del sigr. Antonio Rinaldi, detto Fossano, maestro di ballo di Sua Maestà Imperiale*. St Petersburg.

Borba de Moraes, R. (1969), *Bibliografia brasileira do período colonial*, 2 vols. Rio de Janeiro.

Botello, J. (2014), 'Imperio y autobiografía en "El vellocino de oro", de Lope de Vega', *Romance Notes* 54.2: 161–8.

Bouffard, M. (2019), 'Les habillements de l'Académie royale de musique: une chasse-gardée bien française', in M. Bouffard, J.-M. Vinciguerra, and C. Schirm (eds.), *Un air d'Italie: L'Opéra de Paris de Louis XIV à la Révolution*, exhibition catalogue. Paris.

Boyer, A. (1764), *The royal dictionary abridged. In two parts. I. French and English. II. English and French. Containing Many Thousand words more than any French [...]*, vol. 2. London (ECCO).

Brea, R. (2019), 'Cuando la verdad estalla', *Pausa: periódico digital* (29 June): https://www.pausa.com.ar/2019/06/cuando-la-verdad-estalla/.

Bressand, F. C. (1692), *JASON, | Singe=Spiel/ | auf | Dem Braunschw. Schauplatz | vorgestellet | im Jahr 1692. | [...] In Verlegung Caspar Grubers/Buchhändl. in Braunschw. | Druckts Heinrich Hessen in Helmstädt*. Braunschweig.

Bressand, F. C. (1695), *Die | Unglückliche Liebe | Des | Tapffern | JASONS, | In einem | Singe=Spiel/ | Auff | Dem Hamburgischen Schau=Platz | vorgestellet. | Im Jahr 1695.* Hamburg.

Bressand, F. C. (1715), *Die an des JASONS Untreu sich | rächende | MEDEA, | In einem | Singe=Spiel | vorgestellet | Auf dem Grossen Braunschweigischen | THEATRO. | Im Jahr 1715. | Braunschweig. | In Verlegung Christoph Friedrich Fickels/Buchh.* Braunschweig.

Bressand, F. C. (1724), *Die | An des | JASONS Untreu | sich rächende | MEDEA, | In einer OPERA | vorgestellet | Auf dem | Grossen Braunschweigischen | THEATRO, | In der | Sommer=Messe | Anno 1724. | Wolffenbüttel/Druckts Christian Bartsch/Hertzogl. Privil. Hof=| und Cantzley=Buchdrucker.* Braunschweig.

Bret, D. (1997), *Maria Callas: The Tigress and the Lamb.* London.

Brito, M. C. de (1996), 'Ópera e teatro musical em Portugal no século XVIII: una perspectiva ibérica', in *Teatro y Musica en España (siglo XVIII), Actas del Simposio Internacional.* Salamanca.

Brncić Becker, C. (2018), 'Metadrama: reescrituras y falsificaciões en Shakespeare, Barrales y Radrigán', *Alpha* 47: 75–80.

Brown, J. R. (2005), *The Shakespeare Handbook's Macbeth.* Basingstoke.

Brown, L. (1993), *Ends of Empire: Women and Ideology in Early Eighteenth-Century English Literature.* Ithaca and London.

Browning Halley, A. (1959), 'Five Dramas of Ludwig Tieck hitherto Unpublished: A Critical Edition', 2 vols. Unpublished PhD thesis, University of Cincinnati.

Brunetti, C. (1768), *Jason, o la conquista del vellocino. Zarzuela heroica, que han de representar las dos Compañias de Comicos de Madrid en el Teatro del Principe este año de 1768. Puesto en musica por don Cayetano Bruneti, músico de la Real Capilla de Su Majestad.* Madrid.

Buarque de Holanda, C. and P. Pontes (1975), *Gota d'água.* Rio de Janeiro.

Budasz, R. (2008), *Teatro e música na América portuguesa: convenções, repertório, raça, gênero.* Curitiba.

Burden, M. and J. Thorp (eds.) (2014), *The Works of Monsieur Noverre translated from the French: Noverre, His Circle, and the English/Lettres sur la danse.* Hillsdale.

Burdett, S. C. (2016), 'Martial Women in the British Theatre'. Unpublished PhD thesis, University of York.

Burgtheater Wien (1994), *Programmbuch 124,* F. Grillparzer, *Das goldene Vlies.* Vienna.

Burke, E. (1757), *A Philosophical Enquiry into the Origin of our Ideas of the Sublime and Beautiful.* London.

Burke, E. (1968), *Reflections on the French Revolution* [1790], ed. C. Cruise O'Brien. Harmondsworth.

Cahusac, L. de (2004), *La danse ancienne et moderne ou Traité historique de la danse* [1754], ed. N. Lecomte, L. Naudeix, and J.-N. Laurenti. Paris.

Calderón de la Barca, P. (attrib.) (1664), *Auto famoso, El divino Jasson de don Pedro Calderon,* in *Navidad y Corpus Christi festejados por los mejores ingenios de España.* Madrid, 9–26.

Calderón de la Barca, P. (1726), *Los tres mayores prodigios,* in *Parte segunda de comedias verdaderas del celebre poeta español D. Pedro Calderón de la Barca […] Nuevamente corregidas.* Madrid, 449–516.

Calderón de la Barca, P. (1760), *Comedia famosa. Los tres mayores prodigios.* Barcelona.

Calderón de la Barca, P. (1760–3), *Comedias del celebre poeta español D. Pedro Calderón de la Barca […] que saca a luz D. Juan Fernandez de Apontes,* vol. 6. Madrid.

Calderón de la Barca, P. (1763), *Comedia famosa. Los tres mayores prodigios.* Barcelona.

Calderone, A. (1983), 'Catalogo delle commedie di magia rappresentate a Madrid nel Secolo XVIII', in E. Caldera (ed.), *Teatro di magia*. Rome, 236–46.

Campbell, T. (1834), *Life of Mrs Siddons*, 2 vols. London.

Campos García Rojas, A. (2011), 'Medea en los libros de caballerías hispánicos: libros, mito y ejemplaridad', *Acta poética* 32: 115–43.

Cano, B. (2012), *Medea: basada en la obra de Eurípides*. Ciudad Real.

Carey, D. and L. Festa (2009), 'Introduction', in D. Carey and L. Festa (eds.), *Postcolonial Enlightenment: Eighteenth-Century Colonialisms and Postcolonial Theory*. Oxford, 1–34.

Casanova, J. (1843), *Mémoires de Jacques Casanova de Seingalt écrits par lui-même*, vol. 4. Paris.

Castro Filho, C. (2016), *Eu mesma matei meu filho: poéticas do trágico en Eurípides, Goethe e García Lorca*. Coimbra.

Cernuschi, A. (1993), 'La Musique projetée dans *Pygmalion* de Rousseau ou l'enjeu du principe d'alternance entre paroles et musique aux origins du mélodrame', *Equinoxe* 9: 37–55.

Chapelain, J. (1638), *Les Sentiments*. Paris.

Chardonnet-Darmaillacq, D. (2014), 'Repenser la réforme du costume au XVIIIe siècle: quand les enjeux pratiques priment sur les enjuex esthétiques', in A. Verdier and D. Doumergue (eds.), *Le costume de scène, objet de recherche*. Cirey-lès-Mareilles, 129–38.

Chase, G. (1939), 'Barbieri and the Spanish Zarzuela', *Music & Letters* 20: 32–9.

Chayanova, O. (1927), *Teatr Maddoksa v Moskve 1776–1805* [*Maddox Theater in Moscow 1776–1805*]. Moscow.

Chazin-Bennahum, J. (1983), 'Cahusac, Diderot and Noverre: Three Revolutionary French Writers on Eighteenth-Century Dance', *Theatre Journal* 35: 169–78.

Chazin-Bennahum, J. (1988), *Dance in the Shadow of the Guillotine*. Carbondale.

Chazin-Bennahum, J. (2005), *The Lure of Perfection: Fashion and Ballet, 1780–1830*. London.

Chompré, P. (1766), *Dictionnaire abrégé de la fable*, 10th edn. Paris.

Christout, M.-F. (1987), *Le ballet de cour au XVIIe siècle*. Geneva.

Christout, M.-F. (2005), *Le ballet de cour de Louis XIV (1643–1672), mises en scène*. Paris.

Cicognini, G. A. (1649), *Giasone, dramma musicale, del D. Hiacinto Andrea Cicognini, accademico instancabile. Da rappresentarsi in Venetia nel Theatro di San Cassano, nell'anno 1649*. Venice.

Cicognini, G. A. and G. F. Apolloni (1671), *Il novello Giasone dramma per música recitato nel Teatro Novo di Roma in Tardinona l'anno 1671*. Rome.

Cicognini, G. A. and G. F. Apolloni (1676), *Il novello Giasone dramma per música recitato nel Teatro Novo di Roma in Tardinona l'anno 1671*. Rome.

Cláudio, M. (2008), *Medeia: monólogo em nove quadros com prólogo e epílogo*. Lisbon.

Clément, J. M. B. (1779), *Médée: Tragédie en trois actes*. Paris.

Clerico, F. (1792), 'La conquista del vello d'oro. Ballo eroico. Da rappresentarsi nel Teatro grande alla Scala il Carnevale di 1792 composto e diretto dal sig. Francesco Clerico', in *Adrastro Re d'Egitto, dramma per música da rappresentarsi nel Teatro alla Scala il Carnevale dell'anno 1792*. Milan.

Colavito, J. (2014), *Jason and the Argonauts through the Ages*. Jefferson, NC.

Comella, L. F. (1793), *Función tragico-comica que en obsequio del público de Madrid representa la Compañía de Manuel Martinez el dia 5 de Agosto de 1793. Su autor Don Luciano Francisco Comella. Principia con la pieza de música en un acto intitulada 'El Puerto de Flandes'. Despúes se sigue con el drama heroyco en otro acto 'La escosesa Lambrum'*. n.p.

Corneille, P. (1764), *Theatre de Pierre Corneille*, vol. 1.

Corneille, P. (1980), *Médée*, in *Œuvres complètes*, ed. G. Couton, vol. 2. Paris.

Corneille, P. (1987), 'Discours de l'utilité et des parties du poème dramatique' [1660], in *Œuvres complètes*, ed. G. Couton, vol. 3. Paris, 117–41.

Correia, H. (2006), *Desmesura: exercícios com Medeia*. Lisbon.

Corti, L. (1998), *The Myth of Medea and the Murder of Children*. Westport, CT.

Costa Miranda, J. da (1984), 'Sul teatro di Metastasio nel settecento portoghese', *Italianistica* 13: 223–7.

Cotarelo y Mori, E. (1896), *Francesca Ladvenant y Quirante: primera dama de los teatros de la corte*. Madrid.

Coupé, J.-M.-L. (1795), *Médée*, in *Théâtre de Sénèque. Traduction nouvelle, enrichie de Notes historiques, littéraires et suivie du Texte latin, corrigé d'après les meilleurs Manuscrits*, vol. 2. Paris, 5–96.

Cronk, N. (2002), *The Classical Sublime: French Neoclassicism and the Language of Literature*. Charlottesville, VA.

Csengei, I. (2012), *Sympathy, Sensibility and the Literature of Feeling in the Eighteenth Century*. New York.

Cullhed, A. (2006), '"Hur grufligt - - - - O Natur! – – hur ljuft, at vara Mor!" Moderskapets blick i Bengt Lidners operalibretto Medea', *Samlaren* 127: 5–40.

Cullhed, A. (2011), *Hör mänsklighetens röst: Bengt Lidner och känslans spark*. Lund.

Cullhed, A. (2013), 'A World of Fiction: Bengt Lidner and Global Compassion in Eighteenth-Century Sweden', in G. Rydén (ed.), *Sweden in the Eighteenth-Century World: Curious Cosmopolitans*. Farnham, 299–324.

Cullhed, A. (2017), 'A New Medea: Staging Conjugal Passion in Eighteenth-Century Europe', in C. Niekerk and M. Nenon (eds.), *Lessing Yearbook* XLIV. Göttingen, 89–106.

Cullmann, H. (2016), 'Von *Médée* zu *Medea*. Wandlungen einer Opern-Partitur', in H. Geyer and M. Pauser (eds.), *Luigi Cherubini: Vielzitiert, Bewundert, Unbekannt*. Sinzig, 275–89.

Curtius, M. C. (1753), 'Abhandlung von der Absicht des Trauerspiels', in *Aristoteles Dichtkunst, ins Deutsche übersetzet, Mit Anmerkungen und besondern Abhandlungen, versehen, von Michael Conrad Curtius*. Hanover.

Cypess, S. M. (1996), 'Myth and Metatheatre: Magaña's *Malinche and Medea*', in F. Dauster (ed.), *Perspectives on Contemporary Spanish American Theatre*. Lewisburg, 37–52.

Cypess, S. M. (2005), '"Mother" Malinche and Allegories of Gender, Ethnicity and National Identity in Mexico', in R. Romero and A. Nolacea Harris (eds.), *Feminism, Nation and Myth: La Malinche*. Houston, 14–27.

Dabhoiwala, F. (2012), *The Origins of Sex: A History of the First Sexual Revolution*. New York.

Dahms, S. (1991), 'Jean Georges Noverre, Medea and Jason', in C. Dahlhaus and S. Döhring (eds.), *Pipers Enzyklopädie des Musiktheaters*, vol. 4. Munich and Zürich, 476–8.

Dahms, S. (2010), *Der konservative Revolutionär. Jean Georges Noverre und die Ballettreform des 18. Jahrhunderts*. Munich.

Damasceno, L. (2003), 'The Gestural Art of Reclaiming Utopia: Denise Stoklos at Play with the Hysterical-Historical', in D. Taylor and R. Costantino (eds.), *Holy Terrors: Latin American Women Perform*. Durham, NC, 152–78.

Darchia, I., et al. (eds.) (2018), *Proceedings of the International Conference: 'Medea in World Artistic Culture', Ivane Javakhishvili Tbilisi State University, Tbilisi, 17–20 September, 2017*. Tbilisi.

Davies, T. (1780), *Memoirs of the Life of David Garrick, esq*. London.

de Góes, C. (2012), *Medea en promenade*, dir. Guta Stresser. Distribution Viagem à Lua.

de la Cruz Cano, R. (1768), *Briseida: zarzuela heroica en dos actos*. Madrid.

Delaumosne, Abbé de (1893), *Delsarte's System of Oratory*, 4th edn. New York.

De Lucca, V. (2013), 'Dressed to Impress: The Costumes for Antonio Cesti's Orontea in Rome (1661)', *Early Music* 41: 461–75.

De Lucca, V. (2019), 'Costumes for Balli in Late Seventeenth-Century Roman Operas', in P. Dotlačilová and H. Walsdorf (eds.), *Dance Body Costume*. Prospektiven 2. Leipzig, 79–101.

Delctanville, T. (1794), *A new French dictionary, in two parts: the first, French and English; the second, English and French: Containing, I. Several Hundred Words not to* [...]. London (ECCO).

Delvig, A. (1959), *Polnoye sobraniye stihotvoreniy* [*Complete Collection of Poems*]. Leningrad.

Derzhavin, G. R. (1864), 'Vodopad', in *Sochineniya Derzhavina s ob"yasnitel'nymi primechaniyami YA. Groota* [*Works of Derzhavin with Notes by J. Groot*], vol. 1. St Petersburg, 457–80.

Despréaux, J. E. (1784), *Médée et Jason, ballet terrible orné de danse*. Paris.

Dictionnaire critique de la langue française. Tome premier, A–D / par M. l'abbé Feraud [...] (1787). Paris: http://catalogue.bnf.fr/ark:/12148/cb351538037.

Dictionnaire de l'Académie françoise (1762), 4th edn. Paris.

Dictionnaire de l'Académie française. Tome 1 / revu, corr. et augm. par l'Académie elle-même (1798). Paris: http://catalogue.bnf.fr/ark:/12148/cb35474154c.

Diderot, D. (1875-7), *Entretien sur le fils naturel* [1757], in J. Assézat and M. Tourneux (eds.), *Œuvres complètes de Diderot: Revues sur les éditions originales: Etude sur Diderot et le mouvement philosophique au XVIIIe siècle*. Paris.

Díez Borque, J. M. (1995), 'Sobre el teatro cortesano de Lope de Vega: *El vellocino de oro*, comedia mitológica', in J. Canavaggio (ed.), *La comedia: seminario hispano-francés*. Madrid, 155–77.

Dionísio, E. (1992), *Antes que a noite venha*. Lisbon.

Dobie, M. (2010), *Trading Places: Colonization and Slavery in Eighteenth-Century French Culture*. Ithaca and London.

Doiron, N. (2012), 'La vengeance d'une déesse. La Médée de Pierre Corneille', *Poétique* 171.3: 321–36.

Dolce, L. (1560), *Le tragedie di Seneca, tradotte da m. Lodovico Dolce*. Venice.

Dolle, V. (2014), 'A manera de introducción. La representación de la Conquista en el teatro latinoamericano de los siglos XX y XXI: constantes transnacionales y variantes nacionales', in V. Dolle (ed.), *La representación de la Conquista en el teatro latinoamericano de los siglo*. Heidelsheim, xi–xxxii.

Donat, M. (2005), 'Drama Queens', *The Guardian* (19 August): https://www.theguardian.com/music/2005/aug/19/classicalmusicandopera.edinburghfestival2005.

Doni, G. B. (1763), *Trattato della musica scenica/Lyra Barberina amphichordos: accedunt eiusdem opera* [1640], ed. A. F. Gori and G. B. Passeri. Florence.

Doran, R. (2015), *The Theory of the Sublime from Longinus to Kant*. Cambridge.

Dotlačilová, P. (2014), 'Varšavský rukopis, známý a neznámý', *Živá hudba* 5: 140–56.

Dotlačilová, P. (2017), 'Picturing the Horror: Costume for Furies on the French Stage from 1650 to 1766', in G. Boyes (ed.), *Terpsichore and her Sisters: The Relationship between Dance and other Arts. Conference Proceedings of Early Dance Circle*. Cambridge, 53–68.

Dotlačilová, P. (2019), 'Louis-René Boquet's Work for Opera and Ballet in the Second Half of the Eighteenth Century', in P. Dotlačilová and H. Walsdorf (eds.), *Dance Body Costume*. Prospektiven 2. Leipzig, 102–58.

Dotlačilová, P. (2020), *Costume in the Time of Reforms: Louis-René Boquet Designing Eighteenth-Century Ballet and Opera*. PhD thesis, Stockholm University.

Dotlačilová, P. (2021), 'Visible and Invisible Hands: Costume-Making Practices of Italian Music Theatre in the Early Modern Era', in R. Illiano (ed.), *Performing Arts and Technical Issues*. Turnhout, 309–40.

Doubrovsky, S. (1963), *Corneille et la dialectique du héros*. Paris.

Draghi, A. (1680), *La pazienza di Socrate con due mogli. Scherzo drammatico per música. Alle augustissime Maestà imperiali nel Carnovale dell'anno M. DC. LXXX*. Prague.

Drake, J. D. (1971), 'The 18th-Century Melodrama', *The Musical Times* 112.1545: 1058–60.

Dratwicki, B. (2019), 'Empoi ou genre', in S. Boussou, P. Denécheau and F. Marchal-Ninosque (eds.), *Dictionnaire de l'Opéra de Paris sous l'Ancien Régime (1669–1791)*, vol. 2. Paris, 496–504.

Dryden, J. (1912), 'On Comedy, Farce, and Tragedy', preface to *An Evening's Love; or, The Mock Astrologer* [1671], in *Dryden's Dramatic Poesy and Other Essays*, ed. G. Watson. London and New York, 77–86.

Dubos, J. B. (1719), *Réflexions critiques sur la poésie et sur la peinture*. Paris.

Dularidze, T. (2007), 'The Argonauts' Voyage in the Transitional Period of Georgian Literature (the 18th–19th Centuries)', *Phasis* 10.2: 27–31. https://phasis.tsu.ge/index.php/PJ/issue/view/308.

Eastman, C. (2012), 'Beware the Abandoned Woman: European Travelers, "Exceptional" Native Women, and Interracial Families in Early Modern Atlantic Travelogues', in T. Bowers and T. Chico (eds.), *Atlantic Worlds in the Long Eighteenth Century: Seduction and Sentiment*. Basingstoke, 135–47.

Ellis, M. (1996), *The Politics of Sensibility: Race, Gender and Commerce in the Sentimental Novel*. Cambridge.

Engel, J. J. (1785–6), *Ideen zu einer Mimik*, 2 vols. Berlin.

Escalante Varona, A. (2018), 'El Neoclasicismo dramático español, entre dos poéticas: *El Sigerico*, de Manuel Fermín de Laviano', in J. L. Eugercios Arriero, S. García García, and M. Piqueras Flores (eds.), *Letras anómalas: estudios sobre textos y autores hispánicos más allá del canon*. Madrid, 115–33.

Esquer Torres, R. (1965), 'Las prohibiciones de comedias y autos sacramentales en el siglo XVIII', *Segismundo* 2: 187–226.

Euripides (1506), *Hecuba, et Iphigenia in Aulide, Euripidis tragoediae, in latinum translatae Erasmo interprete*. Paris.

Euripides (1507), *Hecuba, et Iphigenia in Aulide, Euripidis tragoediae, in latinum translatae Erasmo interprete*. Venice.

Euripides (1543), *Hecuba, et Iphigenia in Aulide, Euripidis tragoediae, in latinum translatae Erasmo Roterodamo interprete; Medea eiusdem, Georgio Buchanano scoto interprete*. Paris.

Euripides (1747), *Tragedie, trasportate dalla greca nell'italiana favela da Monsignor Christoforo Guidiccioni*. Lucca.

Euripides (1778), *Tragédies d'Euripide, traduites par M. Prevost Oreste*. Paris.

Euripides (1781–3), *The Tragedies of Euripides translated by R. Potter*, 2 vols. London.

Euripides (1782), *Tragédies d'Euripide, traduites par M. Prevost Oreste*. Paris.

Euripides (1988a), *Medéia; As bacantes*, trans. M. da Gama Kury. São Paulo.

Euripides (1988b), *Medéia; Hipólito; As troianas*, trans. M. da Gama Kury. São Paulo.

Euripides (1991), *Medéia; Hipólito; As troianas*, trans. M. da Gama Kury. Rio de Janeiro.

Euripides (1998), *Medéia; As bacantes; As troianas*, trans. D. Jardim Jr. Rio de Janeiro.

Euripides (2001), *Medea*, in *Cyclops, Alcestis, Medea*, ed. and trans. D. Kovacs [1994, repr. with corr.]. Cambridge, MA.

Euripides (2005), *Medéia*, trans. M. Silveira and J. Silveira Gonçales. São Paulo.

Euripides (2010), *Medeia*, trans. T. Vieira and O. M. Carpeaux. São Paulo.

Fabbricatore, A. B. (2017), *La Querelle des pantomimes. Danse, culture et société dans l'Europe de Lumières*. Rennes.

Feijoo, J. B. (1742–60), 'El origen de la fábula en la historia', in *Cartas eruditas y curiosas*, vol. 1. Madrid, 320–9.

Felsenstein, F. (1999), *English Trader, Indian Maid: Representing Gender, Race, and Slavery in the New World: An Inkle and Yarico Reader*. Baltimore.

Felsenstein, F., J. I. Marsden, M. Choudhury, and N. Bhattacharya (2014), 'Colman's *Inkle and Yarico*: Four Critical Perspectives', in J. Swindells and D. F. Taylor (eds.), *The Oxford Handbook of the Georgian Theatre, 1737-1832*. Oxford, 688–705.

Fernández de Moratín, L. (1991), *Viaje a Italia (1793–97)*, ed. B. Teherina. Madrid.

Ferrer Valls, T. (1993), *Nobleza y espectáculo teatral (1535-1622): estudio y documentos*. Valencia.

Ferrero, M. V. (2002), 'Stage and Set', in L. Bianconi and G. Pestelli (eds.), *Opera on Stage*. Chicago.

Festa, L. (2006), *Sentimental Figures of Empire in Eighteenth-Century Britain and France*. Baltimore.

Fielding, H. (1755), 'The Grub Street Opera', in *The Dramatic Works of Henry Fielding, Esq., In three volumes*, vol. 2. London (ECCO).

Findeizen, N. (2008), *History of Music in Russia from Antiquity to 1800*, vol. 1. Oxford.

Fischer, C. (1931), *Les costumes de l'Opéra*. Paris.

Fischer-Lichte, E. (2002), *History of European Drama and Theatre*, trans. J. Riley. London.

Fischer-Lichte, E. (2004), 'Thinking About the Origins of Theatre in the 1970s', in E. Hall, F. Macintosh, and A. Wrigley (eds.), *Dionysus Since 69*. Oxford, 329–60.

Fleitas, V. (2019), '*Medea va*: una versión que potencia la vigencia de un clásico', *El diario* (Paraná): http://www.eldiario.com.ar/35756-medea-va-una-version-que-potencia-la-vigencia-de-un-clasico/.

Foppa, G. (1793), 'La conquista del vello d'oro. Ballo eroico pantomimo', in *Tito e Berenice, dramma per música di Giuseppe Foppa da rappresentarsi nel nuovo e nobilissimo Teatro detto La Fenice la fiera dell'Ascensione dell'anno 1793*. Venice, 25–37.

Foster, S. L. (1996), *Choreography and Narrative: Ballet's Staging of Story and Desire*. Bloomington.

Franco Perpetuo, I. (2006), 'Municipal e Sesc recebem montagens brasileiras', *Folha de São Paulo: Guia da Folha* (13 October), 78.

Francus, M. (2012), *Monstrous Motherhood: Eighteenth-Century Culture and the Ideology of Domesticity*. Baltimore.

Frantz, P. (1998), *L'esthétique du tableau dans le théâtre du XVIIIe siècle*. Paris.

Frenzel, E. (1983), *Stoffe der Weltliteratur. Ein Lexikon dichtungsgeschnittlicher Längsschnitte*, 6th edn. Stuttgart.

Fyvie, J. (1908), *Tragedy Queens of the Georgian Era*. London.

García de la Huerta, V. (1779), 'Traduccion en romance endecasílabo. Medea a Jason', in *Obras poeticas del Don Vicente Garcia de la Huerta, oficial primero de la Real Bibliotheca, etc.* Madrid, 301–19.

García Garrosa, M. J. (1990), *La retórica de las lágrimas: la comedia sentimental española, 1751-1802*. Valladolid.

Gellert, C. F. (2000), 'Inkle und Yariko', in U. Bardt and B. Witte (eds.), *Gesammelte Schriften*, vol. 1: *Fabeln und Erzählungen*. Berlin, 70–4.

Gess, N., T. Hartmann, and D. Hens (eds.) (2015), *Barocktheater als Spektakel: Maschine, Blick und Bewegung auf der Opernbühne des Ancien Régime*. Paderborn.

Glaser, H. A. (2001), *Medea: Frauenehre—Kindsmord—Emanzipation*. Frankfurt a. M.

Glover, R. (1761), *Medea*. Dublin.

Glover, R. (1792), *Medea: A Tragedy, Adapted for Theatrical Representation, as Performed at the Theatre-Royal, Drury-Lane. Regulated from the Prompt-Book, By Permission of the Manager*. London.

Glushkovskij, A. (2010), *Vospominaniya baletmejstera* [*Memoirs of a Choreographer*], 2nd edn. St Petersburg.

Goez, J. F. von (1783), *Versuch einer zalreichen Folge leidenschaftlicher Entwürfe für empfindsame Kunst- und Schauspiel-Freunde. Erfunden, gezeichnet, geäzt und mit Anmerkungen begleitet von J. F. von Göz*. Augsburg.

Goff, B. and M. Simpson (2015), 'New Worlds, Old Dreams? Postcolonial Theory and Reception of Greek Drama', in K. Bosher, F. Macintosh, J. McConnell, and P. Rankine (eds.), *The Oxford Handbook of Greek Drama in the Americas*. Oxford, 30–52.

Gomes dos Santos, M. (1963–4), 'Buchanan e o ambiente coimbrao do século XVI', *Humanitas* 15–16: 261–327.

Gómez de Ciudad Real, Á. (1546), *El vellocino dorado, y la historia de la orden del Tuson que primero compuso en verso latino Alvar Gomez señor de Pioz* [...] *traduzido agora nuevamente en muy elegante prosa castellana, por el Bachiller Juan Bravo* [...] *Assi mismo el summario delos Catholicos Reyes don Fernando y doña Isabel, con la tomada de Granada, y de otros pueblos que valerosamente conquistaron sacado de la obra grande de las cosas memorables de España que escrivio Lucio Marineo Siculo*. Toledo.

Goncourt, E. de (1893), *La Guimard, d'après les registres des menu-plaisirs de Bibliothèque de l'Opéra*. Paris.

González, A. (2000), 'Medea mapuche de Radrigán clama en mapudungún', *La nación* (Santiago de Chile) (7 June), 38.

Gotter, F. W. (1775), *Medea. ein [sic] mit Musik vermischtes Drama*. Gotha.

Gotter, F. W. (1776), *Medea. Ein Musicalischen Drama vom Herrn Gotter die Musik vom Herrn Georg Benda*. Hamburg: https://www.loc.gov/resource/musschatz.17569.0/?sp=2.

Gotter, F. W. (1782), *Medea. Verfaßt vom Herrn Gotter die Musik vom Herrn Georg Benda*. Innsbruck.

Gotter, F. W. and G. Benda (2018), *Medea. Version 1784*, ed. J. Krämer. Spektrum des europäischen Musiktheaters in Einzeleditionen 3. Kassel.

Gouvêia Júnior, M. M. (2014), *Medeias romanas: Medeae Romae*. Belo Horizonte.

Gozzi, G. (1758), *Medea* [1746], in *Opere in versi e in prosa del signor conte Gasparo Gozzi veneziano dedicate a sua Eccellenza il sig. Daniele Farsetti*, vol. 1. Venice, 99–176.

Grillparzer, F. (2015), *Das goldene Vlies. Dramatisches Gedicht in drei Abteilungen. Der Gastfreund. Die Argonauten. Medea*. Berlin.

Grimm, F. M. (1812), *Correspondance littéraire, philosophique et critique* [...] *depuis 1753 jusqu'en 1760*, ed. J. B. A. Suard. 6 vols. Paris.

Gubkina, N. (2003), *Nemeckij muzykal'nyj teatr v Peterburge v pervoj treti XIX veka* [*German Musical Theatre in St. Petersburg in the First Third of the 19th Century*]. St Petersburg.

Guedes Ferreira, A. M. (2013), 'A Medeia segundo Bocage', in C. Pimentel and P. Mourão (eds.), *A literatura clássica ou os clássicos na literatura*. Lisbon, 95–108.

Guest, I. (1996), *The Ballet of Enlightenment: The Establishment of the Ballet d'Action in France 1770–1793*. London.

Gukovskij, G. K. (2013), 'Rasin v Rossii 18 veka' ['Racine in Russia in the 18th Century'], *18 vek.* [*18th century*] 27: 434–78. First published 1927, 'Racine en Russie au XVIIIe siècle: la critique et les traducteurs', *Revue des Études Slaves* 7.1.2: 75–93: https://www.persee.fr/issue/slave_0080-2557_1927_num_7_1?sectionId=slave_0080-2557_1927_num_7_1_7374.

Habermas, J. (1989), *The Structural Transformation of the Public Sphere: An Inquiry into a Category of Bourgeois Society* [1962], trans. T. Burger. Cambridge.

Hall, E. (1989), *Inventing the Barbarian: Greek Self-Definition through Tragedy*. Oxford.

Hall, E. (1999), 'Medea and British Legislation before the First World War', *Greece & Rome* 46.1: 42–77.

Hall, E. (2000), 'Medea on the Eighteenth-Century London Stage', in E. Hall, F. Macintosh, and O. Taplin (eds.), *Medea in Performance, 1500–2000*. Oxford, 49–74.

Hall, E. (2002), 'The Singing Actors of Antiquity', in P. Easterling and E. Hall (eds.), *Greek & Roman Actors: Aspects of an Ancient Profession*. Cambridge, 3–38.

Hall, E. (2008), 'Ancient Pantomime and the Rise of Ballet', in E. Hall and R. Wyles (eds.), *New Directions in Ancient Pantomime*. Oxford, 363–77.

Hall, E. (2013), *Adventures with Iphigenia in Tauris: A Cultural History of Euripides' Black Sea Tragedy*. New York.

Hall, E. (2014), 'Divine and Human in Euripides' *Medea*', in D. Stuttard (ed.), *Looking at Medea: Essays and a Translation of Euripides' Tragedy*. London, 139–55.

Hall, E. (2018), 'Lioness, Goldsmith and Pontic Voyager: The Georgian Provenance of Euripides' Medea', in I. Darchia et al. (eds.), *Medea in World Artistic Culture*. Tbilisi.

Hall, E. and F. Macintosh (2005), *Greek Tragedy and the British Theatre 1660–1914*. Oxford.

Hall, E., F. Macintosh, and O. Taplin (eds.) (2000), *Medea in Performance, 1500–2000*. Oxford.

Halturin, Y., V. Kuchurin, and Y. Rodichenkov (2015), *Nebesnaya nauka: Evropejskaya alhimiya i rossijskoe rozenkrejcerstvo v XVII–XIX vekah* [*Celestial Science: European Alchemy and Russian Rosicrucianism in the 17th–19th Centuries*]. St Petersburg.

Hambridge, K. and J. Hicks (eds.) (2018), *The Melodramatic Moment: Music and Theatrical Culture, 1790–1820*. Chicago and London.

Harris-Warrick, R. (2016), *Dance and Drama in French Baroque Opera: A History*. New York.

Harvey, D. A. (2012), *The French Enlightenment and Its Others: The Mandarin, the Savage, and the Invention of the Human Sciences*. New York.

Hazlitt, W. (1816), 'Mrs Siddons', *The Examiner* (16 June).

Head, M. (2018), 'Benevolent Machinery: Techniques of Sympathy in Early German Melodrama', in K. Hambridge and J. Hicks (eds.), *The Melodramatic Moment: Music and Theatrical Culture, 1790–1820*. Chicago and London, 151–70.

Heavey, K. (2015), *The Early Modern Medea: Medea in English literature, 1558–1688*. New York.

Hederich, B. (1724), 'Medea', in *Gründliches Lexicon mythologicum* [...]. Leipzig, cols. 1238–45.

Hederich, B. (1741), 'Medea', in *Gründliches Lexicon mythologicum* [...]. Leipzig, cols. 1238–45.

Hederich, B. and J. J. Schwabe (1770), 'Medea', in *Gründliches mythologisches Lexicon* [...], *sorgfältigst durchgesehen, ansehnlich vermehret und verbessert von Johann Joachim Schwaben*. Leipzig, cols. 1539–45.

Herr, C. (2000), *Medeas Zorn: eine 'starke Frau' in Opern des 17. und 18. Jahrhunderts*. PhD thesis, University of Bremen. Herbolzheim.

Heßelmann, P. (2002), *Gereinigtes Theater? Dramaturgie und Schaubühne im Spiegel deutschsprachiger Theaterperiodika des 18. Jahrhunderts*. Frankfurt a. M.

Hettner, H. (1970), *Literaturgeschichte der Goethezeit* [1876], ed. J. Anderegg. Munich.

Hill, B. (1989), *Women, Work and Sexual Politics in Eighteenth-Century England*. Oxford.

Hillerkus, M. (2017), 'Mellefonts Ehescheu als Männlichkeitskrise. Zum Konfliktfeld von Ehe und Sexualität in Lessings *Miss Sara Sampson*', in C. Niekerk and M. Nenon (eds.), *Lessing Yearbook* XLIV. Göttingen, 107–27.

Hodermann, R. (1894), *Geschichte des Gothaischen Hoftheaters 1775–1779*. Hamburg and Leipzig.

Hoffer, P. C. and N. E. H. Hull (1981), *Murdering Mothers: Infanticide in England and New England 1558–1803*. New York.

Hoffmann, F. B. and L. Cherubini (1797), *Médée, Tragédie en trois actes, en vers*. Paris.

Hogarth, W. (1753), *The Analysis of Beauty*. London.

Hölderlin, F. (1796–8), 'Hyperions Schicksalslied', in *Sämtliche Gedichte*: https://www.textlog.de/17824.html.

Hölderlin, 'Hyperion's Song of Fate', trans. J. G. Paton: https://www.lieder.net/lieder/get_text.html?TextId=22407.

Horace (1753), *The Works of Horace translated into English Prose, as near the Original as the different Idioms of the Latin and English Languages will allow. With the Latin text*, 2 vols., 4th edn. London.

Horace (1929), *Satires, Epistles and Ars Poetica*, trans. H. R. Fairclough (rev. and repr.). Cambridge, MA.

Horowitz, J. M. (2014), 'Ovid in Restoration and Eighteenth-Century England', in J. F. Miller and C. E. Newlands (eds.), *A Handbook to the Reception of Ovid*. Chichester, 355–70.

Hörster, M. A. and M. de Fátima Silva (2019a), 'Hélia Correia's *A de Cólquida* (The Woman from Colchis)', in A. Pociña Pérez, A. López, C. Ferreira Morais, M. de Fátima Silva, and P. Finglass (eds.), *Portraits of Medea in Portugal during the 20th and 21st Centuries*. Leiden, 144–57.

Hörster, M. A. and M. de Fátima Silva (2019b), 'Medea in the Society of Entertainment: A Reading of Mário Cláudio's *Medeia*', in A. Pociña Pérez, A. López, C. Ferreira Morais, M. de Fátima Silva, and P. Finglass (eds.), *Portraits of Medea in Portugal during the 20th and 21st Centuries*. Leiden, 200–15.

Houssaye, A. (1857), *Men and Women of the Eighteenth Century*, vol. 2. New York.

Hylland Eriksen, T. (2010), *Ethnicity and Nationalism: Anthropological Perspectives*, 3rd edn. London.

Istel, E. (1906), *Die Entstehung des deutschen Melodramas*. Berlin and Leipzig.

Izmajlov, A. E. (1819), 'Medea, peredelka tragedii Longepierra' ['Medea, the Transformation of Longepierre's Tragedy'], *Blagonamerenny* 11: 329.

Jardine, A. (1788), *Letters from Barbary, France, Spain, Portugal, &c by an English Officer*, 2 vols. London.

Jaucourt, M. (1751), 'Esclavage', in D. Diderot and J. le Rond d'Alembert, *Encyclopédie ou Dictionnaire raisonné des sciences, des arts et des métiers*, vol. 5. Paris: https://gallica.bnf.fr/ark:/12148/bpt6k50537q/f972.item.r=esclavage.

Jenny, U. (1996), 'Die ewige Kindermörderin', *Der Spiegel* (5 February): https://www.spiegel.de/kultur/die-ewige-kindermoerderin-a-35b1d4e0-0002-0001-0000-000008872060.

Johnson, C. (1731), *The Tragedy of Medæa*. London.

Jones, V. (ed.) (1990), *Women in the 18th Century: Construction of Feminity*. London.

Kapanadze, G. (1998), 'Birth of the New Opera', *The Georgian Theatre's Day*, 14.1.

Karamzin, N. (1984), *Pis'ma russkogo puteshestvennika* [*Letters from a Russian Traveller*]. Leningrad.

Karatygin, P. A. (1929), *Zapisky* [*Memoirs*]. Leningrad.

Karsenti, T. (2016), 'Quels tragiques pour Médée?', *SKÉN & GRAPHIE* 4: 33–41.

Kenkel, K. (1979), *Medea-Dramen: Entmythisierung und Remythisierung: Euripides, Klinger, Grillparzer, Jahnn, Anouilh*. Studien zur Germanistik, Anglistik und Komparatistik 63. Bonn.

Kerhoas, M.-J. (2007), 'Les dessins de costumes de scène de 1750 à 1790 dans les collections patrimoniales françaises'. Unpublished PhD thesis, University of Tours.

Kerstein, L. (1984), *Four Centuries of Ballet: Fifty Masterworks*. New York.

Kheraskov, M. (1895), *Rossiada. Poema v 12-ti pesnyah* [*Rossiada. Poem in 12 Songs*]. St Petersburg.

Kheraskov, M. (1961), *Izbrannye proizvedeniya* [*Selected Works*]. Moscow and Leningrad.

Kidd, C. (1999), *British Identities Before Nationalism: Ethnicity and Nationhood in the Atlantic World, 1600–1800*. Cambridge.

Kinney, D. and E. Styron (n.d.), *Ovid Illustrated: The Reception of Ovid's Metamorphoses in Image and Text*: http://ovid.lib.virginia.edu/ovidillust.html.

Klein, I. (2005), *Puti kul'turnogo importa: Trudy po russkoj literature XVIII veka* [*Ways of Cultural Import: Works on Russian Literature of the 18th Century*]. Moscow.

Klepikov, S. (1964), 'Russkie gravirovannye knigi 17–18 vekov' ['Russian Engraved Books of the 17th–18th Centuries'], *Kniga. Issledovaniya I materialy* [*Book. Researches and Materials*] 9: 141–77.

Kleshchevich, O. V. (2017), *Ieroglifika Petergofa. Alhimicheskie allyuzii v simvolike Petergofskogo sadovo–parkovogo ansamblya* [*Hieroglyphics of Peterhof. Alchemical Allusions in the Symbolism of the Peterhof Garden and Park Ensemble*]. St Petersburg.

Klest, J. G. (1752), *Medea | Wurde | an dem hocherfreulichen Geburths-Feste | [...] Johann Friedrichs, | Fürstens zu Schwartzburg, [...] | Welches | am 8. Januar. 1752. | Zu des Hochfürstl. Hauses Vergnügen [...] erschienen, auf gnädigsten Befehl | [...] in nachstehenden Singe-Spiel |unterthänigst aufgeführt/ | Von der Fürstl. Hof-Capelle. | Rudolstadt, gedruckt mits Löwischer Wittwe sel. Schriften 1752*. Rudolstadt.

Klinger, F. M. von (2012), *Werke: Historisch-kritische Gesamtausgabe*, vol. 7: *Medea in Korinth, Medea auf dem Kaukasos, Aristodymos*, ed. K.-H. Hartmann, U. Profitlich, and M. Schulte. Berlin and Boston.

Knott, S. and B. Taylor (eds.) (2005), *Women, Gender and Enlightenment*. Basingstoke.

Koni, F. (1840), 'Vospominaniay o moskovskom teatre pri M. E. Medokse. Pocherpnuto iz neizdannyh zapisok S. N. Glinki i iz ustnyh rasskazov starozhilov' ['Memories of the Moscow Theatre at M. Maddox. Taken from S. N. Glinka's unpublished notes and from oral stories of old–timers'], in *Panteon i repertuar* [*Pantheon and Repertory*], part 1, dep. 2, 89–102.

Korndorf, A. S. (2011), *Dvorcy Himery. Illyuzornaya arhitektura i politicheskie allyuzii pridvornoj sceny* [*Palaces of the Chimera. Illusory Architecture and Political Allusions of the Court Scene*]. Moscow.

Koselleck, R. (1985), 'The Historical-Political Semantics of Asymmetric Counterconcepts', in *Futures Past: On the Semantics of Historical Time*, trans. K. Tribe. Cambridge, MA, 159–97.

Koselleck, R. (2002), 'The Eighteenth Century as the Beginning of Modernity', in *The Practice of Conceptual History: Timing History, Spacing Concepts*, trans. T. S. Presner. Stanford, 154–69.

Krämer, J. (1998), *Deutschsprachiges Musiktheater im späten 18. Jahrhundert: Typologie, Dramaturgie und Anthropologie einer populären Gattung*, 2 vols. Studien zur deutschen Literatur 149/150. Tübingen.

Krämer, J. (2018), 'Preface', in J. Krämer (ed.), F. W. Gotter and J. A. Benda, *Medea: Ein mit Musik vermischtes Melodram/Melodrama. Version 1784*, trans. M. L. McCorkle. Kassel XXVII–XLV.

Krämer, J. (2019), 'Johann Friedrich Schink und das Melodram', in B. Jahn and A. Košenina (eds.), *Johann Friedrich Schink (1755–1835): Dramaturg—Bühnendichter—Theaterkritiker*. Hamburger Beiträge zur Germanistik 62. Berlin, 9–35.

Krämer, J. (2022), 'Der Abdruck der Musik im Text. Überlegungen zum Status von Melodramen-Libretti des 18. Jahrhunderts am Beispiel von *Medea* (Gotter/Benda)', in B. Leßmann and T. Venzl (eds.), *Das Singspiel im 18. Jahrhundert. Interdisziplinäre Studien*. Jahrbuch Aufklärung 34. Hamburg, 33–63.

Krasovskaya, V. (1981), *Zapadnoyevropeyskiy baletniy teatr: Ocherky istorii: Epoha Noverra* [*West European Ballet Theatre: Essays of the History: Noverre's Epoch*]. Leningrad.

Krasovskaya, V. (2008), *Russkij baletnyj teatr ot vozniknoveniya do serediny XIX veka* [*Russian Ballet Theatre from the Beginning to the Middle of the 19th Century*]. St Petersburg.

Kravitt, E. F. (1976), 'The Joining of Words and Music in Late Romantic Melodrama', *The Musical Quarterly* 62.4: 571–90.

Kühn, U. (2001), *Sprech-Ton-Kunst: Musikalisches Sprechen und Formen des Melodrams im Schauspiel- und Musiktheater (1770–1933)*. Theatron 35. Tübingen.

Kunz, I. (2007), 'Inkle und Yariko. Der Edle Wilde auf den deutschsprachigen Bühnen des ausgehenden 18. Jahrhunderts'. Unpublished PhD thesis, LMU Munich.

La Gorce, J. de (1986), *Berain, dessinateur du Roi-Soleil*. Paris.

La Gorce, J. de (1997), *Féeries d'opera: Décors, machines et costumes en France 1645–1765*. Paris.

La Gorce, J. de (2011), *Dans l'atelier des menus plaisirs du roi: Spectacles, fêtes et cérémonies aux XVIIe et XVIIIe siècles*. Paris.

La Vega, A. de (1566), *Comedia llamada: Tholomea*, in *Las tres famosissimas comedias del ilustre poeta y representante Alonso de La Vega*. Valencia.

Lada-Richards, I. (2010), 'Dead but not Extinct: On Reinventing Pantomime Dancing in Eighteenth-Century England and France', in F. Macintosh (ed.), *The Ancient Dancer in the Modern World: Responses to Greek and Roman Dance*. Oxford, 19–38.

Lafarga, F. (2010), 'La traducción de las tragedias francesas', *CES* 18: 115–27.

Lange, C. (1964), 'La ópera y las casas de ópera en el Brasil colonial', *Boletín Interamericano de música* 44: 3–11.

Latishev, A. (dir.) (2017), *Medea*. Linterna Films, La Feria Producciones, Temporal Films.

Lauriola, R. (2019), 'The Reception of Medea in the 20th and 21st Centuries', in A. Pociña Pérez, A. López, C. Ferreira Morais, M. de Fátima Silva, and P. Finglass (eds.), *Portraits of Medea in Portugal during the 20th and 21st Centuries*. Leiden, 83–110.

Le Bel, J. L. (1769), *Art poétique d'Horace [...]*. Paris.

Le Duc, A. (2013), *La Zarzuela. Les origines du théâtre lyrique national en Espagne, 1832–1851*. Sprimont.

Le Picq, C. (1772), 'Ballo primo: Medea e Giasone', in *Sismano nel Mogol, dramma per música da rappresentarsi nel Regio-Ducal Teatro di Milano nel Carnovale dell'anno 1773 [...] La poesía è del sig. De Gamera poeta del Regio-Ducal di Torino; compositore della música il celebre sig. Giovanni Paisiello maestro di cappella napolitano*. Milan.

Le Picq, C. and D. Ricciardi (1771), *Giasone e Medea: ballo trágico*, in *Adriano in Siria, dramma per música*. Venice, 27–32.

Lecercle, F. (2000), 'Médée, la volupté d'un geste lent', in *Le Fait de l'analyse 8: La Maladie sexuelle*: 213–32.

Lecercle, F. (2001), 'Médée et la passion mortifère', in F. Lecercle and S. Perrier (eds.), *La Poétique des passions à la Renaissance, Mélanges offerts à Françoise Charpentier*. Paris, 239–55.

Lehmann, H.-T. (2013), *Tragödie und dramatisches Theater*. Berlin.

Leloir, M. (1951), *Dictionnaire du Costume*. Paris.

Leopold, S. (1998), 'Herrin der Geister - Tragische Heroine: Medea in der Geschichte der Oper', in A. Kämmerer, M. Schuchard, and A. Speck (eds.), *Medeas Wandlungen: Studien zu einem Mythos in Kunst und Wissenschaft*. Heidelberg, 129–42.

Lepskaya, L. A. (1996), *Repertuar krepostnogo teatra* [*The Repertoire of the Sheremetevs' Serf Theatre*]. Moscow.

Lermontov, M. Yu (2014), 'Ya k vam pishu (Valerik)' ['I am Writing to You (Valerik)'], in *Polnoe sobranie sochinenij* [*Complete Works*], vol. 1. St Petersburg, 328–35.

Lessing, G. E. (1987), *Werke und Briefe in 12 Bänden*, vol. 11/1: *Briefe von und an Lessing 1743–1770*, ed. H. Kiesel, G. Braungart, and K. Fischer. Frankfurt a. M.

Lessing, G. E. (1990), *Werke und Briefe in 12 Bänden*, vol. 5/2: *Werke 1766–1769*, ed. W. Barner. Frankfurt a. M.

Lessing, G. E. (2003), *Miß Sara Sampson*, in *Werke und Briefe in 12 Bänden*, vol. 3: *Werke 1754–1757*, ed. C. Wiedemann, W. Barner, and J. Stenzel. Frankfurt a. M.

Lessing, G. E. (2010), *Hamburgische Dramaturgie*, part 30, in *Werke und Briefe in 12 Bänden*, vol. 6: *Minna von Barnhelm, Hamburgische Dramaturgie, Werke 1767–1769*, ed. K. Bohnen (1985). Berlin.

Levin, S. R. (1979), 'Medea on the Eighteenth-Century Stage: A Study in the Assimilation of Classical Tragedy'. Unpublished PhD thesis, Indiana University Bloomington.

Licevoj letopisnyj svod (2014), *Licevoj letopisnyj svod 16 veka* [*Illustrated Chronicle of Ivan the Terrible*]. *Vsemirnaya istoriya* [*The World History*], vol. 1, *Istoriya razrusheniya velikoj Troi* [*The History of the Destruction of the Great Troy*]. Moscow.

Lichtenstein, J. (1993), *The Eloquence of Color: Rhetoric and Painting in the French Classical Age*. Berkeley.

Lidner, B. (1936–7), *Medea* [1784], in *Samlade skrifter*, vol. 2, ed. H. Elovson et al. Stockholm, 279–342.

Llewellyn, N. (1990), 'Illustrating Ovid', in C. Martindale (ed.), *Ovid Renewed: Ovidian Influences on Literature and Art from the Middle Ages to the Twentieth Century*. New York, 151–66.

Lockhart, E. (2018), 'Forms and Themes of Early Melodrama', in K. Hambridge and J. Hicks (eds.), *The Melodramatic Moment: Music and Theatrical Culture, 1790–1820*. Chicago and London, 25–42.

Lomonosov, M. (1952), 'Kratkoe rukovodstvo k ritorike na pol'zu lyubitelej sladkorechiya' ['A Quick Guide to Rhetoric for the Benefit of Sweet-Talkers', 1744], in *Polnoe sobranie sochinenij* [*Complete Works*], vol. 7. Moscow and Leningrad.

Longepierre, H.-B. de (1694), *Médée, tragédie*. Paris: https://gallica.bnf.fr/ark:/12148/bpt6k10900405.r=M%C3%A9d%C3%A9e%20Longepierre%2C?rk=42918;4.

Longepierre, H.-B. de (2000), *Médée* [1694], ed. E. Minel. Paris.

Lope de Rueda (1567), *Comedia llamada Armelina*, in *Las quatro comedias y dos coloquios pastoriles*. Valencia.

López Montaner, A. (2006), 'Medea o la desesperada conquista del fraude', *Ana López Montaner: actriz Universidad Católica de Chile, mágister en Artes U. de Chile, profesora de dramaturgía* (24 November): http://analopezmontaner.blogspot.com/2006/11/medea-o-la-desesperada-conquista-del.html.

Lourenzo, M. (2009), *Medea dos fuxidos*. A Coruña.

Lü, Y. (2009), *Medea unter den Deutschen: Wandlungen einer literarischen Figur*. Freiburg i. Br., Berlin et al.

Lü, Y. (2010), 'Transformations of Medea on the Eighteenth-Century German Stage', in H. Bartel and A. Simon (eds.), *Unbinding Medea: Interdisciplinary Approaches to a Classical Myth from Antiquity to the 21st Century*. Abingdon, 148–60.

Lucía Megías, J. M. (1997), 'Hacia la edición crítica de *Flores de filosofía*: la *collatio externa* y los modelos de compilación sapiencial', in S. Furtuño Llorens and T. Martínez Romero (eds.), *Actes del VII Congrés de l'Associació Hispànica de Literatura Medieval*, vol. 2. Castelló de la Plana, 353–74.

Luserke-Jaqui, M. (2002), *Medea: Studien zur Kulturgeschichte der Literatur*. Tübingen.

Lütteken, L. (1998), *Das Monologische als Denkform in der Musik zwischen 1760 und 1785*. Wolfenbütteler Studien zur Aufklärung 24. Tübingen.

Luzker, P. (2017), 'Eudossa vs. Atenaide: o proiskhozhdenii libretto Dzh. Bonekki, Evdoksiyavenchannaya' ['Eudossa vs. Atenaide: On the Origin of the Libretto by J. Bonecchi, "Eudoxia Crowned"'], *Early Music Quarterly* 2.76: 6–11.

Lysell, R. (1996), 'Edith Clever – En klassisk Medea', *Upsala Nya Tidning* (22 March).

Lysell, R. (2004), 'Känslans stasis och modersgestaltens framträdelseformer hos Bengt Lidner – ett romantikens perspektiv', *Sjuttonhundratal* 1: 131–48.

McCleave, S. (2007), 'Marie Sallé, a Wise Professional Woman of Influence', in L. Matluck Brooks (ed.), *Women's Work: Making Dance in Europe before 1800*. Madison, 160–81.

Macintosh, F. (ed.) (2010), *The Ancient Dancer in the Modern World: Responses to Greek and Roman Dance*. Oxford.

Macintosh, F. (2013), 'Choruses, Community, and the Corps de Ballet', in J. Billings, F. Budelmann, and F. Macintosh (eds.), *Choruses, Ancient and Modern*. Oxford, 309–26.

Macintosh, F. (2018), 'Epic Transposed: The Real and the Hyper-Real during the Revolutionary Period in France', in F. Macintosh, J. McConnell, S. Harrison, and C. Kenward (eds.), *Epic Performances from the Middle Ages into the Twenty-First Century*. Oxford, 476–92.

Macintosh, F., C. Kenward, and T. Wrobel (2016), *Medea: A Performance History*. Oxford, interactive eBook.

McIntyre, I. (1999), *Garrick*. Harmondsworth.

McKenzie, R. (1998), 'Women in Seventeenth-Century Russian Literature', in R. J. Marsh, C. Kelly, and A. Cross (eds.), *Gender and Russian Literature: New Perspectives*. Cambridge, 41–54.

Magaña, S. (1967), *Los argonautas*. Mexico City.

Magaña, S. (1985), *Cortés y la Malinche (los argonautas)*, in *Moctezuma II*. Mexico City.

Mahling, C.-H. (1993), 'Original und Parodie: Zu Georg Bendas *Medea und Kason* und Paul Wranitzky's *Medea*', in C. Heyter-Rauland and C.-H. Mahling (eds.), *Untersuchungen zu Musikbeziehungen zwischen Mannheim, Böhmen und Mähren im späten 18. und frühen 19. Jahrhundert*. Mainz, 244–95.

Mahotina, A. (2011), *Panegiricheskaya programma I ee hudozhestvennee voploshchenie v iskusstve gosudarstvennyh prazdnestv epohi Ekateriny II* [*Panegyric Programme and its Artistic Embodiment in the Art of State Festivals of the Epoch of Catherine II*], vol. 2. Moscow.

Maikov, V. I. (1867), 'Elisej ili razdrazhennyj vakkh' ['Elysee or Irritated Bacchus'], in *Sochineniya i perevody* [*Writings and Translations*], vol. 1. St Petersburg, 297–524.

Malein, A. I. (1918), 'Ostrovsky i antichnaya komediya' ['Ostrovsky and the Antique Comedy'], *Biryuch Petrogradskih gosudarstvennyh teatrov* [*Biryuch of the Petrograd State Theatres*] 8: 35–8.

Marinelli, G. (1791), *La vendetta di Medea. Dramma per música da rappresentarsi nel nobilissimo Teatro di San Samuele il Carnovale dell'anno 1792*. Venice.

Marmontel, J.-F. (1763), *Poétique françoise*, vol. 2. Paris.

Marmontel, J.-F. (2005a), 'Mœurs', in *Éléments de littérature* [1787], ed. S. Le Ménahèze. Paris, 721–38.

Marmontel, J.-F. (2005b), 'Vraisemblance', in *Éléments de littérature* [1787], ed. S. Le Ménahèze. Paris, 1164–79.

Martinelli, G. (1783), *Teséo. Dramma per música da cantarsi nella Real Villa di Queluz per celebrare il felicissimo giorno natalizio del serenissimo signore D. Giuseppe príncipe del Brazile, li [sic] 21 agosto 1783. Il drammatico componimento è di Gaetano Martinelli; la música è di Girolamo Francesco de Lima*. Lisbon.

Martínez Cabezón, M. E. (2014), 'El mito de Medea en las letras hispanas (siglos XIII–XVII)'. Unpublished PhD thesis, Universidad de La Rioja.

Martínez Redondo, J. (2017), 'El surgimiento del concierto público en Madrid (1767–1808)'. Unpublished PhD thesis, Universidad de la Rioja.

Maslov, A. (2010), 'K voprosu o znacheniir russkih perelozhenij "Troyanskoj Istorii" Gvido de Kolumna' ['Notes on the Significance of Russian Adaptations of Guido delle Collone's "Historia Troiana"'], *Vestnik Nizhegorodskogo universiteta imeni N.I. Lobachevskogo* [*Vestnik of Lobachevsky University of Nizhni Novgorod*] 6: 215–21.

Massar, P. D. (1970), 'Costume Drawings by Stefano della Bella for the Florentine Theater', *Master Drawings* 8.3: 243–66; 297–317.

Melchinger, S. (1980), *Die Welt als Tragödie*, vol. 2: *Euripides*. Munich.

Menéndez y Palayo, M. (1896), *Obras de Lope de Veja, publicadas por la Real Academia Española*, vol. 6: *Comedias mitológicas; comedias históricas de asunto extranjero*. Madrid.

Ménestrier, C.-F. (1682), *Des Ballets anciens et modernes, selon les régles du théâtre*. Paris.

Metastasio, P. (1736), *Alexandre na India. Drama para música para se representar em Lisboa na Sala da Academia na Praça da Trindade. A poesía he do Senhor Abbade Pedro Mestatasio; a música he toda nova do Senhor Caetano Maria Schlassi*. Lisbon.

Metastasio, P. (1737), *L'Olimpiade, drama per música* [...] *dedicato alla nobilta di Portogallo*. Lisbon.

Milcent, J.-B.-G.-M. de (1813), *Médée et Jason*. Paris.

Minato, N. (1678), *La conquista del vello d'oro. Festa teatrale nelle felicissime nozze della maestà d'Eleonora, arciduchessa d'Austria, Regina di Polonia, con l'altezza serenissima di Carlo, Duca di Lorena, et Baar, etc.* Vienna.

Minato, N. (1717), *La conquista del vello d'oro. Drama per música da rappresentarsi nel Teatro dell'illustrissimo Pubblico di Reggio in occasione della fiera l'anno 1717*. Reggio.

Miranda Cancela, E. (2002), 'Medea: otredad y subversión en el teatro latinoamericano contemporáneo', in C. Morenilla Talens and F. de Martino (eds.), *El perfil de les ombres: el teatre clàssic al marc de la cultura grega i la seua pervivència dins la cultura occidental*. Bari, 317–31.

Miranda Cancela, E. (2020), *Dionisio en las Antillas*. Madrid.

Miravel y Casadevante, J. de (1753), *El gran diccionario histórico, o miscellanea curiosa de la historia sagrada y profana*. Paris.

Montero, R. (1997), *Medea*. La Habana.

Moreira de Azevedo, J. (1877), *O Rio de Janeiro: sua história, monumentos, homens notáveis, usos e curiosidades*, 2 vols. Rio de Janeiro.

Morelly, É. G. (1778), *L'Hymen vengé, en 5 chants*. London and Paris.

Moreno Jashés, A. (1999), *Medea*. Santiago de Chile.

Moreno Jashés, A. (dir.) (2019), *Medea*. Jirafa.

Morreco Brescia, R. (2010), 'O Teatro Efémero na América Portuguesa: do teatro do Siglo de Oro ao teatro "ao gosto português"', *Nuevos mundos* 10: https://journals.openedition.org/nuevomundo/60143.

Morse, R. (1996), *The Medieval Medea*. Cambridge.

Moser, C. (2018), 'The Concept of Barbarism in Eighteenth-Century Theories of Culture and Sociogenesis', in M. Winkler, with M. Boletsi, J. Herlth, C. Moser, J. Reidy, and M. Rohner, *Barbarian: Explorations of a Western Concept in Theory, Literature, and the Arts*, vol. 1: *From the Enlightenment to the Turn of the Twentieth Century*. Stuttgart, 45–144.

Moser, C. and M. Boletsi (eds.) (2015a), *Barbarism Revisited: New Perspectives on an Old Concept*. Boston.

Moser, C. and M. Boletsi (2015b), 'Introduction', in C. Moser and M. Boletsi (eds.), *Barbarism Revisited: New Perspectives on an Old Concept*. Boston, 11–28.

Mourey, M.-T. (2011), 'La tentation de la Pologne: le "manuscrit de Varsovie"', in M.-T. Mourey and L. Quentin (eds.), *Jean-Georges Noverre (1727–1810): Danseur, chorégraphe, théoricien de la danse et du ballet: Un artiste européen au siècle des Lumières*. Musicorum 10. Tours, 133–54.

Mourey, M.-T. and L. Quentin (eds.) (2011), *Jean-Georges Noverre (1727–1810): Danseur, chorégraphe, théoricien de la danse et du ballet: Un artiste européen au siècle des Lumières*. Musicorum 10. Tours.

Mozart, W. A. (1962–77), *Mozart: Briefe und Aufzeichnungen*, ed. W. A. Bauer, O. E. Deutsch, and J. H. Eibl, 7 vols. Kassel.

Mozart, W. A. (1985), *The Letters of Mozart and his Family*, trans. E. Anderson, 3rd edn. New York.

Murphy, A. (1801), *The life of David Garrick, esq.* London.

Nadareishvili, K. (2007), 'Medea in the Context of Modern Georgian Culture', *Phasis* 10: 2–30.

Napoli, C. (2011), 'Literaturnaya sud'ba Medei v Rossii' ['The Literary Fate of Medea in Russia'], in O. Lebedeva and T. Pecherskaya (eds.), *Obrazy Italii v russkoj slovesnosti: Po itogam Vtoroj mezhdunarodnoj nauchnoj konferencii Mezhdunarodnogo nauchno-issledovatel'skogo centra «Russia—Italia» - «Rossiya—Italiya», Tomsk—Novosibirsk, 1–7 iyunya 2009* [*Images of Italy in Russian Literature: According to the Results of the Second International Conference of the International Research Center 'Russia–Italia' - 'Russia-Italy', Tomsk—Novosibirsk, June 1–7, 2009*]. Tomsk, 415–29.

Nery, R. V. (2008), 'E lhe chamam uma nova corte', in R. V. Nery (ed.), *As músicas luso-brasileiras no final do antigo regime*. Lisbon, 255–334.

Nielsen, W. C. (2015), 'Rousseau's *Pygmalion* and Automata in the Romantic Period', in A. Esterhammer, D. Piccitto, and P. Vincent (eds.), *Romanticism, Rousseau, Switzerland: New Prospects*. Basingstoke, 68–83.

Nikiforova L. (2022), 'Eighteenth-century visual media: the New Argonauts ballet and the celebration of the Chesme victory in 1770' ΠΡΑΞΗΜΑ. *Journal of Visual Semiotics*, 2.32: 136–56. DOI:10.23951/2312-7899-2022-2-136-156.

Nikoloutsos, K. P. (2015), 'Cubanizing Greek Drama: José Triana's *Medea in the Mirror* (1960)', in K. Bosher, F. Macintosh, J. McConnell, and P. Rankine (eds.), *The Oxford Handbook of Greek Drama in the Americas*. Oxford, 333–58.

Noble, A. H. (2006), 'Social Convention and Performance Choices in Three Interpretations of Lady Macbeth'. Unpublished PhD thesis, University of Birmingham.

Noël, F. J. M. (1810), *Dictionnaire de la fable*, 2 vols., 3rd edn. Paris.

Nogueira Coelho, M. C. de M. (2013), 'Five Medeas: Euripides in Brazil', *Bulletin of the Institute of Classical Studies Supplement* 126: 359–80.

Noverre, J.-G. (1760), *Lettres sur la Dance, et sur les Ballets*. Lyon.

Noverre, J.-G. (1776), *Recueil de Programmes de Balletts de M. Noverre* [...]. Vienna.

Noverre, J.-G. (1784), *Giasone, e Medea. Ballo eroico-tragico d'inventione dal Sig. Noverre rimesso in scena dal Sig. Vestris; dato in Venezia dal Sig. le-Picq; e adesso messo in scena dal Sig. Domenico Le-Fevre nel nobilissimo Teatro di San Benedetto, il Carnovale dell'anno 1784, in Osmane, dramma per música. Da rappresentarsi nel nobilissimo Teatro di S. Benedetto il Carnovale dell'anno 1784. Dedicato al nobile signore John Fitz-Gerald Esq*. Venice, 23–9.

Noverre, J.-G. (1803–4), *Lettres sur la danse, sur les ballets et les arts*. St Petersburg.

Noverre, J.-G. (1804), *Médée, ballet tragi-pantomime, de la composition de M. Noverre* [...] *Remis à ce Théâtre par MM. Gardel et Vestris*. Paris.

Noverre, J.-G. (1807), *Lettres sur les arts imitateurs en général et sur la danse en particulier*, 2 vols. Paris.

Noverre, J.-G. (1930), *Letters on Dancing and Ballets* [1803], trans. C. W. Beaumont from the rev. enlarged edn. at St Petersburg. London.

[Noverre, J.-G. and J.-J. Rodolphe] (1763), *Médée et Jason. Ballet tragique* in *Didon abandonnee: tragedie en musique: representee sur le Theatre ducal de Stoutgart le jour de la naissance de Son Altesse Serenissime le duc regnant de Wirtemberg et Teck &c. &c.* Stuttgart, 75–89: https://www.loc.gov/resource/musschatz.18168.0/?sp=40.

Nussbaum, F. A. (2003), *The Limits of the Human: Fictions of Anomaly, Race, and Gender in the Long Eighteenth Century.* Cambridge.

Nye, E. (2008), 'Choreography is Narrative: The Programmes of the Eighteenth-Century "Ballet d'action"', *Dance Research* 26.1: 42–59.

Nye, E. (2011), *Mime, Music and Drama on the Eighteenth-Century Stage: The Ballet d'Action.* Cambridge.

Nye, E. and F. Thépot (2007), 'Dramaturgie et musique dans le ballet-pantomime "Médéé et Jason" de Noverre et Rodolphe', *Revue d'histoire du théâtre* 236: 305–23.

Olavo, A. (1961), *Além do rio (Medea)*, in A. D. Nascimento (ed.), *Drama para negros e prólogo para brancos: antologia de teatro negro-brasileiro.* Rio de Janeiro.

Oliveira, J. de (2016), *Kseni, a estrangeira/Kseni, die fremde.* Naxos: VIDVD0041.

Olivo, D. (2010), '*Medea* y la orfandad vacuña', *Poliedo: cultura y perspectiva* (26 July): https://poliedrodigital.blogspot.com/2010_07_26_archive.html.

Oostveldt, B. van and S. Bussels (2017), 'The Sublime and French Seventeenth-Century Theories of the Spectacle: Toward an Aesthetic Approach to Performance', *Theatre Survey* 58: 209–32.

Ordbok öfver svenska språket (= SAOB) (1903), 'Barbar', vol. 2. Lund, col. B 298: https://www.saob.se/artikel/?unik=B_0161-0148.bo4C&pz=5.

Outram, D. (1995), *The Enlightenment.* Cambridge.

Ovid (1977), 'Heroides XII: Medea to Jason', in *Heroides, Amores*, trans. G. Showerman [1914], rev. G. P. Goold, 2nd edn. Cambridge, MA, 142–159.

Pais Brandão, F. H. (1998), *Sob o olhar de Medeia.* Lisbon.

Paiva dos Santos, J. da (2015), 'The Darkening of Medea: Geographies of Race, (Dis)placement, and Identity in Agostinho Olavo's *Além do Rio (Medea)*', in K. Bosher, F. Macintosh, J. McConnell, and P. Rankine (eds.), *The Oxford Handbook of Greek Drama in the Americas.* Oxford, 400–16.

Palazzi, G. (1726), *Medea e Giasone dramma per música da rappresentarsi nel Teatro di Sant'Angelo nel Carnovale dell'anno 1726.* Venice.

Palazzi, G. (1749), *Il vello d'oro, dramma per música da rappresentarsi nel Teatro Tron di S. Cassiano nel Carnovale dell'anno 1749.* Venice.

Parsons, C. (1909), *The Incomparable Siddons.* New York.

Paso, R. (2016), *Perversión Medea: perversión y destrucción de Medea, representada por cinco putas en una institución mental madrileña.* San Fernando.

Perdichizzi, V. (2008), 'Le manteau de Timanthe dans la tragédie classique: échos théoriques et répercussions scéniques à l'époque modern', in L. Comparini and M. Vuillermoz (eds.), *Montrer/Cacher: La représentation et ses ellipses dans le théâtre des XVIIe et XVIIIe siècles.* Chambéry, 37–63.

Pérez de Moya, J. (1599), *Filosofía secreta.* Zaragoza.

Pigna, G. V. (1554), *I Romanzi*, vol. 1. Vinegia.

Pinault Sørensen, M. (2001), 'Barbarian and Savage: Representations', in M. Delon and P. Stewart (eds.), *Encyclopedia of the Enlightenment*, vol. 1. London and New York, 160–3.

Piot, A. (2014), 'Recherches sur Louis-René Boquet (1717–1814)'. Unpublished Master's thesis, École du Louvre.

Pletnyov, P. A. (1822), *Dramaticheskoye iskusstvo gospozhi Semyonovoy* [*Madam Semyonova's Dramatic Art*]. Sorevnovatel'prosvetscheniay i blagotvoritel'nosty [The Works of the Society of Russian Literature Lovers] 5. St Petersburg.

Pociña Pérez, A. (1996), 'Tres dramatizaciones del tema de Medea en el siglo de oro español: Lope de Vega, Calderón de la Barca y Rojas Zorrilla', in A. Pociña Pérez and J. M. García González (eds.), *Pervivencia y actualidad de la cultura clásica*. Granada, 287–314.

Poeplau, A. (2012), *Selbstbehauptung und Tugendheroismus: Das dramatische Werk Friedrich Maximilian Klingers zwischen Sturm und Drang und Spätaufklärung*. Würzburg.

Pogozhev, V., A. Molchanov, and K. Petrov (eds.) (1892), *Arhiv direkcii Imperatorskih teatrov* [*Archive of the Directorate of Imperial Theatres*], vol. 1, part 3. St Petersburg.

Pollard, T. (2017), *Greek Tragic Women on Shakespearean Stages*. Oxford.

Postel, C. H. (1695), *Medea | In Einem | Singe=Spiel| vorgestellet. | Im Jahr CHRisti 1695.* [Hamburg].

[Puisieux, P.-F de] (1750), *La Femme n'est pas inférieure à l'homme, traduit de l'anglois*. London.

Purkiss, D. (2000), 'Medea in the English Renaissance', in E. Hall, F. Macintosh and O. Taplin (eds.), *Medea in Performance, 1500-2000*. Oxford, 32–48.

Pushkareva, N. (2012), *Chastnaya zhizn' russkoj zhenshchiny XVIII veka* [*Private Life of a Russian Woman of the 18th Century*]. Moscow.

Pushkin, A. (1962), 'Moi zamechania o russkom teatre' ['My Remarks about Russian Theatre'], in *Sobranie sochinenij* [*Collected Works*], vol. 6. Moscow.

Radishchev, A. (1941), 'O cheloveke, ego smertnosti I bessmertii' ['About Human Being, His Mortality and Immortality'], in *Polnoe sobranie sochinenij* [*Complete Works*], vol. 2. Moscow.

Radrigán, J. (2004), *Medea mapuche*, in *Crónicas del amor furioso*. Santiago de Chile, 141–55.

Ralph, R. (1985), *The Life and Works of John Weaver*. London.

Ramírez Hein, C. (2000), 'Medea habla en mapadungun', *La tercera* (Santiago de Chile) (1 June): 15.

Rasetti, A. (1745), *La conquista del vello d'oro, drama per música da rappresentarsi nel Regio Teatro di Torino nel Carnolvale del 1745*. Turin.

Real, M. (2018), 'Um estudo sobre *Medeia*, de Mário Cláudio', in C. S. Gomes Xavier Luís, A. A. da Costa Luís, and M. Real, *Vida e obra de Mário Cláudio*. Porto, 223–33.

Reddy, W. (2001), *The Navigation of Feeling: A Framework for the History of Emotions*. Cambridge.

Rembovsky, K. (trans.) (1794), *Prevrashcheniya Ovidievy s primechaniyami i istoricheskimi ob'yasneniyami* [*Ovid's Metamorphoses with Notes and Historical Explanations*], vol. 2. Moscow.

Riaza, L. (2006), *Medea es buen chico* [1984], in *Teatro escogido*. Madrid, 191–242.

Ricciardi, D. (1785), *Giasone e Medea: primo ballo. La música del primo ballo è tutta nuova del celebre sig. Giuseppe Horbman*, in *Giuno Bruto dramma per música da rappresentarsi nel nobilissimo Teatro delle Dame l'anno 1785.* n.p.

Rice, J. A. (2003), *Empress Marie Therese and Music at the Viennese Court, 1792-1807*. Cambridge.

Rigby, C. E. (1996), *Transgressions of the Feminine: Tragedy, Enlightenment and the Figure of Woman in Classical German Drama*. Heidelberg, 173–97.

Río Torres-Murciano, A. (2010), 'Argonautas celestiales: mito y alegoría en *El divino Jasón*', in A. R. Pricco and S. M. Moro (eds.), *Perviviencia del mundo clásico en la literatura: tradición y relecturas*. Coimbra, 47–58.

Ríos, J. (1961), *La selva*, in *Teatro*. Lima, 377–524.

Rocha Pereira, M. H. (1963–4), 'O mito de Medeia na poesía portuguésa', *Humanitas* 15–16: 348–66.

Rohner, M. (2016), 'Verhandlungen des Barbarischen in Inkle und Yariko-Adaptionen aus dem 18. Jahrhundert', in M. Rohner and M. Winkler (eds.), *Poetik und Rhetorik des Barbarischen*. Swiss Review of General and Comparative Literature 45. Bielefeld, 51–62.

Rojas Zorilla, F. de (1645), *Los encantos de Medea*, in *Segunda parte de las comedias de don Francisco de Rojas Zorilla*. Madrid, 154r–169r.

Rojas Zorilla, F. de (1651), *Los encantos de Medea: comedia famosa*. Madrid.

Rojas Zorilla, F. de (1680), *Los encantos de Medea*, in *Comedias*, vol. 2. Madrid, 154v–169r.

Rojas Zorilla, F. de (1704), *Comedia famosa, Los encantos de Medea de D. Francisco de Roxas*, in *Jardin ameno de varias y hermosas flores, cuyos matizes son doze comedias escogidas de los mejores ingenios de España, y las ofrece a los curiosos un aficionado. Parte XIX*. Madrid, 211r–225v.

Rojas Zorilla, F. de (*c.* 1705), *Los encantos de Medea. Comedia famosa de don Francisco de Rojas*. n.p.

Rojas Zorilla, F. de (1742), *Los encantos de Medea*. Madrid.

Rojas Zorilla, F. de (*c.* 1750), *Los encantos de Medea*. Salamanca.

Rojas Zorilla, F. de (*c.* 1760), *Comedia famosa, Los encantos de Medea*. Salamanca.

Rojas Zorilla, F. de (*c.* 1790), *Comedia famosa, Los encantos de Medea*. Madrid.

Rojas Zorilla, F. de (1792), *Comedia famosa, Los encantos de Medea*. Salamanca.

Rojas Zorilla, F. de (*c.* 1799a), *Comedia. Los encantos de Medea*. Madrid.

Rojas Zorilla, F. de (*c.* 1799b), *Comedia. N. 68. Los encantos de Medea de don Francisco de Roxas*. Madrid.

Rosovetsky, S. (1994), 'Odno iz stilevyh techenij russkoj belletristiki vtoroj poloviny 16 – nachala 18 v. i provincial'nyj knizhnik Fedor Zlobin' ['One of the Stylistic Trends in Russian Fiction of the Second Half of the 16th to the Beginning of the 18th Century and Provincial Scribe Fyodor Zlobin'], in *Knizhnye centry Drevnej Rusi. XVII vek: Raznye aspekty issledovaniya* [*Book Centers of Medieval Russia. 17th Century: Different Aspects of Research*]. St Petersburg, 315–79.

Round, N. G. (1974–7), 'Las traducciones medievales, catalanas y castellanas, de las Tragedias de Séneca', *Anuario de estudios medievales* 9: 187–227.

Rubio y Ortega, B. (1797), *Medea cruel: tragedia nueva. Ira igual no puede haber a la ira de una mujer*. Madrid.

Russell, T. W. (1946), *Voltaire, Dryden and Heroic Tragedy*. New York.

Russo, P. and M. A. Smart (1994), 'Visions of Medea: Musico-Dramatic Transformations of a Myth', *Cambridge Opera Journal* 6.2: 113–24.

Ryan, C. (2020), 'Colonus in England's Green and Pleasant Lands: William Mason's Caractacus and His Use of Sophocles', *International Journal of the Classical Tradition* 28.4: 1–24.

Sadler, G. and S. Thompson (2015), 'The Italian Roots of Marc-Antoine Charpentier's Chromatic Harmony', *Analecta musicologica. Veröffentlichungen der Musikgeschichtlichen Abteilung des Deutschen Historischen Instituts in Rom*, Band 52: 546–70.

Sala Valldaura, J. M. (2010), 'El teatro, entre el primer y el Segundo siglo XVIII', in A. Egido and J. E. Laplana (eds.), *La luz de la razón: literatura y cultura del Siglo XVIII. A la memoria de Ernest Lluch*. Madrid, 97–120.

Salazar Bondy, S. (1952), '*Medea* de Juan Ríos', in *Espacio* (Lima) 1, 2–22.

Salvaneschi, L. M. (1992), *Medea de Moquehua*. Buenos Aires.

Sanches, P. A. (1995), 'Denise Stoklos estréia sua *Des-Medéia*', *Folha de São Paulo* (29 September): 9.

Sánchez Jiménez, A. (2002), '"Dorado animal": una nueva metáfora colonial y el *Vellocino de oro* de Lope de Vega', *Bulletin of Hispanic Studies* 84: 287–305.

Sanna, S. (1999), *Von der ratio zur Weisheit. Drei Studien zu Lessing*. Bielefeld.

Santaliz, P. (1992), *El castillo interior de Medea Camuñas*, in *Teatro*. San Juan, 65–106.

Santos Simões, H. dos (2002), *O disfarce como tema em António José da Silva: contribuições para a leitura de Os encantos de Medeia*. Lisbon.

Sasportes, J. (2011), *Storia della danza italiana: dalle origini ai nostri giorni*. Venice.

Schimpf, W. (1988), *Lyrisches Theater: Das Melodrama des 18. Jahrhunderts*. Palaestra 282. Göttingen.

Schink, J. F. (1782), *Dramaturgische Fragmente*, vol. 3, part 1. Graz, 659–94.

Schlegel, A. W. (1923), *August Wilhelm Schlegels Vorlesungen über dramatische Kunst und Literatur*, vols. 1–2, ed. G. V. Amoretti. Bonn.

Schmierer, B. (2005), *Motivation in Medea-Tragödien der Antike und der Neuzeit*. Epistemata 556. Würzburg.

Schwarz-Danuser, M. (1997), 'Melodram', in *Die Musik in Geschichte und Gegenwart*, 2nd edn. Sachteil 6. Kassel, cols. 67–99.

Schweitzer, Z. (2007), 'Sexualité et questions de genre dans les Médée renaissantes et classiques', in *Revue Silène. Centre de recherches en littérature et poétique comparées de Paris Ouest-Nanterre-La Défense*, 1–13: http://www.revue-silene.com/f/index.php?sp=liv&livre_id=89.

Schweitzer, Z. (2015), '"Mais son cœur était fait pour aimer la vertu": sentiment moral et violence dans les tragédies de *Médée*', in B. Guion (ed.), *Le Sentiment moral*. Paris, 219–32.

Schweitzer, Z. (2016), '"Que Médée ne tue point ses Enfans aux yeux du Peuple": la question du représentable dans les *Médée* écrites pour la scène, XVIe–XVIIIe siècle', in *Médée. Versions et interprétations d'un mythe. Cahiers du théâtre antique. Cahiers du GITA* 20. Besançon, 197–210.

Scodel, R. (2010), *An Introduction to Greek Tragedy*. Cambridge.

Seneca (1631), *Malthaei Raderi [...] ad Senecae Medeam Commentarii*. Munich.

Seneca (1713), *L. Annaei Senecae Tragoediae [...] cum notis Thomae Farnabii*. Amsterdam.

Seneca (1728), *L. Annaei Senecae Tragoediae cum notis integris Johannis-Frederici Gronovii [...] itemque observationibus nonnullis hugonis Grotii. Omnia recensuit [...] Johannes Casparus Schröderus*. Delphi.

Seneca (1748), *L. Annaei Senecae Tragoediae [...] cum notis Thomae Farnabii*. Padua.

Seneca (1785), *L. Annaei Senecae Tragoediae [...] cum notis Thomae Farnabii*. Zweibrücken.

Seneca (1795), *Théâtre de Seneque, par M. L. Coupé*, 2 vols. Paris.

Seneca (1993), *Medéia*, trans. G. D. Leoni. Rio de Janeiro.

Seneca (2018), *Medea*, in *Hercules, Trojan Women, Phoenician Women, Medea, Phaedra*, ed. and trans. J. G. Fitch (rev. edn.). Cambridge, MA.

Shakespeare, W. (1963), *The Winter's Tale*, ed. J. H. P. Pafford. London.

Shalev, Z. (2011), *Sacred Words and Worlds: Geography, Religion and Scholarship, 1550–1700*. Leiden.

Silva, F. L. Sousa da (2016), 'De exílio em exílio: um diálogo entre Eurípides e Clara de Góes na peça *Medeia en promenade*', in *Abralic: XIV Congresso Internacional. Fluxos e correntes: tránsitos e traduçoes literárias*. Porto Alegre: http://www.abralic.org.br/anais/arquivos/2015_1455988678.pdf.

Silva, J. C. da (1782), *Composições dramáticas do senhor abade Pedro Metastazio*. Lisbon.

Silva, M. de F. (2019a), 'Os encantos de Mediea by António José da Silva: A Comedy Version of a tragic Theme (18th Century)', in A. Pociña Pérez, A. López, C. Ferreira Morais, M. de Fátima Silva, and P. Finglass (eds.), Portraits of Medea in Portugal during the 20th and 21st Centuries. Leiden, 45–64.

Silva, M. de F. (2019b), 'A Portuguese Medea: Eduarda Dionísio, Antes que a noite venha', in A. Pociña Pérez, A. López, C. Ferreira Morais, M. de Fátima Silva, and P. Finglass (eds.), Portraits of Medea in Portugal during the 20th and 21st Centuries. Leiden, 123–43.

Silveira, E. B. (2015), 'Os encantos de Medeia: a transformação do mito trágico ao cômico', Webmosaica 7.1: 114–16.

Silventi, M. C. (2010), 'El escorpión blanco, una recreación de Medea', in A. R. Pricco and S. Moro (eds.), Pervivencia del mundo clásico en la literatura: tradición y relecturas. Coimbra, 345–55.

Siviter, C. F. I. (2016), 'Rewriting History Through Performance of Tragedy 1799–1815'. Unpublished PhD thesis, University of Warwick.

Smart, C. (1757), The Works of Horace, translated into verse. With a prose interpretation for the help of students. And occasional notes, 4 vols. London.

Smith, M. D. (1990), 'Le Barbier's "Un Canadien et sa femme pleurant sur le tombeau de leur enfant": An Emblem of Respect for the Dead in the Aftermath of the French Revolution', Notes in the History of Art 9.3: 19–23.

Sografi, S. A. (1789), Gli Argonauti in Colco o sia la conquista del vello d'oro, dramma per música del signor A. S. Sografi. Da rappresentarsi nel nobilissimo Teatro di San Samuele il Carnovale dell'anno 1790. Venice.

Sografi, S. A. (1793), Giasone, e Medea, dramma per música da rappresentarsi nel Real Teatro di San Carlo nel dì 4 de noviembre 1793. Per festeggiarsi il glorioso nome di sua maestà la Regina. Dedicato alla real maestà di Ferdinando 4, nostro amabalissimo sovrano. Lisbon.

Sotelo Inclán, J. (1957), Malintzin (Medea americana): drama en tres actos. Mexico City.

Stabler, J. (2005), 'The Shakespearean Sublime and the Reception of Byron's Writing', Revue de l'Université de Moncton 2005: 27–39.

Staff Writer (2006), 'Kseni – a estrangeira, a nova ópera de Jocy de Oliveira', Estadão (São Paulo) (5 October): 47.

Standen, E. A. (1989), 'Jean-Jacques-François Le Barbier and Two Revolutions', Metropolitan Museum Journal 24: 255–74.

Steele, R. (1711), The Spectator 11 (13 March): http://www2.scc.rutgers.edu/spectator/text/march1711/no11.html.

Steele, R. (1719), Bibliothèque des dames, contenant des Règles générales pour leur conduite dans toutes les circonstances de la vie, traduit de l'anglois par Mr. Janiçon [1676]. Amsterdam.

Stenhammar, J. (1793), 'Sång öfver Segern vid Svensksund Den IX Juli MDCCXC', in Svenska Akademiens Handlingar Ifrån År 1786, IV (1809), [293]–305: https://litteraturbanken.se/f%C3%B6rfattare/SvenskaAkademien/titlar/SvenskaAkademien4/sida/293/faksimil

Stephan, I. (2006), Medea: Multimediale Karriere einer mythologischen Figur. Cologne.

Stoklos, D. (1995), Des-Medéia. São Paulo.

Stuttard, D. (ed.) (2014), Looking at Medea: Essays and a Translation of Euripides' Tragedy. London.

Stuurman, S. (2017), The Invention of Humanity: Equality and Cultural Difference in World History. Cambridge, MA and London.

Svensson, C. (2009), 'Lidner och det främmande: Det försvunna kulturmötet i Lidners opera *Milot och Eloisa*', in A. Cullhed, O. Fischer et al. (eds.), *Poetens monopolium: Lidner 250 år*. Lund, 261–78.

Tanner, M. (1993), *The Last Descendant of Aeneas: The Hapsburgs and the Mythic Image of the Emperor*. New Haven.

Taylor, A. (2012), 'Catherine the Great: Coleridge, Byron, and Erotic Politics on the Eastern Front', *Romanticism and Victorianism on the Net* 61: https://id.erudit.org/iderudit/1018597ar.

Taylor, G. (2000), *The French Revolution and the London Stage, 1789–1805*. Cambridge.

Ter-Nedden, G. (1986), *Lessings Trauerspiele. Der Ursprung des modernen Dramas aus dem Geist der Kritik*. Germanistische Abhandlungen 57. Stuttgart.

Terrier, A. (ed.) (2015), *L'Opéra comique et ses trésors*. Lyon.

Tessier, A. (1926), 'Les habits d'opéra au XVIII siècle: Louis Boquet, dessinateur et inspecteur général des Menus-Plaisirs', *La Revue de l'Art* 49: 272–4.

Thomson, J. (1744), 'Summer', in *The Seasons*. London (ECCO).

Tolivar Alas, A. C. (1988), 'Traducciones y adaptaciones españolas de Racine en el s. XVIII', *Estudios de Investigación franco-española* 1: 177–90.

Trancart, A. (1772), *Medea und Jason, ein tragisches Ballet*. Munich.

Triana, J. (1991), *Medea en el espejo. La noche de los asesinos. Palabras comunes*. Madrid.

Tvorogov, O. (1971), 'Drevnerusskij perevod "Troyanskoj Istorii" Gvido de Kolumnaiizdanie 1709 goda' ['Old Russian Translation of the "Trojan History" by Guido de Columna and Edition of 1709'], in *Trudy Otdela drevnerusskoj literatury* [*Works of the Old Russian Literature Department*], vol. 26: 64–71. St Petersburg.

Tvorogov, O. (1972), *Troyanskie skazaniya: Srednevekovye rycarskie romany po russkim rukopisyam 16–17-go vekov* [*Trojan Legends: Medieval Knightly Novels Based on Russian Manuscripts of the 16th and 17th Centuries*]. Leningrad.

Urchueguía, C. (2015), *Allerliebste Ungeheuer. Das deutsche komische Singspiel 1760–1790*. Frankfurt a. M.

Uriot, J. (1763a), *Beschreibung der Feyerlichkeiten, welche bey Gelegenheit des Geburtsfestes Sr. Herzogl. Durchlaucht […] 1763. angestellet worden*. Stuttgart.

Uriot, J. (1763b), *Descriptions des fêtes donnée pendant les quatorze jours à l'occasion de jour de naissance de S.A.S. Monseigneur le Duc*. Stuttgart.

Valberkh, I. (2010), *Iz arhiva baletmeystera: dnevniki. Perepiska. Szenarii* [*From a Choreographer's Archive: Diaries. Letters. Playwrights*]. St Petersburg.

van der Veen, J. (1955), *Le Mélodrame musical de Rousseau au romantisme*. The Hague.

Verdier, A. (2006), *Histoire et poétique de l'habit de théâtre en France au XVIIe siècle*. Vijon.

Vigel, F. (2000), *Zapiski* [*Memoirs*]. Moscow.

Vigor, J. (1777), *Letters from a Lady, who Resided Some Years in Russia, to her Friend in England*. London: https://archive.org/details/lettersfromalad00vigogoog/page/n94.

Vogel, J. C. (1786), *La toison d'or. Tragédie lyrique en trois actes, dedié Monsieur le Chevalier Gluck, mise en musique par Mr. Vogel. Représentée por la première fois par l'Accademie Royale de Musique le 5 septembre 1786*. Paris.

Vogt, P. (2015), 'The Conceptual History of Barbarism: What Can We Learn from Koselleck and Pocock?', in C. Moser and M. Boletski (eds.), *Barbarism Revisited: New Perspectives on an Old Concept*. Boston, 125–38.

Waeber, J. (ed.) (1997), *Pygmalion: scène lyrique*. Geneva.

Waeber, J. (2005), *En musique dans le texte: Le mélodrame de Rousseau à Schoenberg*. Paris.

Waeber, J. (2018), 'Afterword: Looking Back at Rousseau's *Pygmalion*', in K. Hambridge and J. Hicks (eds.), *The Melodramatic Moment: Music and Theatrical Culture, 1790–1820*. Chicago and London, 191–8.

Wagner, H. L. (1777), *Briefe die Seylerische Schauspielgesellschaft und Ihre Vorstellungen zu Frankfurt am Mayn betreffend*. Frankfurt.

Wahrman, D. (2004), *The Making of the Modern Self: Identity and Culture in Eighteenth-Century England*. New Haven and London.

Ward, M. (2019), 'Assemblage Theory and the Uses of Classical Reception: The Case of Aristotle Knowsley's Oedipus', *Classical Receptions Journal* 11: 508–23.

Warton, T. (1781), *The History of English Poetry*. London.

Weickmann, D. (2007), 'Choreographer and Narrative: The Ballet d'Action of the Eighteenth Century', in M. Kant (ed.), *The Cambridge Companion to Ballet*. Cambridge, 51–64.

Wheeler, R. (2000), *The Complexion of Race: Categories of Difference in Eighteenth-Century British Culture*. Philadelphia.

Wigzell, F. (1998), 'Reading the Future: Women and Fortune-Telling in Russia (1770–1840)', in R. J. Marsh, C. Kelly, and A. Cross (eds.), *Gender and Russian Literature: New Perspectives*. Cambridge, 75–91.

Wiles, D. (2020), *The Players' Advice to Hamlet: The Rhetorical Acting Method from the Renaissance to the Enlightenment*. Cambridge.

Winkler, A. (2001), 'Medea-Libretti: Eine stoffgeschichtliche Untersuchung in Kompositionen von Cavalli bis Liebermann'. Unpublished PhD thesis, Paderborn University.

Winkler, M. (2009), *Von Iphigenie zu Medea: Semantik und Dramaturgie des Barbarischen bei Goethe und Grillparzer*. Tübingen.

Winkler, M. (2018), 'Theoretical and Methodological Introduction', in M. Winkler, with M. Boletsi, J. Herlth, C. Moser, J. Reidy, and M. Rohner, *Barbarian: Explorations of a Western Concept in Theory, Literature, and the Arts*, vol. 1: *From the Enlightenment to the Turn of the Twentieth Century*. Stuttgart, 1–44.

Winkler, M., with M. Boletsi, J. Herlth, C. Moser, J. Reidy, and M. Rohner (2018), *Barbarian: Explorations of a Western Concept in Theory, Literature, and the Arts*, vol. 1: *From the Enlightenment to the Turn of the Twentieth Century*. Stuttgart.

Winter, M. H. (1974), *The Pre-Romantic Ballet*. London.

Wiseman, S. (2008), ' "Perfectly Ovidian"? Dryden's "Epistles", Behn's "Oenone", Yarico's Island', *Renaissance Studies* 22.3: 417–33.

Woesler, W. (1978), 'Lessings Miß Sara Sampson und Senecas Medea', in R. D. Schade and J. Glenn (eds.), *Lessing Yearbook X*. Munich, 75–93.

Wokler, R. (1987), *Rousseau on Society, Politics, Music and Language*. New York and London.

Wortman, R. (2006), *Scenarios of Power: Myth and Ceremony in Russian Monarchy from Peter the Great to the Abdication of Nicholas II*. Princeton.

Wygant, A. (2007), *Medea, Magic, and Modernity in France: Stages and Histories, 1553–1797*. Aldershot and Burlington.

Wygant, A. (2010), 'Revolutionary Medea', in H. Bartel and A. Simon (eds.), *Unbinding Medea: Interdisciplinary Approaches to a Classical Myth from Antiquity to the 21st Century*. Abingdon, 136–47.

Yelizarova, N. (1944), *Teatry Sheremetevyh* [*The Sheremetevs' Theatres*]. Moscow.

Yushkov, I. (1806), 'Stihi na tancovanie gospozhi Kolosovoj i vyzov publikoj po okonchanii baleta Medeya i Yazon' ['Rhymes on the Dance of Mrs. Kolosova and a Call by the Public after the Ballet Medea and Jason'], *Lyceum*, Part 2, Number 1.

Zanobi, A. (2014), *Seneca's Tragedies and the Aesthetics of Pantomime*. London.

Zedler, J. H. (1739), *Grosses Vollständiges Universal-Lexicon Aller Wissenschaften und Künste [...]*, vol. 20. Halle-Leipzig.

Zorin, A. (2016), *Poyavlenie geroya. Iz istorii russkoj emocional'noj kul'tury konca 18–nachala 19 veka* [*Appearance of the Hero. From the History of Russian Emotional Culture of the Late 18th to Early 19th Centuries*]. Moscow.

Manuscript Sources

Chapter 3

Medea (1819). Tragediya v pyati dejstviyah v stihah, peredelannaya s francuzskogo teatra Lonzhp'era. Pozvolyaetsya 29 yanvarya 1819. Predstavlena v pervyj raz v Sankt–Peterburgskom Bol'shom teatre 15 maya 1819 v benefis gospozhi Semyonovoj [Five-act tragedy in verse. Translated from French (Longepierre). Put on 29 January 1819. Performed for the first time in St Petersburg Bolshoy Theatre on 15 May in favour of Madam Semyonova]. [Translators S. Marin (1st act); A. Delvig (2nd act); N. Gnedich (3rd act); P. Katenin (4th act); A. Pomorsky (5th act)]. Manuscript. St Petersburg State Theatre Library.

Medea and Jason (1802). Melodrama v odnom dejstvii. Perevod s nemeckogo [F. Gotter]. [One-act melodrama. Translation from German [F. Gotter].] [Translator N. Sandunov.] Manuscript. St Petersburg State Theatre Library.

Vsevolodski-Gerngross, V. N. Kartoteka repertuarnaya Peterburgskim, Moskovskim, i provoncialnym teatram, sostavl'ennaya po Sankt–Peterburgskim i Moscowskim vedo-mostyam i drugim istochnikam [Repertoire card-catalogue for St Petersburg, Moscow and provincial theaters, compiled from St Petersburg and Moscow vedomosti and other sources]. St Petersburg State Theatre Library.

Chapter 4

Anon. (1782–4), *Theatro comico portuguez ou Colecções das óperas portuguezas* […]. Lisbon, Biblioteca nacional, cod-1365-2.

Agramont y Toledo, J. de (1750), *Recobrar por una letra el tesoro de los cielos, y mágica de Nimega*. Madrid, BnE, mss/16529 (s. xviii); mss/16266, 38r–131v.

Andreozzi, G. (1793b), *Giasone e Medea: drama per música del Sig. D. Gaetano Andreozzi*. Lisbon, Instituto Português do Património Cultural, Departamento de Musicologia, ms.

Calderón de la Barca, P. (1785), 'Loa para la comedia de Los tres mayores prodigios', Madrid: Biblioteca Histórica Municipal de Madrid, ms. Tea 1-186-68-A.

Fermín de Laviano, M. (*c.* 1760), *No se evita un principio si se falta a la deidad, y mágico Fineo*. Madrid, Biblioteca histórica de Madrid, ms. Tea 1-131-3.

Lisbon, Biblioteca nacional de Portugal, cod-1365-2.

Lisbon, Biblioteca nacional de Portugal, ms. M.M 142//2, 3, 9.

Madrid, Biblioteca histórica municipal, ms. Tea 1-186-68-A.

Madrid, Biblioteca histórica municipal, Mus 54–2.

Madrid, Biblioteca nacional de España, mss/16279.

Madrid, Biblioteca nacional de España, mss/16882.

Madrid, Biblioteca nacional de España, mss/22565, fols. 98r–126r.

Madrid, Biblioteca nacional de España, mss/71945.

Madrid, Biblioteca nacional de España, mss/13756.

Madrid, Biblioteca nacional de España, mss/14244/8.

Madrid, Biblioteca nacional de España, mss/17533.

Seville, Biblioteca Universitaria, Fondo Antiguo, ms. A 250/109(3bis).

Chapter 8

Mémoire de Peintures et dorures faittes sur les habits pour les menus plaisirs du Roy pour les spectacles donnés a la cour pendant l'année 1763. Les dits ouvrages faits par ordre de Monsieur de la ferté Intendant et controlleur des menus plaisirs et affaires de la chambre du Roy et sous la conduitte de Boquet peintre et dessinateur des menus plaisirs du Roy, Archives Nationales, F-Pan O/1/3008.

Programme des Opéras representée devant leur majestés ou État de costumes pour les spectacles de la Cour 1754–1770, Archives Nationales, F-Pan O/1/3266.

Théorie et pratique de la danse simple et composé par Mr. Noverre/Programmes de Grands Ballets Historiques, Héroiques, Poetiques, Nationnaux, Allégoriques et Moraux de la Composition de M. Noverre/Musique des Ballets composée d'après les Programmes de M. Noverre Habits de Costume pour l'Exécution des Ballets de Mr. Noverre dessigné par M. Boquet. 11 vols. 1766. PL-Wu, Inw.zb.d. 20818-20828.

Index

For the benefit of digital users, indexed terms that span two pages (e.g., 52–53) may, on occasion, appear on only one of those pages.